EXPLORING DISCOVERY

ALA Editions purchases fund advocacy, awareness, and accreditation programs for library professionals worldwide.

EXPLORING
DISCOVERY

THE FRONT DOOR TO YOUR LIBRARY'S LICENSED AND DIGITIZED CONTENT

EDITED BY
KENNETH J. VARNUM

An imprint of the American Library Association
Chicago 2016

KENNETH J. VARNUM is senior program manager for discovery, delivery, and learning analytics at the University of Michigan Library. In this role, he is responsible for the library's discovery interfaces (the "MLibrary" single search tool, ArticlesPlus, Search Tools, etc.), link resolution and content delivery interfaces, and the library's evolving and emerging learning analytics infrastructure. Varnum received a master's degree from the University of Michigan's School of Information and a bachelor of arts degree from Grinnell College. Over his two decades working with public-facing technology in academic, corporate, and special libraries, he has gained a deep appreciation and understanding of the need to tailor systems and interfaces to the local user base. In addition to numerous articles and chapters, he wrote *Drupal in Libraries* (2012), compiled the Library Information Technology Association guide *The Top Technologies Every Librarian Needs to Know* (2014), and edited Lorcan Dempsey's *The Network Reshapes the Library* (2014). He blogs at rss4lib.com and can be found on Twitter at @varnum.

© 2016 by the American Library Association

Extensive effort has gone into ensuring the reliability of the information in this book; however, the publisher makes no warranty, express or implied, with respect to the material contained herein.

ISBN: 978-0-8389-1414-4 (paper)

Library of Congress Cataloging-in-Publication Data

Names: Varnum, Kenneth J., 1967- editor.
Title: Exploring discovery : the front door to your library's licensed and digitized content / Kenneth J. Varnum, editor.
Description: Chicago : ALA Editions, an imprint of the American Library Association, 2016. | Includes bibliographical references and index.
Identifiers: LCCN 2015043425 | ISBN 9780838914144 (paper)
Subjects: LCSH: Electronic information resource searching. | Federated searching. | Information retrieval—Computer programs. | User interfaces (Computer systems) | Libraries—Special collections—Electronic information resources. | Electronic information resources—Management.
Classification: LCC ZA4230 .E97 2016 | DDC 025.5/24—dc23 LC record available at http://lccn.loc.gov/2015043425

Book design in the Bembo Std and Proxima Nova typefaces by Alejandra Diaz.
Imagery © Meowu/Shutterstock, Inc.

♾ This paper meets the requirements of ANSI/NISO Z39.48–1992 (Permanence of Paper).
Printed in the United States of America

20 19 18 17 16   5 4 3 2 1

Dedicated to my father,
who has not only given me new ways of getting to where I'm going,
but helped me find new destinations to aim for.

CONTENTS

PART III
INTERFACES

PART IV
CONTENT AND METADATA

INTRODUCTION

We are in a new age of discovery. Not the one recalled from high school history books, where exploration of the physical world proceeded apace, but an age in which the incredible breadth and depth of knowledge is just as mysterious to the typical researcher. Where centuries ago, explorers set out to find the edges of the known world, so information seekers today are setting out to find the edges of knowledge so they can build upon them. Much as the new technologies of that era enabled those explorers to go farther, go faster, and make discoveries that redefined their world, so do today's technologies enable researchers to explore ever-vaster realms of information more efficiently than ever before, and make new discoveries in the heretofore hidden realms of someone else's studies.

This new age of discovery builds on decades of advancements in handling metadata and full text in digital formats, natural language processing, keyword searching, and information science. The pace of change in the last half-century has been dizzying, enabling library technologists to enable discovery across multiple scales, with tools and processes specific to each. There was a period of centuries when a comprehensive index of books was simply a chronological list of published works, maintained by individuals and copied by hand or, eventually, by the printing press. Discovery required going someplace, often several places, to find both the index and the items.

First, there is discovery writ large. As the twentieth century dawned, we entered the age of the subject-based card catalog, in which there were several indices to printed books: title, author, a few hand-selected subject words. As we entered the current century, it became plausible to describe searching the entire contents of most printed works available in the world. Google Books and HathiTrust provide search and display capabilities for a significant proportion of the information contained in printed books.

In parallel processes, article-level discovery has emerged as a technologically driven tool. From early hand-maintained indices to individual publications in the nineteenth century, we arrived at the mass-produced subject guides to articles and journals in the form of the venerable *Readers Guide to Periodical Literature*, a staple of my secondary education. Rapidly, as the information technology age burst upon us at the turn of the millennium, not just the indexes but the full text of the articles themselves became accessible to computer-driven indexing and search technologies. Products such as Google Scholar, Summon, and Primo Central are the brands the library world has come to see as the providers of article-level (and, for e-books, chapter-level) discovery. Second, there is discovery writ small. There is even more innovation here, because the tools are purpose-built for specific needs, even if they share a common infrastructure and application computer code. The variety of materials managed and collected by individual libraries is expansive, and purpose-built discovery tools are still needed to provide in-depth access to them. Where the relatively small number of items in a unique collection in one library might get lost in the ocean of all human knowledge, once the collection surfaces through a large-scale discovery tool, the items can then be found in smaller-scale, purpose- or collaboratively built interfaces. Libraries and archives have been busy working on custom interfaces to large-scale discovery tools and, equally important, discovery tools and interfaces that are focused on the specialized items of a single collection.

Thus, the concept of "discovery" covers scales from billions of items in the large, web-scale systems to thousands, or even just hundreds of items at the other end of the scale. This book therefore approaches the topic with commensurate breadth, and explores both tools that have been made to enable in-depth access to relatively narrow information silos and tools that enable exploration of broad swathes of digital and off-line content. What cutting-edge tools and services are emerging from the growing suite of discovery interfaces and indexes? Where is "discovery" going, and what tools and techniques are emerging as standard elements in the library technology toolbox? By providing a series of case studies illustrating the interfaces and technologies that can be used by libraries today, this book attempts to explore answers to these questions.

PART I

VENDED DISCOVERY SYSTEMS

CHAPTER ONE

COLLABORATIVE GROWTH TOWARD DISCOVERY

Becoming Stronger through Change

MARGARET HELLER AND HONG MA

I n 2014 and 2015, Loyola University Chicago Libraries migrated to Alma and Primo from Ex Libris's Voyager integrated library system (ILS) and the WebVoyage online public access catalog (OPAC), WorldCat Local, and a suite of electronic resource tools from Serials Solutions. We chose the radical act of leaving the past behind and deliberately changing all our systems at once. We grounded the project in a collaborative selection and implementation process with user experience data–driven decision-making. While the project is in the implementation phase at the time of writing, we can convey a number of best practices from the literature and suggestions for similar projects.

MOVING TO WEB-SCALE AND LIBRARY SERVICES PLATFORMS

The first commercial web-scale discovery (WSD) products came to the market in 2009, though the concept goes back farther to earlier federated search systems. Athena Hoeppner defines WSD as a pre-harvested central index coupled with a richly featured discovery layer providing a single search across a library's local, open access, and subscription collections (2012). The WSD contains two major components: a central index and a discovery layer. Major WSD products are WorldCat Local (now called WorldCat Discovery Service), Summon, Primo, and EBSCO Discovery Service (EDS). These products began as independent from the specific library systems, but that is changing, as we will see.

Increasingly by 2010, academic libraries started evaluating and adopting web-scale discovery services. Most institutions used WSD as a tool for consolidated article search and kept their legacy OPAC for locating local collections. This tendency is partially due to the hesitation of reference librarians to introduce WSD to users, especially graduate students and other researchers in specific subject domains. While the tools are easy to use and cover a lot of disciplines, their subject coverage is not always clear and relevancy rankings are proprietary algorithms, leading to information overload and dissatisfaction with known item searching (Thomsett-Scott and Reese 2012).

Providing access to resources is increasingly challenging as libraries offer information resources in all formats. Library users' expectations and needs require the library to provide an easy way to access all these collections in a comprehensive and timely manner. Given the complexity of managing multiple information resource formats, the legacy ILS and OPAC are no longer adequate to manage all aspects of selection, acquisition, cataloging, discovery, and fulfillment. To make up for the absence of necessary functions in the ILS, Loyola University Chicago Libraries (which includes eight physical locations in the Chicago area and Rome, Italy) implemented a variety of ancillary products such as link resolvers, electronic resource management (ERM) systems, digital asset management systems, and web-scale discovery services. Installing, configuring, maintaining, and integrating systems in such a disintegrated environment are challenging.

The solution to this is to reimagine the ILS to match what WSD did for the OPAC. Marshall Breeding named what was popularly known as "next-generation ILS" as library services platforms (LSP) (2011). LSPs aim to provide a more comprehensive approach to managing library collections than a traditional ILS. They can handle diverse print and electronic formats of content in unified workflows to simplify library operations (figure 1.1). They use new cloud computing models, such as fully web-based multi-tenant and software as a service (SaaS). LSPs emphasize managing library collections through shared metadata rather than traditional local bibliographic databases. Theoretically, LSPs are decoupled from discovery services. One vendor's LSP could power another vendor's WSD, however synchronizing library holdings with multiple/different knowledgebase may be difficult or impossible, and so in that way retains the nature of an ILS with OPAC attached. WSD products have evolved and improved in expanding content coverage as well as features, relevancy ranking, and so the LSP adds in seamless integration with library patron services.

FIGURE 1.1 ───

Transformation of legacy ILS and siloes to library services platform

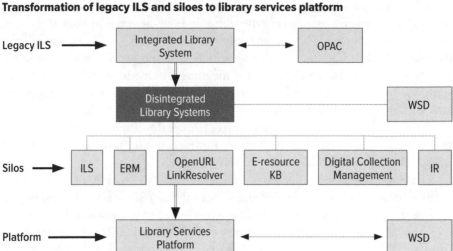

CHOOSING THE RADICAL SOLUTION

We say replacing a traditional ILS and OPAC with an LSP and WSD is radical because it forces library staff across the board to examine the root of their practices and make changes where necessary. Not all practices will change—for instance, bibliographic data may still be encoded in MARC—but other practices such as approaches to library instruction or copy cataloging may change dramatically. Managing this change is a challenge, and our journey to choosing an LSP and WSD is a good example of effective and ineffective ways to approach this.

One of the major risks of migrating systems is making a particular portion of the staff feel that they must make all the changes, or that they have no say in the changes. For example, the Auraria Library in Colorado believes their transition to WorldCat Local in 2009 failed for this reason, and a later migration to Summon was successful because they started by understanding fundamental practices and workflows in a collaborative process (Sommerville 2013). Other experiences shared in the literature bear this out. For instance, Fabbi recommends organizational learning with a participatory focus to reimagine a technical services department (2009). A truly participatory project requires that the participants be able to decline the project at all, which was the experience of one institution which in 2012 voted not to implement any discovery layer (Ellero 2013).

Like other academic libraries at the advent of WSD in 2010, Loyola University Chicago did a short investigation and decided to try WorldCat Local. In 2010, the initial solution was to keep a traditional OPAC (WebVoyage), and implement WorldCat Local as an article discovery tool. At the same time, we had been looking for a long-term solution for managing all different formats in a unified workflow by monitoring the trends in next-generation library systems. However, public service librarians felt left out of the process and unhappy with the results. Usability testing revealed serious flaws in the accessibility of resources, which was partly due to the tool not meeting the needs of technical services staff, who did not feel confident in their ability to work with it, because of the lack of local control, and reliance on master bib records which anyone in the OCLC community could modify. Furthermore, development was not up to our current needs, including the process for ingesting local library content and the OCLC knowledge base for electronic resources.

The experiences of other libraries mesh with our own. Much of the literature focuses on the effect that implementing a WSD service has on public service staff, but we can draw from their experiences to understand the potential effects of an LSP and WSD on all library staff. Because public service librarians must work with end users, they have to be comfortable with the tool, which example after example shows is not always the case. Edith Cowan University described librarian perceptions of their 2009 migration to Summon as "culture shock" with a lack of initial trust and not enough time to adjust (Howeard and Wiebrands 2011).

In fact, as Dave Pattern points out, WSD systems are not meant to be particularly comfortable for librarians, since they are designed for the needs of the average user (2012). Most library users have already made the radical shift that libraries are only just now making. When Google Scholar became available a decade ago, users took to it immediately because it offered a search experience that was more appealing than library-provided interfaces, which was alarming to librarians who cautioned people away from using something not as powerful as library-provided tools (York 2005). Students are so used to the Google Scholar experience that a discovery layer may not tempt them back. A 2015 study of Summon found that while overall users were satisfied with the tool, graduate students reported that they preferred specialized databases for their subject work, or Google Scholar for general searching (Lundigran, Manuel, and Yan 2015). That said, another study of student searching in Google Scholar and a federated search tool found that students do prefer the research experience in the federated tool, though they have a limited understanding of the differences between the two (Georgas 2014).

A limited understanding of how discovery layers work has created massive shifts for instruction and reference librarians, on which population most of the literature focuses. In theory, it is no longer necessary to spend so much class time on how to search in a database interface, and class time should be devoted to higher-level skills such as evaluating and using information (Cmor and Li 2012). In fact, the advent of discovery layers has in some ways directly contributed to the Association of College Research Libraries (ACRL) developing Information Literacy Frameworks to replace the Information Literacy Standards (Seeber 2015). As Pete Coco points out, the convenience of a discovery layer belies its complexity—finding articles is easy enough, but understanding and using them still requires instruction and information literacy. Librarians can use the opportunity to teach the discovery layer in creative ways (2012). Buck and Steffy suggest that instruction librarians must know whether the tool is appropriate to a certain class by knowing what is in it, making sure students understand the tool at the level that is appropriate, using active learning techniques, teaching refining techniques to manage information overload, and working with colleagues to share successful techniques over time (2013).

Not all users or librarians will change their practices radically, or even at all. Ninety percent of instruction librarians at the Association of Research Libraries (ARL) institutions would bypass the discovery layer in favor of a specialized database for subject-specific classes (Kulp, McCain, and Scrivener 2014). That said, limited data exists about how advanced researchers and librarians actually use discovery layers, and furthermore how this changes when the traditional OPAC is no longer available. Anecdotally, however, we have heard from faculty that they plan to use the discovery layer for current awareness rather than searching in each database interface. Known–item searching is a weakness in discovery layers, since they rely on relevancy algorithms and post-search filtering, which is frustrating for searchers such as librarians with a solid understanding of Boolean logic and left-anchor searches. At Loyola, a priority for implementation is creating an advanced search in Primo that meets the needs of both librarians and advanced users. Alma, which is the library services platform powering Primo, is of course available to Loyola librarians to take advantage of its robust repository search, but we want to ensure that users are able to perform their own advanced searches without relying on staff access to another interface.

MAKING GOOD CHOICES

Identifying user needs should underpin implementation of a WSD or an LSP. Techniques such as query log analysis and web analytics have a role in the development and testing of discovery layers (particularly from the vendor side), since these allow us to see that, for instance, users start with simple searches and use facets to limit their results (Diamond, Price, and Chandrasekar 2013; Durante and Wang 2012). Users work with idiosyncratic methods and favorite tools that might not be the most efficient but are comfortable for them. It is our job to figure out what works for our users and either adapt our systems accordingly or teach them better practices (Daigle 2013).

Testing early is more effective than testing at the end of the project (Krug 2006, 134). In the case of implementing a new discovery layer, this means well before the project is under way in whatever system the library is currently using, as well as systems the library is considering using. Gallaway and Hines (2012) suggest "competitive usability" as a method to select the next-generation catalog or discovery system. But knowing what questions to ask in competitive usability should be informed by knowledge of users' current practices. Without the baseline from the legacy OPAC search it is difficult to understand what has improved or how instructional material should be changed (Jarrett 2012).

The Loyola University Libraries Web Team started routine usability testing of the library website, catalog, and other services in 2013. We followed the method outlined by Steve Krug in *Rocket Surgery Made Easy* (2010), which emphasizes lightweight routine testing and fixing of errors. These routine tests uncovered errors or confusing aspects of the library website in general, but most importantly for discovery, the tests found it impossible to locate e-books or digital collections when starting from WorldCat Local. This realization prompted a meeting of all the departments that touched WorldCat Local to understand the features and limitations of WorldCat Local. These tests made it clear that while the traditional OPAC worked for students, they did not enjoy searching it and tended to choose WorldCat Local without understanding why, or what the differences between the two were. While we made a number of changes to the library website interface to provide help and context clues, it was clear from testing that maintaining two systems in parallel was not a good use of our time. (A 2014 debate between Dianne Cmor and Rory Litwin came to roughly the same conclusion.)

One example of how our testing led us to know an LSP was right for us was that of theses and dissertations, which were cataloged in the ILS up until 2012, at which point they were cataloged in the institutional repository. Older dissertations and theses in the catalog had no link associated with them, and the newer ones were not at all discoverable without searching the repository, which was almost unknown to average users. To provide complete access, it would have been necessary to catalog all the new dissertations, as well as add the links to the older records. Harvesting the institutional repository into WorldCat Local certainly helped with finding these items, but it still left the management of them spread across multiple systems.

Other intractable issues included constant miscommunications between the discovery layer and the link resolver that made it impossible to trust its results. We attempted to improve this, but determined that going forward we would only try to use a discovery layer with a tightly integrated link resolver. All of these usability findings made us determined to select a system with integrated resource management, access, and discovery so that we could focus on presenting our resources to the best of our ability without having to spend so much time massaging rough edges between systems. These pre-identified limitations left a limited number of available systems as contenders.

COLLABORATIVE SELECTION PROCESS

In 2014 when the libraries began the process of developing a new three-year strategic plan, the dean of libraries decided to initiate a process to select and implement an LSP. We evaluated the following candidates: OCLC WorldShare Management Services (WMS)/WorldCat Discovery Service, Ex Libris Alma/Primo, and ProQuest Intota/Summon. We determined that Alma and Primo should replace the current Voyager ILS and WorldCat Local. The evaluation process involved people from all library departments to ensure we included concerns from all aspects of library work. Our four years of experience using WorldCat Local, routine user studies, and feedback gathering helped to clarify the expectation for systems under evaluation.

The dean of libraries appointed a Next-Gen ILS Exploratory Committee (chaired by the head of library systems) and public service/technical service subcommittees in January 2014. There were purposely overlaps between the main committee and the subcommittees. The main committee involved personnel from campus IT as stakeholders from outside the libraries. The collaborative selection process started with educating all library staff about LSPs and WSDs with an overview of novel terminology and concepts (such as cloud computing, service-oriented architectures (SOA), SaaS, and multi-tenant computing), coordinating vendor webinars, and encouraging participation of related presentations in conferences. Similar to any system evaluation process, the main committee developed a request for proposal (RFP) and sent it to three vendors, reviewed RFP responses from the vendors, and developed customized scripts for the on-site vendor demo. All library staff were invited to attend the on-site demo and asked to fill in the survey for each LSP demo. In addition to the interaction and communication with the vendors, we interviewed peer institutions which recently implemented these candidates LSPs. It was essential to have participation in the process by all staff in a variety of functional areas. In July 2014 the committee summarized pros and cons based on information gathered and produced a report, including a recommendation to select Alma and Primo, for library administration to make a decision. After a couple of follow-up discussions between library administration and the committee, the Loyola Libraries made the final decision to choose Alma/Primo in October 2014, and signed the contract in December 2014.

COLLABORATIVE IMPLEMENTATION PROCESS

The pre-implementation phase started immediately after signing the contract. Ex Libris delivered a project schedule on December 31, 2014. The implementation phase started with a kickoff meeting on January 16, when an Ex Libris implementation team came on-site and did a complete project overview with all library staff. The dean appointed the head of library systems as project manager. We formed an executive group focused on policy, vision, planning, coordinating, and communicating decision making. We formed a series of working groups to focus on migration and implementation details: Access Services, Acquisition and Resource Management, ERM, Primo/Discovery, and Systems, as well as an electronic resources access and troubleshooting group midway through the process. Representation on the implementation team included librarians and staff from across functional areas of the library and from branch libraries (Law and Health Sciences), with overlaps between groups. The largest group was the Primo group. It contained staff from a variety of library departments (Reference, Technical Services, Systems, and Special Collections). After the first implementation meeting the Loyola team and Ex Libris's team held weekly calls to manage the project, and each working group started watching video trainings, as well as completing a variety of forms to prepare the initial migration, which took place after Ex Libris's on-site systems analysis workshop in late January. The chairs of each working group took the lead on implementation tasks, so that the majority of the decision making was decentralized from the project leader and in the hands of functional areas. Ex Libris used Basecamp as a project management tool, and Loyola used an institutional Box subscription to share files and manage the project internally.

The nature of collaboration and a decentralized model can make things happen in an efficient way. However, due to the different contexts of and needs expressed by multiple campuses, the radical shift in approach did not always go smoothly. For example, the Health Science Library uses a separate EZProxy server. There are resources shared by all campuses, as well as resources limited to health science users. The built-in solution in Alma required that all patrons be loaded into predefined network groups to gain access to the specific licensed resources, but not all health science patrons could be loaded into Alma since the hospital system is owned by a different corporate entity and their staff information system was not accessible. Accessing this data is a high-priority goal for the future. In order to resolve this challenge, we reached out to other institutions for advice and learned a great deal about the structure of Alma and Primo. Eventually, we identified an acceptable solution. While this put us behind our agreed-upon time line with Ex Libris, in the end the main campus libraries and the Health Sciences Library better understood each other's needs.

Usability testing continued throughout the implementation process. We started with an informal card-sorting exercise, and once Primo was available we did four rounds of usability testing with students, both undergraduate and graduate. The card-sorting exercise took place in a busy area of the library and invited students to describe the process they would take to access an item in the catalog. This helped us determine which Primo jargon would work—other Primo studies have found that while searching Primo is intuitive, its language is not, nor are terms for standard library practices such as holds (Comeaux 2012). Doing the card-sorting exercise led directly to changes in the request area of user interface, including removing or moving vendor-provided labels and page elements with CSS and JQuery to remove visual clutter and improve flow. Alma provides robust display logic that allows only the most appropriate services for intercampus or interlibrary loan to be displayed in Primo, and card sorting helped us to understand the most effective ways to use that display logic.

Our usability testing continued to follow the Krug model. The first round used the questions from an earlier WorldCat Local and Voyager testing session to see how the user experience changed. The second round incorporated questions raised by the first round as well as staff testing in Primo. Both sessions uncovered errors and areas for improvement, but the most heartening result was that in staff discussions about our implementation choices we could point directly to our usability testing as justification for these choices. Later rounds of testing continued to test questions about access and labeling as well as customizations to the user interface. We created two versions with a different set of customizations and labeling and tested these with five students on one day, and then picked the most popular results out of these two tests for an additional test before opening the interface for a public beta in late June 2015. Our results generally match those in the Primo usability testing literature—post-search facets used for filtering are clear to students, but the scope of the search is not clear (Comeaux 2012), and metadata errors will create confusion (Nichols et al. 2014).

We could act on results of tests quickly because of the cross-departmental collaborative nature of our Primo team. The electronic resources librarian spotted a problem with ProQuest database activation and made a plan to fix it without needing to wait for an error report from public service staff, but while still ensuring public services staff understood the technical issues. Reference staff could likewise relay information about changes in instructional practices to access services staff. While going forward we will return to testing all library web services with a slightly different group of staff running the testing, and we will be able to use the collaborative ties formed in our implementation team to ensure we are gathering testing scenarios and creating solutions with the appropriate people. While we are confident in our testing to give us a roadmap for future development, we will maintain a regular testing schedule as our student population changes and the features of Primo change.

One of the struggles with implementing a discovery layer, particularly one on top of an LSP, is identifying the most effective ways of providing reliable access to resources. Learning how to navigate the complex relationships between a variety of data sources such as the Alma repository, the Primo Central index, and a new link resolver requires new ways of thinking about how we provide access. One example is when to make edits to the holdings, which rely on indexing mechanisms over which we have limited control. Primo Central has a 5–10-day delay for new resources to be available to users for searching, and publishing our local holdings information to Primo Central involves a 4–5-day delay. Learning all this takes ongoing collaboration between public and technical services to test and fix issues in the product over time (Silton 2014). For that reason we decided after Primo was available that we needed a group to address e-resource access issues and troubleshooting in a structured way, and so formed a new working group with members pulled from across departments and campuses. This has been a valuable group to work together to learn the system and make choices together that we will all understand in the future. The new group will continue when Alma/Primo goes live, and will establish a structure to deal with access issues efficiently during implantation, build knowledge, establish a model for ongoing maintenance and support, and coordinate problem reporting and solving. Frequent releases and changes in resource coverage will require monthly meetings to stay on top of changes (Boyer and Besaw 2012), and so going forward we plan to maintain these collaborative ties between departments in order to stay knowledgeable on both the public and technical sides about Primo and Alma. This is a new model for our libraries, but it already has been successful enough that we feel it is worth continuing.

CONCLUSION

Radical changes mean uneasy times for those living through them. But when approached with the right attitude they can strengthen an institution and improve its practices. Going into the project with a user-centered, inclusive process grounded in evidence and data will not alleviate all stress and uncertainty, but can provide a framework for decision-making that will give everyone confidence.

References

Boyer, Ginny M., and Megan Besaw. 2012. "A Study of Librarians' Perceptions and Use of the Summon Discovery Tool." *Journal of Electronic Resources in Medical Libraries* 9, no. 3: 173–83. doi:10.1080/15424065.2012.707056.

Breeding, Marshall. 2011. "The Systems Librarian: A Cloudy Forecast for Libraries." *Computers in Libraries* 31, no. 7: 32.

Buck, Stefanie, and Margaret Mellinger. 2011. "The Impact of Serial Solutions' Summon on Information Literacy Instruction: Librarian Perceptions." *Internet Reference Services Quarterly* 16, no. 4: 159–81. doi:10.1080/10875301.2011.621864.

Buck, Stefanie, and Christina Steffy. 2013. "Promising Practices in Instruction of Discovery Tools." *Communications in Information Literacy* 7, no. 1: 66–80.

Cmor, Dianne, and Xin Li. 2012. "Beyond Boolean, towards Thinking: Discovery Systems and Information Literacy." *Library Management* 33, nos. 8/9: 450–57. doi:10.1108/01435121211279812.

Cmor, Dianne, and Rory Litwin. 2014. "Should We Retire the Catalog?" *Reference & User Services Quarterly* 53, no. 3: 213–16.

Coco, Pete. 2012. "Convenience and Its Discontents: Teaching Web-Scale Discovery in the Context of Google." *ACRLog.* January 27. http://acrlog.org/2012/01/27/convenience -and-its-discontents-teaching-web-scale-discovery-in-the-context-of-google/.

Comeaux, David J. 2012. "Usability Testing of a Web-Scale Discovery System at an Academic Library." *College & Undergraduate Libraries* 19, nos. 2–4: 189–206. doi:10.1080/10691316. 2012.695671.

Daigle, Ben. 2013. "Getting to Know You: Discovering User Behaviors and Their Implications for Service Design." *Public Services Quarterly* 9, no. 4: 326–32. doi:10.1080/15228959. 2013.842416.

Diamond, Ted, Susan Price, and Raman Chandrasekar. 2013. "Actions Speak Louder Than Words: Analyzing Large-Scale Query Logs to Improve the Research Experience." *The Code4Lib Journal* no. 21 (July). http://journal.code4lib.org/articles/8693.

Durante, Kim, and Zheng Wang. 2012. "Creating an Actionable Assessment Framework for Discovery Services in Academic Libraries." *College & Undergraduate Libraries* 19, nos. 2–4: 215–28. doi:10.1080/10691316.2012.693358.

Ellero, Nadine P. 2013. "An Unexpected Discovery: One Library's Experience with Web-Scale Discovery Service (WSDS) Evaluation and Assessment." *Journal of Library Administration* 53, nos. 5–6: 323–43. doi:10.1080/01930826.2013.876824.

Fabbi, Jennifer L. 2009. "'Discovery' Focus as Impetus for Organizational Learning." *Information Technology & Libraries* 28, no. 4: 164–71.

Gallaway, Teri Oaks, and Mary Finnan Hines. 2012. "Competitive Usability and the Catalogue: A Process for Justification and Selection of a Next-Generation Catalogue or Web-Scale Discovery System." *Library Trends* 61, no. 1: 173–85.

Georgas, Helen. 2014. "Google vs. the Library (Part II): Student Search Patterns and Behaviors When Using Google and a Federated Search Tool." *Portal: Libraries and the Academy* 14, no. 4: 503–32. doi:10.1353/pla.2014.0034.

Hayman, Richard, and Erika E Smith. 2015. "Sustainable Decision Making for Emerging Educational Technologies in Libraries." *Reference Services Review* 43, no. 1: 7–18. doi:10.1108/RSR-08–2014–0037.

Hoeppner, Athena. 2012. "The Ins and Outs of Evaluating Web-Scale Discovery Services." *Computers in Libraries* 32, no. 3: 6–10, 38–40.

Howeard, David, and Constance Wiebrands. 2011. "Culture Shock: Librarians' Response to Web Scale Search." Paper presented at the ALIA Information Online Conference, Sydney, N.S.W. http://ro.ecu.edu.au/cgi/viewcontent.cgi?article=7208&context=ecuworks.

Jarrett, Kylie. 2012. "Findit@flinders: User Experiences of the Primo Discovery Search Solution." *Australian Academic & Research Libraries* 43, no. 4: 278–87.

Krug, Steve. 2006. *Don't Make Me Think: A Common Sense Approach to Web Usability.* 2nd ed. Berkeley, CA: New Riders.

———. 2010. *Rocket Surgery Made Easy: The Do-It-Yourself Guide to Finding and Fixing Usability Problems.* Berkeley, CA: New Riders.

Kulp, Christina, Cheryl McCain, and Laurie Scrivener. 2014. "Teaching Outside the Box: ARL Librarians' Integration of the 'One-Box' into Student Instruction." *College & Research Libraries* 75, no. 3: 298–308. doi:10.5860/cr112–430.

Lundrigan, Courtney, Kevin Manuel, and May Yan. 2015. "'Pretty Rad': Explorations in User Satisfaction with a Discovery Layer at Ryerson University." *College & Research Libraries* 76, no. 1: 43–62. doi:10.5860/cr1.76.1.43.

Mussell, Jessica, and Rosie Croft. 2013. "Discovery Layers and the Distance Student: Online Search Habits of Students." *Journal of Library & Information Services in Distance Learning* 7, nos. 1–2: 18–39. doi:10.1080/1533290X.2012.705561.

Nichols, Aaron, Amber Billey, Peter Spitzform, Alice Stokes, and Catherine Tran. 2014. "Kicking the Tires: A Usability Study of the Primo Discovery Tool." *Journal of Web Librarianship* 8, no. 2: 172–95. doi:10.1080/19322909.2014.903133.

Pattern, Dave. 2012. "Relevancy Rules." In *Self-Plagiarism Is Style.* May 6. www.daveyp.com/2012/05/06/relevancy-rules/.

Rose-Wiles, Lisa M., and Melissa A. Hofmann. 2013. "Still Desperately Seeking Citations: Undergraduate Research in the Age of Web-Scale Discovery." *Journal of Library Administration* 53, nos. 2–3: 147–66. doi:10.1080/01930826.2013.853493.

Seeber, Kevin Patrick. 2015. "Teaching 'Format as a Process' in an Era of Web-Scale Discovery." *Reference Services Review* 43, no. 1: 19–30. doi:10.1108/RSR-07–2014–0023.

Silton, Kate. 2014. "Assessment of Full-Text Linking in Summon: One Institution's Approach." *Journal of Electronic Resources Librarianship* 26, no. 3: 163–69. doi:10.1080/1941126X.2014.936767.

Somerville, Mary M. 2013. "Digital Age Discoverability: A Collaborative Organizational Approach." *Serials Review* 39, no. 4: 234–39. doi:10.1016/j.serrev.2013.10.006.

Thomsett-Scott, Beth, and Patricia E. Reese. 2012. "Academic Libraries and Discovery Tools: A Survey of the Literature." *College & Undergraduate Libraries* 19, nos. 2–4: 123–43. doi:10.1080/10691316.2012.697009.

York, Maurice C. 2005. "Calling the Scholars Home: Google Scholar as a Tool for Rediscovering the Academic Library." *Internet Reference Services Quarterly* 10, nos. 3/4: 117–33.

CHAPTER TWO

APPROACHING DISCOVERY AS PART OF A LIBRARY SERVICE PLATFORM

Lessons Learned

NATHAN HOSBURGH

Discovery systems such as Summon, EBSCO Discovery Service, Primo, and WorldCat Discovery Services have become part of academic libraries' standard toolbox. The Olin Library at Rollins College in Winter Park, Florida, became an early adopter of Serials Solutions Summon Service in 2009, enhancing access to print and electronic material. Although this has led to general improvements over the fractured searching of the traditional online catalog, database list, A–Z journal list, and digital repository, we recognized that the disparate systems hampered our ability to deliver a superior discovery experience and effectively provide other library services for our patrons.

Therefore, we did not begin by examining discovery tools, but new library systems. Our goal was to streamline data and resource management and enable further deconstruction of information silos that developed in the library. We previously used a SIRSI Integrated Library System for decades in addition to other systems that operated more or less in isolation from each other. Integration between them meant pushing and pulling data from one system to another, resulting in information lag and inconsistencies across systems. All of this impacted the discovery experience for end users.

While we investigated new library systems, it became apparent that we needed a revolutionary change versus an evolutionary change. We required a holistic system, one in which back-end processes seamlessly integrated into the front-end discovery layer. After the investigation process, we decided to replace our SIRSI integrated library system (ILS), Serials Solutions electronic resources management system (ERMS), and Summon discovery layer with Ex Libris Alma/Primo. This chapter will detail our motivations for change, investigation, selection process, preparation, and implementation of the Alma/Primo system as well as offer a framework for evaluating when a system architecture no longer meets current needs.

SYSTEMS BACKGROUND AND MOTIVATIONS FOR CHANGE

As Anita Cassidy points out, an information systems strategy must be coherent, consistent, and directional, offering positive changes of some kind rather than endorsing the status quo. Such a strategy should also be future-driven, focused on solving problems, and anticipating user needs.

"Through the planning process, the organization can proactively balance conflicting forces and manage the direction of Information Systems rather than continually building upon the current investment in a reactionary mode" (Cassidy, 2006).

As early as 2008, it became clear to Olin Library staff that something had to be done with systems in place at that time, particularly the SIRSI ILS. An outside firm, R2 Consulting, analyzed the selection-to-access workflows in the library and found the SIRSI system to be a significant impediment to the future growth of library services at Rollins (R2 Consulting, 2008). The library had run various iterations of the SIRSI system since 1995: Horizon, Unicorn, and finally Symphony. This progression in the ILS did not keep pace with the advancement of other library technologies, making it difficult to integrate this core system with other key components such as web-scale discovery, course reserves, digital collections, and the institutional repository. Most urgently, the physical server hardware that housed SIRSI had reached its end of life and began to exhibit early signs of impending failure. At the same time, SIRSI was running on a Solaris 9 Unix operating system (originally released in 2002), placing it into the extended support period of its life cycle. Therefore, the continuing support contract carried with it a surcharge.

When Rollins adopted Summon, it was the first hosted "web scale discovery" service to market and there were no real competitors. Summon served Rollins well over the years, offering more "Google-like" search capabilities across the library's various print and electronic resources—and beyond. This tool supplanted the SIRSI online public access catalog (OPAC), opening up discovery beyond what could be traditionally housed in the catalog. The library was reasonably satisfied with the discovery experience afforded by Summon and the discovery service, in and of itself, was not a driving force for change.

The library also utilized the Serials Solutions electronic resources management system (ERMS), which included a suite of services: 360 Resource Manager, 360 Link Resolver, and 360 Core A-Z Journal List. All of these pieces working in tandem with Summon created a tightly integrated set of tools for managing and providing access to print and e-journals, e-books, databases, and the underlying content, such as articles, book chapters, reference entries, and so on. Unfortunately, this high degree of integration among Serials Solutions components did not extend across all of our resources. We continued to run the SIRSI ILS, composed mostly of books and e-books that were not contained within Serials Solutions' knowledge base. Running two core but disparate library systems required intensive data transfer of MARC records that were added, deleted, or modified from SIRSI to Summon in order to keep our holdings synchronized. Acquisitions information was also tracked in both systems. This situation increased the potential for errors, inconsistencies, and information lag.

SIRSI and Serials Solutions formed the backbone of our library systems architecture, yet there were separate peripheral components that factored into the picture. In archives and special collections, we have used the open-source Archon software for archival finding aids—descriptive guides for archival print collections. For our digital special collections, we have relied on OCLC's CON-TENTdm software. Since 2008, we have also been using OCLC ILLiad, a proven application for handling interlibrary loan activities. In order to provide users with secure authentication and access to our licensed resources from outside the library's computer network, we have relied on OCLC's EZproxy web proxy server. One of the newest additions to our constellation of systems is the institutional repository, locally known as Rollins Scholarship Online (RSO), which is hosted on the Digital Commons Bepress platform. In addition to these library systems, there are also important campus systems such as the Banner enterprise resource planner (ERP) and Blackboard learning management system (LMS) which are critical to the educational mission of the college, but are not as closely tied to the library systems as we would like.

Working with a scattered information systems architecture is less than optimal, yet most academic libraries find themselves in a similar situation. Libraries have started with core components, such as the ILS, and added various software over the years to handle specific services such as interlibrary loan or specialized sets of material such as digital collections and institutional repositories. When considering discovery as an aspect of a complete library system, we should not approach it as if it were simply an "add on" like an addition to a home. If executed poorly, home additions look as though they have been slapped on—they are neither aesthetic nor functional. From a systems architecture perspective, the discovery piece is similar to a home addition. Whether it sits on top of or alongside the existing structure, it should be integrated seamlessly into a cohesive whole.

INVESTIGATING SYSTEMS AND DECISION-MAKING

Before I arrived at Rollins College in 2013, a "Next-Gen ILS Task Force" had been formed and was charged with investigating options for a new library system, including the possibility of a new discovery layer. This initial charge included certain prominent factors:

- The new system should have a lower annual cost than the total existing expenses associated with all current systems.
- Focus on the overall ease of use and effectiveness for the end user, particularly undergraduates.
- Enable more efficient staff time through the reduction of duplicate data entry.
- Enable more effective integration with other campus-wide applications such as Banner and Blackboard.

The current SIRSI system was deemed "increasingly outmoded" and other library systems were offered up as options, although this was by no means an exhaustive list. The original task force also solicited input from Olin Library staff in fall 2012 for specifications for a new library system. While this type of input is a good idea, in this case, it resulted in general statements such as "less labor-intensive," "more intuitive," and "less complicated and clunky" and also combined specifications for both an ILS and discovery into one list which was confounding to some degree.

Early in 2014, I was asked to revive the search for a new library system and cochaired the task force along with Jonathan Harwell, the head of collections and systems. As discovery and systems librarian, I began intensive research on library service platforms on the market at that time. There were a number of useful publications that served as guideposts in the investigation (Ken Chad Consulting 2012; Breeding 2013; helibtech 2015), but the most important source of information was Carl Grant's 2012 article in *Information Standards Quarterly* entitled "The Future of Library Systems: Library Services Platforms" (Grant 2012). Grant observes that many libraries are critically examining the effectiveness of their ILS, which has long been a core component driving many of the services provided by libraries. Next-generation library systems have come to be known collectively as "library services platforms," conveying that the new systems extend beyond the traditional scope of the ILS (largely designed to manage print collections), integrating a variety of workflows necessary for managing both print and digital items. While some vendors have taken an evolutionary approach to developing next-generation systems, effectively building on existing products, others have taken a more revolutionary approach by designing completely new products from the ground up.

Rollins College's current ILS vendor, SIRSI, released "BLUEcloud," a cloud-based library services platform around the same time the library began its investigation in earnest again. Although BLUEcloud might have been a natural option in the progression of SIRSI products, it would not have enabled us to save money or meet our other goals. Built on the existing SIRSI architecture and structured around the traditional catalog, it did not appear to offer the e-resource management and discovery capabilities inherent in other key systems, such as Serials Solutions Summon and 360 Suite. Although BLUEcloud was touted as a cloud-based, Software-as-a-Service (SaaS), this was not a major selling point for us. We wanted a cloud-based service, but one that was proven among academic libraries and would expand our capabilities beyond those of the traditional catalog and ILS.

After reading Grant's article, it became apparent that in order to achieve the type of integration and consolidation of disparate systems that we desired, a fundamental change was needed. It did not make sense to expend the time and effort of migrating to a new library services platform unless that single platform could take the place of a collection of software and services we were paying for and managing separately. There were a few systems at the time that had the potential to take us where we wanted to go: OCLC WorldShare, Ex Libris Alma, and ProQuest Intota. As current Serials Solutions/ProQuest customers, Intota would have been a strong contender, but because Intota was still being developed, we could not consider it as a viable option. Aging physical hardware and software associated with the SIRSI system meant that we had to take action sooner rather than later.

Since we were able to narrow potential choices down to two systems early on, this streamlined the selection process. When we brought the two vendors in for product demos and compared their relative strengths, weaknesses, features, and functionality, it was easier to identify the points at which they differed most. This kind of investigation can be very time-consuming, but we had the advantage of being more nimble than many other institutions. We are a small private institution with a single campus and single library serving that campus. There is no larger governing body overseeing the activities of the college, nor were we pursuing the selection of a new library system as part of a consortial effort.

CHOOSING THE LIBRARY SERVICES PLATFORM AND DISCOVERY LAYER

Rollins asked both vendors to come to campus for half-day demonstrations of their respective products, including discovery: OCLC presented WorldShare and their new discovery layer, WorldShare Discovery Services (WDS), while Ex Libris presented Alma and their discovery layer, Primo. At this stage of the process, we were leaning towards OCLC WorldShare because we were already using a few of their products. WorldShare had also been adopted by hundreds of academic institutions of various sizes and had been on the market for a couple of years. We heard good things about the system from peer institutions across the region and believed that, if it satisfied their needs, it would satisfy ours as well. Ex Libris was more of an unknown for us. We had never used any Ex Libris systems previously and they did not have as great a market share with Alma as OCLC had with WorldShare. Because OCLC was more forthcoming with their pricing initially, we suspected that fewer institutions chose Ex Libris because they were more expensive. However, we were aware of a number of institutions that had selected Alma and were satisfied, including the Orbis-Cascade Alliance in the northwest United States. The Ex Libris legacy ILS systems were also well regarded as was their discovery layer, Primo.

During the OCLC WorldShare demonstration, we found its greatest strength was the cataloging component due to the seamless integration with WorldCat. When we saw a presentation of the ERM, known as License Manager, we were unconvinced that it could take the place of our Serials Solutions ERM. Over the years, we had come to appreciate the best-in-breed, robust functionality included in the ERM and relied on it heavily for managing our subscriptions and for feeding content into Summon for discovery. The lack of ERM functionality in WorldShare meant that we would likely have to keep Serials Solutions, undermining the purpose of such a systems migration.

The WorldShare Discovery Services (WDS) interface was also a disappointment. Part of this was due to the user interface and the inadequacy of certain search mechanisms such as robust faceting and advanced searching. The overwhelming preponderance of books within search results was also a serious concern. At Rollins, our users expect to discover the most relevant results, not limited to books and including a healthy mixture of articles, book chapters, and other non-monographic material. However, across various searches we saw similar results—a higher proportion of monographic content—on our beta WDS site as well as with other institutions running WDS in a production environment. When we gathered feedback from our librarians, everyone was unanimously unimpressed.

We were aware that OCLC and EBSCO formed a partnership and that EBSCO Discovery Service (EDS) was a front-end option when using World-Share. Although we were dismayed with WDS, we didn't want to completely give up on WorldShare, so we brought in EBSCO for a separate demo of EDS. EBSCO's product was an improvement over WDS, but it would have cost us as much as we were paying for Summon and would have meant another disparate system outside of the single library services platform, which we hoped would be all-encompassing.

Although cost was a concern for us, cost savings was not our ultimate goal, nor were we intent on settling for the least expensive product. The initial quote for Alma was much higher than WorldShare, therefore some work had to be done at the negotiation table in order to arrive at a bundled price that would allow Alma/Primo to compete with Worldshare as a viable option. If Ex Libris could not bring their price down into the realm of OCLC's price, we made it clear that they would no longer be under consideration. Although ExLibris appeared to offer a more robust system, the price of WorldShare was very attractive. The bundled price for WorldShare included OCLC services for cataloging and interlibrary loan, which we were paying for separately at that time. OCLC supplied us with a worksheet designed to compare the collective systems in our library to WorldShare over the next three years. By adapting this worksheet and applying it to the ExLibris system, we were able to compare each system to current services and compare each potential system with each other. This was extremely helpful in that we could see which services could be replaced by functionality in the new system and how that actually affected the bottom line in terms of cost. It also enabled us to differentiate between upfront costs during the first year associated with the migration and continuing costs in future years.

Once we negotiated an acceptable price for Alma/Primo, the task force compared the two systems across a range of features and functionality based on our experience with the products during the demos and feedback from other staff within the library. Although there were many issues involved, discovery turned out to be the deciding factor: Primo was very similar to Summon while WorldShare Discovery Services was unacceptable and EBSCO Discovery Services would have meant paying separately for discovery and potentially running into the problem of a cumbersome "addition" to an otherwise holistic system. Conversely, Alma and Primo were complementary parts of a system designed with end-to-end workflows in mind from acquisitions to discovery. No system is ever perfect, but Alma/Primo turned out to be the clear choice and was endorsed by everyone on the task force.

SUMMON AND PRIMO: DISCOVERY FROM A SYSTEMS PERSPECTIVE

It is beyond the scope of this chapter to perform a full-scale usability study of both Summon and Primo, but it is possible to outline some general differences between the two products from a systems perspective and how this will likely impact discovery and total system functionality going forward.

Activating Resources

By activating collections in the Serials Solutions ERM, they can be seamlessly turned on with checkboxes in Summon, 360 link, and the A–Z Journal List. The Summon index lives behind the scenes, yet the content is visible at the publisher, database, and journal title level within the ERMS.

With Primo discovery, the process is more complicated. Alma functions as both the ILS and the ERMS, including MARC records for print and electronic items and all the vendor/publisher, database, and title-level information for individual e-book and e-journal titles. Purchased or licensed databases, packages, and titles must be activated locally in Alma. Primo Central sits between Alma and Primo and functions as the ExLibris knowledge base. It is necessary to take a separate step in the Primo Central activation wizard to turn on resources which have already been activated locally in Alma.

Coverage

The Summon index appears to be more comprehensive than Primo Central in terms of the sheer number of products and collections that Rollins College would be interested in enabling. During the process of activating collections in Primo Central, it was evident that there are often more collections available for activation for a given publisher in Summon than there are in Primo Central. For instance, with the publisher Adam Matthew Digital, there are 67 collections to choose from in Summon, while there are only 17 in Primo Central. While ExLibris certainly continues to index collections from various publishers, they do not appear to have the breadth of content that Serials Solutions has in their knowledge base.

Data Transfer

Up to this point, we had used the SIRSI ILS and Summon, which meant a lag between the time MARC records were created in SIRSI and when those records were discoverable in Summon. This could take anywhere from a few days to a week. The synchronizing of data between the Serials Solutions ERMS and Summon was much better; activations and other changes were reflected the following day.

With Alma/Primo, the publication of records from Alma to Primo is set up as a daily automated job. E-resources that are activated in Alma are published to Primo Central once a week. Therefore, we have gained efficiency with MARC records published to discovery while we have lost efficiency with e-resources published to discovery.

CONCLUSION

Rollins College chose Alma/Primo in June 2014 and formally began the implementation process in January 2015 with a "go-live" date of June 1, 2015. After investigating various library services platforms and discovery layers, we are confident that we chose a system that will enable robust metadata management, streamlined workflows, and a rich, integrated discovery experience. There will certainly be tradeoffs between the best of what our previous systems had to offer and what Alma/Primo offer our library staff and end users, but the overall environment should offer an improved platform that will serve our needs for years to come. Since we will continue to have access to Summon for some time after implementing Primo, we will also find ourselves in the fortuitous situation of being able to compare two fully functional web-scale discovery systems side-by-side (although we will hide Summon from public view). Usability testing will likely provide interesting insights as to the relative strengths and weaknesses of each discovery platform and lend itself to future publication as a separate study.

References

Breeding, M. 2013. "Automation Marketplace 2013: The Rush to Innovate." *The Digital Shift*, April 2. www.thedigitalshift.com/2013/04/ils/automation-marketplace-2013-the-rush -to-innovate/.

Cassidy, A. 2006. *A Practical Guide to Information Systems Strategic Planning.* 2nd ed. Boca Raton, FL: Auerbach.

Grant, C. 2012. "The Future of Library Systems: Library Services Platforms." *Information Standards Quarterly,* 24, no. 4: 4–15. http://doi.org/10.3789/isqv24n4.2012.02.

helibtech. 2015. "Library Services Platforms (LSPs)—The Next Generation of Library Systems." http://helibtech.com/Next+Generation.

Ken Chad Consulting. 2012. "Specification for a Unified (Next Generation) Library Resource Management System." *LibTechRFP,* July: 1–20. https://libtechrfp.wikispaces.com/ Unified+library+resource+management+specification.

R2 Consulting. 2008. *Rollins College Library Workflow Analysis.* www.rollins.edu/library/docs/ planning/R2RollinsWorkflowReportFinal.pdf.

⌘ APPENDIX

FRAMEWORK FOR EVALUATING A SYSTEM ARCHITECTURE

Although it is possible to create a full-blown request for proposal to outline detailed requirements for a library system (Ken Chad Consulting, 2012), it may not be necessary unless required to do so. In any case, it is helpful for libraries to lay out a high-level framework for evaluating a current library system architecture. The relative importance of each of these considerations will vary from one institution to another, but should be generalizable across academic libraries since we deal with very similar activities and processes within the library and with the larger institution. This framework was not formerly in place when Rollins began investigating new library systems, yet the library did consider some of these elements and, in hindsight, these have been identified as important considerations that should aid such an endeavor. The table draws from Anita Cassidy's *A Practical Guide to Information Systems Strategic Planning* and has been expanded and adapted specifically for libraries. It is designed to assist stakeholders in determining how a potential library information system fits their needs and goals in terms of costs, processes, integrations, resources, technology, and overall strategic planning.

COSTS

- ▸ What are the costs of all your current library systems: base costs, hardware, subscription, services/support, necessary peripherals?
- ▸ Are your costs increasing and, if so, by how much? Is the rate of increase sustainable?
- ▸ How does LIS (library information systems) spending compare to similar libraries? What percentage of the total library budget is devoted to LIS?

- ▸ How can we decrease our spending on LIS or spend our money more wisely? Can we reduce the effort and money required throughout the life cycle of systems?
- ▸ Can costs be bundled?
- ▸ What return on investment/value are we obtaining from the investments in LIS?

PROCESSES

- ▸ Do the LIS and associated processes help us deliver services to our users in the most efficient and effective manner?

- ▸ Is the LIS a bottleneck to improvement and growth? Is old software hampering our ability to implement new technology?
- ▸ Is there a current lack of integration between systems?

INTEGRATIONS

- ▸ EDI (electronic data interchange)—Are we able to import/export invoices and orders between our LIS and third parties?
- ▸ Is the LIS able to interface with the college financial system/bursar?

- ▸ Do our proxies and link resolvers work seamlessly to deliver content to our end users?
- ▸ Is it possible to load patron data from the SIS (student information system) into the LIS?

INTEGRATIONS (continued)

▸ Are we able to synchronize holdings between our LIS, OCLC, Google Scholar, and other third-party discovery systems?

▸ Are we able to take advantage of the OAI (Open Archives Initiative) protocol for harvesting data from our institutional repository, digital collections, and so on?

▸ PDA (patron-driven acquisitions)—Is our current system able to effectively handle the complexity and unique workflow of PDA?

RESOURCES

▸ How much time do our IT/systems staff devote towards working on each component of our system? (Take into account both those who work in the library and IT staff working outside the library.)

▸ How does the size of our IT/systems staff compare with other libraries or institutions of similar size?

▸ Do we have the internal skills, time, and so on to take the LIS environment where it needs to be? How much can we do with internal resources and how much should we rely on external resources?

▸ How important is it to have local control over the library system? Often, local control means more physical technology infrastructure, more manpower, and more maintenance. Outsourcing usually means less control; may mean less stable

connections depending on the Internet; but you also now have a dedicated team of experts working on the other side; the vendor is now doing many of the tasks that campus IT/systems administrators would normally be doing.

▸ How important is accessibility without regard to geographic location? Locally controlled systems have traditionally been client-based and are not web-accessible because they are housed on a local network. Hosted/cloud solutions are web-accessible without installing clients and the applications are accessible from virtually anywhere in the world.

TECHNOLOGY

▸ What are the library technology trends over the past 5–10 years and how do those trends affect us?

▸ Open source vs. commercial systems—which is the better option?

▸ Can improved technology reduce operational costs?
  - Simplification
  - Standardization
  - Automation
  - Integration
  - Leveraging
  - Waste reduction

STRATEGIC PLANNING

▸ How does our library system impact student success and retention?

▸ How should the mission of the library/college drive the LIS strategy going forward?

▸ How do changes in library services, research habits, physical space, and so on drive our LIS decision making?

▸ What are end users telling us/demanding of us? What has usability testing shown us?

▸ Is the current system enabling us to extract/compile the information we need for reporting purposes and decision making?

▸ Do our discovery systems engender a sense of trust among our users? Libraries as organizations are based around relationships with our users. Relationships are usually formed around trust. If users cannot trust our discovery systems, they will lose trust in the library as the locus of information discovery and knowledge creation.

▸ Will our current LIS enable us to meet our future goals/challenges?

▸ How does our choice of LIS impact our relationships to other libraries and organizations?

CHAPTER THREE

WHEN YOU RENT
YOUR FRONT DOOR
A Midsize Library's Experiences
Relying on Discovery Vendors

STEPHEN BOLLINGER AND KATE SILTON

The F.D. Bluford Library at North Carolina Agricultural and Technical State University (NCAT) serves an enrollment of 10,000 students and supporting faculty and staff, with an emphasis on supporting faculty research and multiple science, technology, engineering, and mathematics (STEM) PhD granting and related graduate, undergraduate, and distance learning degree programs. Due primarily to the university's STEM focus, the library has historically embraced licensing remote database content and currently expends over 90 percent of its collections budget on electronic resources. Despite the library's enthusiastic embrace of electronic content, achieving robust usage, thereby justifying the expense of licensing these databases, has always been a struggle. In simplifying the user experience to find and use electronic resources, discovery layers appear to be one powerful solution to this problem.

Discovery layers, as the term itself suggests, depend upon several other strata of library-specific technology, which will be referred to as the "technology stack." This stack includes the library's integrated library system (ILS), electronic resources management system, knowledge base, link resolver, institutional repository, and possibly other data sources or custom-developed library systems. While discovery vendors may characterize their products as being able to serve any number of permutations in a given library's technology stack, Bluford Library has discovered through its implementations that the composition and configuration of the stack can have major implications for the efficacy of discovery.

Bluford Library is now on its fourth generation of discovery, the first two being now vendor-discontinued metasearch products, followed by ProQuest's Summon and OCLC's WorldCat Discovery (WCD). While Summon was well received by users and embraced by the library, it first exposed problems in the technology stack. One difficulty arose with interoperability between ProQuest's Summon and EBSCO's LinkSource link resolver product. While anecdotal evidence suggested that transitioning to ProQuest's 360 Link OpenURL resolver might address this issue, existing contracts and the vendor's pricing precluded that option.

However, implementing WCD by itself, atop the library's existing technology stack, would not solve the lingering multi-vendor interoperability complications. Instead, the library's transition to WCD prefaced a transition to OCLC's World-Share Management System (WMS) as its ILS, representing the first time that the technology stack, and the promise of an optimal discovery user experience, was the primary driver for Bluford Library's purchasing decisions.

REALITIES OF DISCOVERY IN A MIDSIZE LIBRARY

Bluford Library can be characterized as a midsize academic library, measured by the size of its staff and the relative size of the institution it serves, with an outsized commitment to licensed remote database content. During the library's two discovery platform selection processes, vendors were consistently incredulous about the high number of e-resource subscriptions the library reported needing to integrate. At a library of Bluford's size, however, it is incredibly difficult to sustain internal software development because recruiting and especially retaining even a lone skilled developer is not a feasible commitment. The university's Information Technology Services (ITS) supports the library in several vital areas but is unable to take on specialized development for a single academic unit such as the library. And although a STEM-focused institution like NCAT has a surfeit of talented students, faculty, and staff, they are not a stable or reliable foundation for the development of fundamental library systems.

This environment leaves a library like Bluford in terms of size and budget essentially entirely dependent on vendors to provide effective interoperability between their own and their competitors' products and ecosystems, since local library software development talent often focused on facilitating data exchange or other limited projects. All of the vendors appear to promise interoperability, but verifying actual production instances of libraries using the same technology stack quickly becomes difficult.

The uniqueness of a library's technology stack especially complicates the evaluation and selection of discovery products, because the sheer number of libraries and the permutations of their individual license subscriptions and technology stacks make it impossible to determine how well they will work in one library's context until only after implementation. Resources such as Marshall Breeding's index of integrated library systems and discovery platforms in libraries (www.librarytechnology.org) often do not reveal the entirety of each library's relevant technology stack, and the discovery vendors themselves are often only dimly aware of the exact composition of their clients' stacks.

THE USE OF PERSONAS TO SELECT DISCOVERY PRODUCTS AND EVALUATE EFFECTIVENESS

When Bluford Library was in the process of selecting its first discovery layer product, the technology stack was not a consideration. Instead, primarily due to the failure of the incumbent metasearch product (360 Search, which was discontinued by the vendor, but also plagued by slow operation and a challenging user interface), the primary lens for evaluation was user-centered, borrowing from Persona-Based Heuristic Evaluation as employed in usability evaluation (Krug 2006). This was because the primary source of complaints about metasearch originated from faculty and graduate students, despite the fact that the library considered it to be a tool best suited for novice searchers and early undergraduates with only basic research needs. In order to address the needs of different user groups, searcher personas, essentially abstracted stereotypical searchers, were created and used to identify information needs and searching tasks (see table 3.1). These personas were then used to compare discovery products implemented at libraries likely to have similar, STEM-focused licensed database content, weighted towards those that could be identified as having the same ILS as Bluford Library.

Originally used by the library's Technology Committee, the personas were guides for each committee member to create a set of query terms and search strings to represent the breadth of subjects represented and varying expertise for each persona's searchers. Search terms and phrases such as "portland cement concrete" or "north carolina history" were then executed in searches of examples of each of the contending discovery products, with the results compared to what the same searches would yield from the appropriate individual database. These personas outlived the product selection process because of their utility in comparing what library subject experts would expect to see in search results in the discovery product versus native remote licensed database interfaces. They helped expose the weaknesses in Bluford Library's technology stack once Summon was implemented, when either expected results failed to link to the proper resource or did not appear.

TABLE 3-1

Personas used in evaluating discovery product effectiveness

Domain Expertise	Persona	Information Needs/Searching Tasks
Expert	‣ Faculty Subject Expert ‣ Advanced Graduate Student	‣ New Items in Discipline ‣ Known Item (Citation) Search ‣ Literature Review ‣ Advanced Research Topics
	‣ Faculty Exploring New, Cross-Discipline Topics	‣ Canonical/Foundational Articles ‣ Literature Review
Novice	‣ New Graduate Student ‣ Undergraduate Researcher	‣ Subject/Discipline Citation ‣ Research Topic Exploration
	‣ Undergraduate Student	‣ Known Item (Course Reserve) Search ‣ Subject/Topic Search for Research Paper ‣ "I'm looking for a book/article on. . . ."

THE SUMMON ERA

Bluford Library implemented Summon in August and September 2011. Due to the ignominious end of Bluford's previous licensed federated search product, the decision was made to brand Summon as "Aggie GOLD Search," in case another discovery vendor change became necessary. This decision proved to be a wise one, as Bluford would change vendors three years later, but continue using the same moniker. The chief work of implementation fell into two main categories: integrating bibliographic data from Millennium into Summon and populating the Serials Solutions knowledge base. (Note: Summon was developed by Serials Solutions, a company later acquired by ProQuest. When Bluford Library initially licensed Summon, Serials Solutions was already owned by ProQuest but still had its own administrative and support sites.)

In order to provide access through Summon to the library's vast collection of e-resources, the library's database, e-journal, and e-book holdings had to be entered into Serials Solutions' Client Center. This process was complicated by the fact that the library used a different vendor, EBSCO, for its A to Z journals list and link resolver. In addition to activating all of these resources, they had to be checked against EBSCO's knowledge base. In some cases, title counts, dates of coverage, and other information did not match up in both knowledge bases. For these resources, the holdings data had to be massaged so that links in Summon would resolve properly. This process was lengthy and was not fully completed when Aggie GOLD Search went live.

While populating the Serials Solutions knowledge base and checking it against EBSCO's knowledge base was a one-time project, ongoing workflows were affected as well. All major e-resources workflows, such as adding a new resource or canceling a resource, had to be updated. Any action required updating information in three places: the library's electronic resources management system, EBSCO A to Z's administrative site, and the Serials Solutions Client Center.

After the initial setup, Aggie GOLD Search was released into production at the beginning of the 2011–2012 academic year. The implementation team immediately received a lot of feedback from library staff regarding the effectiveness of the tool. There were many reports of Summon not reliably linking users with the full text of articles and e-books. This feedback demonstrated the need for an assessment of the tool to determine the causes of link failure. This initial look at Aggie GOLD Search's effectiveness led to an ongoing assessment project.

The first assessment revealed that only 61 percent of full-text links actually led to the full text of an item. It also demonstrated that linking problems tended to occur with particular resource types (chiefly newspaper articles and book chapters) and with particular vendors. In late 2011, Serials Solutions implemented index-enhanced direct linking in Summon, which allowed access to the full text of resources without using the link resolver. This new feature markedly improved the ability of Summon to deliver full text to users. However, not all content providers participated in this program, so it was only a partial solution to link failure. Even at the end of Bluford Library's contract with Summon in August 2014, Aggie GOLD Search was still plagued with ineffective links to newspaper articles. Much of this failure could be attributed to the technology stack problem; by using two different vendors' knowledge bases, there were many instances where the metadata just did not match up to create a resolvable link.

The staff at Bluford Library had great hopes that moving toward a one-vendor environment would resolve some of these woes. OCLC's WorldShare Management System, combined with their WorldCat Discovery (WCD) product, looked like a promising solution to the problems caused by dealing with multiple vendors. Aside from the linking problems described above, the library was quite pleased with Summon, but ultimately decided to switch discovery platforms for the greater good of streamlining the work and providing better access to its significant investment in electronic resources.

THE WORLDCAT DISCOVERY ERA

In August 2014 the library began the transition from Summon to WorldCat Discovery. Due to administrative issues, there was a short period of time between the beginning of the implementation period for WCD and the end of Bluford's contract for Summon. Therefore, the implementation team had to move quickly to deliver a usable discovery experience.

The early stages of implementation revealed that the dream of streamlining workflows might have been overly optimistic. WCD has its own configuration module separate from WMS. This module was used to choose what databases would be searchable in WCD, to configure the accompanying link resolver, and other tasks. Actual full-text content, however, is made accessible using the WorldCat knowledge base, which is managed within WMS. While the move to OCLC's product reduced the duplicate processes in Bluford's old workflows, it still required the use of multiple administrative sites with multiple log-ins. Rather than eliminating the technology stack, the composition of the stack merely changed.

The implementation team used WCD's configuration to decide what resources would be searchable within the new Aggie GOLD Search. WCD uses a combination of a central index and federated searching. This was a profound change from Summon, which uses a central index only. The team's initial plan was to have the default search include as many databases as possible to mimic Summon's coverage. Unfortunately, early testing revealed that searching a large number of databases via federated search significantly increased response time. As a result, the library went live using the WorldCat.org database, EBSCO's Academic Search Complete, and ProQuest Central as default databases.

Another important decision involved whether WCD should search libraries worldwide or NCAT's holdings only. OCLC strongly encourages libraries to make libraries worldwide the default search; they stress that not selecting this option could unnecessarily limit users' access to licensed electronic resources, treated as global rather than local resources by WCD, in search results. While local holdings would be given a higher ranking than resources at other institutions, the implementation team was concerned that this option might lead to a spike in interlibrary loan requests. Despite this concern, Bluford ultimately went live with libraries worldwide as the default option. To date, interlibrary loan requests have not increased noticeably.

Another large piece of the implementation process was entering the library's holdings into the WorldCat knowledge base. This process was lengthy and incomplete when WCD went live. While full-text databases and standard packages were added immediately, the library's large quantity of customized journal packages and individual e-journal subscriptions took a long time to enter. Multiple methods were used to accomplish this goal, including PubGet feeds and manual data entry.

The third significant piece of the implementation process was setting up EZproxy to enable off-campus access. Bluford Library previously used Innovative

Interfaces' Web Access Management for this purpose and opted to use OCLC's hosted EZproxy service moving forward. While OCLC handled most of the EZproxy implementation, the process required a lot of communication between the library and OCLC in order to ensure that everything was accessible from off campus. Also, the IP address of the new proxy server had to be updated with every single content provider. Finally, the library, OCLC, and NCAT's Information Technology Services worked together so that users could authenticate using their campus Active Directory domain credentials.

The implementation team still plans to make more changes to its instance of WCD. In collaboration with public services staff, final decisions need to be made regarding databases included in the default search and regarding the creation of subject groups. As the library's implementation of WMS matures, other changes will likely be required as WCD becomes the primary access point for the library's print holdings as well as its electronic resources. This will be a major transition for the library, as discovery has always been considered only as a gateway to e-resources and databases rather than comprehensive of all library holdings, including print.

Additionally, while the library's technology stack has become intra-vendor rather than inter-vendor, OCLC's Connexion, CONTENTdm, EZproxy, ILLiad, and WorldCat Local all long predate the vision of a unified, seamlessly integrated technology stack that WMS represents. In this scenario, it is still incumbent upon a vendor to resolve interoperability difficulties between disparate systems. That seems more achievable with a single vendor, however, than getting the current field of vendors to facilitate seamless interoperability between any of their products with those of their competitors in any given library's technology stack.

CONCLUSION

The technology stack is integral to the success of library discovery, and therefore often the library itself, regardless of the institution and its resources. However, the shape, size, and impact of the technology stack varies widely from library to library. Other factors, such as the number and types of electronic resources, preexisting vendor contracts, and the availability of in-house developers, affect the composition of the stack. Bluford Library committed to tackling this issue head-on by examining past versions of its stack and resolving to move toward a one-vendor solution. Reducing the number of vendors in the equation can and does eliminate duplicate processes and cut down on linking errors. However, vendors that offer a wide range of products and services come with technology stacks of their own. Even single-vendor stacks contain their own legacy systems, developed separately prior to any notion of integration, which threaten the promise of tightly integrated, smoothly functioning solutions. In the case of midsize and smaller libraries, the vendors appear to be able to handle technology stack integration better than libraries could internally support across multiple vendors.

Small and midsize libraries would also be well served by communicating with peer institutions that have similarly composed technology stacks. However, there is currently no resource available to help these libraries find each other. The creation of a site similar to Breeding's index, that more comprehensively details libraries' technology stacks, could be helpful. Another collaborative solution might be the creation of best practices for navigating technology stack problems.

Ultimately, the technology stack issue is a usability issue. While the problems caused by an unwieldy technology stack can make work unpleasant for library staff, the negative impact on users is far greater. The use of personas to evaluate the tool can inform user-driven priorities for back-end technology stack work. This type of evaluation, combined with a robust collaborative relationship between operational front-line and technology back-end library staff, is essential to the successful deployment of a discovery tool in any library.

Reference

Krug, Steve. 2006. *Don't Make Me Think!: A Common Sense Approach to Web Usability*. Berkeley: New Riders.

CHAPTER FOUR

EXPLORING DISCOVERY AT ROSENBERG LIBRARY

What Happens when a Library, a Museum, and an Archive Get Together to Share a Single Discovery Tool?

T. LOUISE M. KIDDER

WHAT WE ARE

The Rosenberg Library in Galveston, Texas, offers a variety of services and collections to the public. In this, Galveston's public library is really no different from any other public library. What makes the Rosenberg Library—and what it needs from discovery services—unique is its inclusion of two departments that maintain large noncirculating special collections: the Rosenberg Library Museum and the Galveston and Texas History Center.

The current Rosenberg Library building first opened its doors in 1904, thanks mainly to the generous support of the estate of Swiss immigrant Henry Rosenberg. The library was originally established as the Galveston Merchantile Library in 1871, making it the oldest continually operating public library in Texas. The Galveston and Texas History Center is the descendent of the Galveston Historical Society (also founded in 1871), and the Rosenberg Library gained official ownership of its archives in 1931. The library and its associated museum and archives departments have weathered almost a century and a half of economic, political, and meteorological storms.

The library's circulating collections are fairly typical of any public library of its size. Patrons can borrow items like books, videos, and music for their personal informational or entertainment needs. Circulating collections include items for all age groups and interests. A Redbox-like "family media box" includes DVD movies with its own browsing/reservation console; these media box items can also be found via the traditional catalog. The library also offers a variety of digital resources that patrons can access online or through mobile device apps (www .rosenberg-library.org). Patrons typically search for items either by browsing the shelves, asking staff at reference desks for help, or using the online public access catalog (OPAC). The library recently upgraded its OPAC from the basic integrated library system (ILS) patron-side interface to a more customizable platform in hopes of providing a more user-friendly, technologically advanced experience to online library users. Library staff encourage patrons to use the new OPAC and will help patrons figure out how to use it to search for whatever they're looking for. As for those digital resources, many of the e-books and e-media can be accessed right alongside their physical counterparts in the catalog. The public services librarians make extra efforts to inform and educate patrons about their existence and usage.

The Rosenberg Library Museum collections include over 7,200 objects of various types from around the world: paintings, jewelry, pottery, articles of clothing, even a piece of petrified hardtack. Some items are on permanent display, but most items are kept in specialized storage and are only occasionally displayed in free, public exhibits. A museum's raison d'être is often rather different from a public library's, being generally driven by curatorial and conservation duties such as preservation and display. This difference in focus also makes typical museum catalog records rather different from typical library catalog records; information such as physical description or provenance must take center stage here. That said, there are certain segments of metadata that are easily translatable across catalog types, such as title or author/creator—which are coincidentally some of the most commonly pursued search terms in information retrieval/discovery tools.

Access to the actual museum items is more limited, but that doesn't mean that they're secret or completely inaccessible. The public can learn about museum collections and view photos of items through the museum's own version of an OPAC, created using PastPerfect software. The museum began using Past-Perfect collections management software to catalog museum objects in 2006. Prior to this implementation, curators had been using simple Microsoft Excel spreadsheets. They upgraded their software in order to allow access to the entire catalog online in 2013 (www.rosenberg-library-museum.org). Museum staff are contacted a few times per month by patrons who wish to view particularly interesting objects that they discovered via the museum's online catalog. However, this PastPerfect catalog is somewhat "hidden" from typical library patrons, residing as it currently does several link-clicks away from the main Rosenberg

Library web page. Museum staff must often direct patrons to the museum's OPAC to learn more about specific items rather than the other way around. It is a useful information retrieval tool—especially for long-distance researchers or other museums that are interested in potential loan items—but is rarely used as a tool of *discovery*.

What these three types of organizations share is an attention to serving, educating, and—yes—entertaining the public. The Rosenberg Library's mission statement encompasses its library, museum, and archives personalities:

> The Rosenberg Library represents Galveston's past, present, and future, a unique institution serving as the principal repository of Galveston's historical heritage and providing technological and traditional services, all as a continuing source for the community, its children and its children's children.

The Galveston and Texas History Center (GTHC) also includes several collections at various levels of accessibility. Many of the History Center items are essentially reference books as far as library patrons are concerned, available to anyone who visits the library to use them in person. These items are already part of the library's overall catalog, appearing right alongside circulating and traditional reference collections in the OPAC (albeit with Library of Congress call numbers rather than Dewey and a "GTHC" location designation). This arrangement is not terribly unusual among public libraries that house local history or specialized research collections. Unfortunately, the GTHC collections are something like an iceberg—what patrons can see of them in the normal library catalog belies the huge amount of material locked away in the archival vault. This includes material like oral history interviews, business and family papers of locally significant individuals, cemetery records, and even Galveston-themed sheet music. The History Center keeps about 3,000 linear feet of manuscripts, about 100,000 photographs, and several thousand maps. Up until recently, the holdings for these materials could only be accessed using traditional finding aids or via the GTHC website indexes for patrons in-the-know (www.gthcenter .org). Again, all of this information is several link-clicks away from the main library website—and said indexes are unfortunately not keyword-searchable, which is sure to stymie potential users who have learned to rely heavily on the quick and casual "just Google it" method of searching for information. With the GTHC's recent acquisition of CuadraSTAR archives cataloging software, access points for the holdings for these materials are due to change for the better in the very near future.

This meshing of public library, historical archives, and eclectic museum makes the discovery service requirements for the Rosenberg Library unique. Each part of the library has its own set of typical patrons with varying informational needs and varying habits as to how they typically access information about library collections. At the same time, one of the points of a discovery service is, well, *discovery*. A patron searching for local history books in the main OPAC might also be interested in some of the items on display in the museum or available for retrieval in the archives, but unless they already know those things exist how can they be expected to even have the first clue as to how to find information about them? That's why the library decided to attempt to integrate all materials, regardless of collection/department/access method, into a single patron-side discovery tool.

The library had to figure out the best way to integrate these collections while still making it clear to patrons that some of these newly discoverable items are not part of the usual circulating collections in the main library. After all, it would never do to give the impression that a piece of petrified hardtack is just as accessible and borrowable as a book on maritime history, or that an actual painting by local artist Boyer Gonzales is just as accessible and borrowable as a book *about* Boyer Gonzales. Thus the question: how best to update the library's OPAC, integrate nontraditional items for the sake of searchability, and accurately but succinctly indicate accessibility?

WHAT WE DID

The Rosenberg Library launched its SirsiDynix Enterprise OPAC to the public in April 2014 (figure 4.1). Library staff worked closely with the vendor's technical support team over the course of several months to produce a semi-customized interface that they deemed would best serve the library's core patron base. The library had decided to upgrade to Enterprise from Horizon Information Portal (HIP). Why? Well, first and foremost, patron usability. Enterprise offered several usability-enhancing features that library staff hoped would make the online catalog easier for patrons to figure out without the assistance of a librarian or the frustrating experience of being entirely unable to find any wanted information when library staff were unavailable for assistance. For example, misspelled keyword searches either bring up unwanted search results or no results at all in HIP; Enterprise includes a "smart search" feature that helps spelling-impaired patrons (and sometimes library staff) along. Other appealing features were the ability to pull database results via Z39.50 federated search source sets, customizable "rooms" for different age groups or interests, and even social media integration.

It was decided that the launch of the Enterprise platform would be an ideal time to integrate the existing PastPerfect catalog of museum items into the library's main catalog. There were several problems to consider during this process: How to translate non-MARC, non-RDA/AACR2 museum catalog records into ILS-readable records? How to clearly indicate the difference between

FIGURE 4.1 ———

Partial screenshot of the library's current OPAC web page

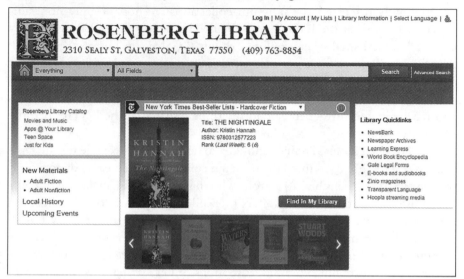

museum objects and typical library items? How to direct interested parties to the museum's own specialized online catalog for more information? And what about simple visual appeal?

In order to accomplish this, museum and library staff worked closely with PastPerfect's technical support staff to devise a means of making these sequestered collections accessible to the public—at least in a digital sense. First, the museum objects' records are exported from PastPerfect in the form of an Excel spreadsheet. These records include two special links; one to the object's full PastPerfect record (including link text language to that effect), and the other to the object's thumbnail image for visual identification in search results. This spreadsheet is then converted to a tab-delimited text file, which is subsequently translated into MARC records using MarcEdit, a terribly useful little piece of file editing/conversion software. These records can then be incorporated into the library's catalog using the ILS import function. Collection, item type, and call number values are assigned to the newly added museum objects at this point.

The end result is a patron-viewable record that includes pertinent information about the object, including a photograph if available, gives the patron an idea of where the object can be found—that is, in the museum collections rather than in the typical circulating, reference, or digital collections—and links the patron to the object's original PastPerfect record, thereby opening a path to the museum-specific OPAC for any further related information needs (such as a larger photograph of the object in question).

WHAT WE WILL DO

As previously discussed, the museum collections are not the only nontraditional collections at the Rosenberg Library. The Galveston and Texas History Center has published several online exhibits ("Galveston History Vignettes") that feature some of the most interesting photographs and postcards in their collections (figure 4.2). The 1900 Storm and Hurricane Ike vignettes are particularly popular. Many patrons have discovered the existence of the archives and have initiated further interaction with or research at the GTHC because of these eye-catching image collections.

The History Center's archives should also be easily discoverable for the same reasons that the library wanted the museum collections to be easily discoverable: they're too often "invisible" to patrons who might otherwise make use of them. The History Center currently offers title indexes for inventoried collections on its own website, which is somewhat separated from the primary library website. Unfortunately, only about half of all the collections in the archives are inventoried and included in the online indexes. Even more unfortunately, one of the most commonly expressed frustrations of GTHC patrons is the lack of subject indexing. If patrons don't know the title of the item or group of items they're looking for, they won't be able to find it among the guides to GTHC holdings. In other words, if a patron doesn't already have a very good idea of what they hope to find, they're unlikely to *discover* any useful information—even if the archives do hold exactly what they need.

FIGURE 4.2 ————————————————————————————————————

Partial screenshot of the GTHC's "Galveston History Vignettes" digital exhibits web page

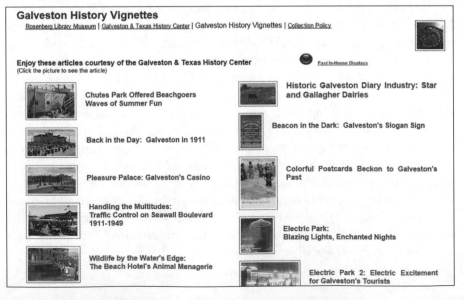

That is not to say that these simple indexes don't serve an important purpose or that the professional archivists of the GTHC can't help patrons find whatever information they're after—quite the opposite, as the History Center staff have to be particularly good at assisting patrons with their information needs in this environment. However, modern technology and associated searching habits being what they are, the History Center decided to pursue a more discovery-friendly way of getting their collections into the public online space.

Due to this limited remote searchability, the leadership of the History Center decided to upgrade their current finding aids-based system to something more akin to the museum's PastPerfect catalog or the library's Horizon catalog: CuadraSTAR. This change was only recently implemented and the History Center staff face an enormous job of cataloging—and in many cases digitizing—all of their heretofore hidden archival treasures. In the interest of increasing the visibility of these collections, these records are also expected to be findable in the main library OPAC. The efforts to address this critical need for discoverability in this vast collection are hampered by two main stumbling blocks that were not involved in the previously discussed library-museum catalog merger.

First, a large portion of the collection is not really "cataloged" in a way that can be easily translated into a traditional library catalog. The types of materials found in special collections are generally more varied than those in traditional library collections, and the ways in which special collections managers must describe and organize their materials are proportionately varied. Special collections are simply less standardized than traditional collections and their catalogs or finding aids necessarily reflect that. Files full of letters, newspaper articles, photos, and ephemera are more difficult to describe and catalog when compared to more typical circulating or display materials like DVD movies or paintings or even early twentieth-century wedding Mardi Gras ball gowns. Getting this information into a standardized, searchable online catalog is not as easy as converting Microsoft Excel spreadsheets into a different file format.

Second, the bulk of the nonbook GTHC collections are still text-based items (notwithstanding those aforementioned 100,000 photographs and online exhibits) which are not yet digitized or indexed for in-item searching. The History Center is determined to digitize and make freely accessible as many of its most interesting holdings as possible as quickly as possible, but this process requires painstaking attention to detail and is necessarily slow. Even those items that have been digitized are generally accessible in PDF or other document formats rather than in scalable image formats. This is in contrast to the eye-catching photos of often beautiful or unusual museum items that are included in both relevant catalogs. An illustrative thumbnail image, whether of a book cover or a watercolor painting, is far more likely to draw the eye of a curious OPAC user than the generic placeholder icon provided for items that lack actual representative thumbnails. This slight disadvantage makes it all the more important that the records for these items in the main library catalogs have descriptive titles, accurate summaries and subject headings, and easy-to-find links to their full GTHC catalog records.

For the library and GTHC staff, one of the appeals of the CuadraSTAR system is its capability to generate MARC records for inclusion in a typical library ILS. These basic MARC records need only be marginally modified for inclusion in the library's catalog. Each record (as with the museum collections) includes a link that points to each individual item's public access record in the GTHC's Cuadra catalog. The Cuadra catalog records may include downloadable files of digitized items. In this way, a patron who might otherwise never even think of looking for pertinent information sources in the archives will be able to easily discover—and in cases involving digitized copies, immediately access—these underutilized resources right alongside the more traditional library materials.

The first item to be added to the main library OPAC in this way was what is known as the "J.O.L.O." book, a bound volume of the records of watches over the Galveston Bay in 1861, including the beginning of the blockade of the Galveston Harbor prior to the First Battle of Galveston at the beginning of the Civil War. The J.O.L.O. group was stationed on top of the still-extant Hendley Building in Galveston's historic Strand district; unfortunately, no one is entirely sure what exactly those initials were meant to stand for. The patron who serendipitously finds this item record in the catalog (by, for example, using the search term "Galveston Harbor" in the Rosenberg Library's most prominent catalog search box) will find not only a book-like catalog record for the item but a link to the more detailed GTHC catalog record which itself includes a complete PDF copy of the item. Some experimenting with link formats, subject headings, and import settings was necessary, but the end result is a delightfully discoverable and accessible item that was previously a part of that vast hidden section of the "iceberg" collections of the archives. Library and History Center staff are looking forward to working together to integrate the rest of the growing GTHC catalog with the library's own OPAC.

The library itself is also planning improvements to its OPAC, mostly having to do with increasing the visibility of the many digital resources it can offer to library cardholders. Its e-book offerings through the popular Overdrive platform (through the Houston Area Digital Media Catalog, a consortium-based service) are already listed alongside physical items using SirsiDynix's eResource Central digital content management tool. The Rosenberg Library also began offering access to downloadable and streaming movies, music, and audiobooks in the "hoopla" platform from Midwest Tape in 2015; part of hoopla's service is providing a monthly collection of ready-to-import MARC records for their newest acquisitions. Having titles from these services show up in catalog search results with more traditional physical materials increases their visibility to library patrons who might not otherwise think to go looking specifically for free library e-books. The library also offers e-books and audiobooks through three other platforms (3M Cloud Library, Recorded Books OneClickdigital, and Tumble-Books); the plan is to attempt to integrate catalog records from these services as well in order to make full use of the OPAC's function as a discovery tool.

Databases, too, have a place in the library's catalog. Federated searching allows users to pull results from some subscription databases as well as library and special collections catalogs. For example, a patron who uses the search term "antioxidants" will find traditional circulating materials like books and DVDs as well as downloadable and streaming e-books and audiobooks in the primary search results tab, plus articles from popular digital magazines such as *Consumer Reports on Health* from EBSCO's MasterFILE Premier database, provided as part of the Texas State Library and Archives Commission's Tex-Share Database Program, in a separate "databases" tab. Unfortunately, current federated search sources are limited and not quite as discovery-friendly as they ought to be in order to provide users with a seamless, single-search tool experience. Basic keyword searches often turn up seemingly unrelated articles, not all search results include abstracts or summaries to help users make quick judgments about their usefulness, and many search results also lack links that take users directly to the source material. Library staff plan to pursue better database integration options in the future. In the meantime, the main Rosenberg Library catalog includes prominent links to the most popular digital resources and how-to guides for their use. The users' need to retrieve information can be met, even if the tool's information *discovery* function is undergoing some significant growing pains.

ONE CATALOG TO RULE THEM ALL

The Rosenberg Library's unusual library/museum/archives organization makes for a unique set of services and materials. It also necessitates uniquely arranged discovery tools in order to help users make the most of the many and varied resources on offer. Rosenberg Library patrons are a diverse group. The needs and habits of historians engaged in academic pursuits, bookworms and movie buffs, children who are learning to read and use technology, tourists hoping to learn more about their chosen vacation destination, genealogists attempting long-distance research, and other types of library users must all be considered in pursuit of well-designed information retrieval and discovery tools. A balance must be found between allowing each department to have its own specialized catalog, suited to its particular collections, and the goal of reducing confusion while at the same time increasing those little incidents of serendipitous discovery that can only be accomplished with one "front door" for all.

PART II

CUSTOM DISCOVERY SYSTEMS

CHAPTER FIVE

GEOSPATIAL RESOURCE DISCOVERY

DARREN HARDY, JACK REED, AND BESS SADLER

Geospatial resource discovery is the simple, common act of finding useful geospatial datasets. Yet, in our current environment, it is a fragmented, mediated endeavor, replete with finding aids, ad hoc strategies, and expert knowledge. The state of geospatial resource discovery is indeed a lack of effective discovery services among a flood of shared geospatial data. In this chapter we discuss our efforts, with Geo-Blacklight (http://geoblacklight.org) and EarthWorks (https://earthworks .stanford.edu), to improve the situation.

GEOPORTALS

The term *geoportal* emerged for a web interface to a geolibrary (De Longueville 2010; Maguire and Longley 2005). Goodchild et al. (1999) define a geolibrary as "a digital library filled with geoinformation and for which the primary search mechanism is place." In effect, today's geoportals are geolibraries. Their goal is to provide a destination for domain-specific collections of geographic information systems (GIS) data (Goodchild, Fu, and Rich 2007). Earlier geolibraries focused on spatial search and data organization (Erwin and Sweetkind-Singer 2009; Goodchild 2004), but not as much on federation and modern search semantics, like query intent processing and faceting (Hearst 2009; Tunkelang 2009). Newer geoportals, such as OpenGeoportal (http://opengeoportal.org) and GeoNetwork (http://geonetwork-opensource.org), use a federated or otherwise harvested catalog of geospatial resources, and they are also built as software designed to be easily installable for others to run geoportals. ESRI Geoportal Server (http://github.com/Esri/geoportal-server) also falls into this category.

Geoportals all have spatial search in common, but the implementations differ. Using a map to define coordinates in which to search is one metaphor, but using place names to specify locations is another. The chosen metaphor has implications on the metadata for geospatial resources, such as having bounding box coordinates or place names in a controlled vocabulary (Bidney 2010).

Limitations

Geoportals have led to increasingly simplified discovery and access to geospatial resources. However, they have suffered from usability issues, lack of federation, and tenuous integration with other applications. For example, they relied on user interaction metaphors from analytic GIS desktop applications, such as multilayered maps and toolbar navigation, that are obstacles for casual users. They also lack flexible faceted refinement and navigation of search results, which are key features of modern search interfaces (Hearst 2009). Our goal with GeoBlacklight is to remove such obstacles for casual users whose primary objective is discovery.

As various disciplines continue to adopt geospatial data as a means for research and development, the volume and complexity of geospatial data grows. Increasingly, the demand to share geospatial data has outpaced the ability to discover shared geospatial resources, thus contributing to resource-intensive mediation for librarians. For example, NASA has massive amounts of geospatial resources and publishes a metadata directory of 35,000 datasets in their Global Change Master Directory (http://gcmd.gsfc.nasa.gov). But, more importantly, they also have dozens of other geoportals that focus on particular dataset categories such as climate and socioeconomic data. This collection of geoportals, however, is effectively a set of simple, unfederated metadata catalogs that do not focus on the specific tasks required for discovery. For example, users search by keyword only to find terse metadata records without any interactive features to evaluate the data or narrow down large result sets via faceted navigation, as is common in modern search semantics (Hearst 2009; Tunkelang 2009). Furthermore, unlike integrated library systems or web searches, it requires searching from publisher to publisher. This lack of federation forces expert knowledge on librarians who need to track all the different publishers' geoportals to create finding aids.[1] The end result is a challenging environment for users who wish to find relevant data quickly, and additional mediation requirements for librarians.

All geoportals rely on metadata for geospatial resources because they are metadata catalogs at their core. Metadata are notoriously difficult to author in the GIS realm and not conducive to automation (Batcheller 2008; Poore and Wolf 2013; Tolosana-Calasanz et al. 2006; Yue et al. 2012). The GIS metadata standards are focused on data evaluation and quality control, rather than search (Durante and Hardy 2015). The Content Standard for Digital Geospatial Metadata (known as FGDC, for the Federal Geographic Data Committee) or the ISO Standards for Geographic Metadata (ISO 19110/19139) are the primary standards and have decades of practice between them (Ahonen-Rainio 2006).

Improvements

We have developed a novel federated discovery service for geospatial resources in a research library setting, based entirely on open-source technologies. Our aim is to provide discovery services with an emphasis on user experience that integrates with other web mapping tools and streamlines the use and organization of geospatial data. Moreover, by concentrating on the user's discovery objective as much as possible, we aim to reduce mediation workloads on librarians. Our hope is that more and more geospatial discovery services adopt interactive, user-focused, task-oriented features that simplify the path to finding relevant available data quickly for users. Next, we discuss how we developed a geospatial resource discovery system, first by discussing the design implications and then our implementation.

DESIGNING FOR GEOSPATIAL RESOURCE DISCOVERY

Design and the design process help us understand the key components and their context upfront to produce a better end product. For example, known technical and usability issues can be addressed from the beginning, and project stakeholders and potential development partners are better informed. To this point, we embarked upon a design process before our development began, and given the state of geoportal design, we decided this was a critical development phase (Reed 2014; Reed, Hardy, and Sadler 2014). We hope that the lessons learned from our design process are applicable to any geospatial resource discovery application.

The use cases for geospatial resource discovery presented unique challenges for creating a great user experience, given the complexity of integrating metadata, federated systems, and user needs. Hardy and Durante (2014) discuss the development of our use cases for curation, resource evaluation and access, and search (figure 5.1). Notably, we focused on a user's ability to quickly evaluate the suitability of a data "layer," the unit of discovery for a geospatial dataset. A key component of evaluation is to visualize a data layer within a web map interface and inspect data attributes, if necessary.

Our design process was a multiphase approach that pulled from industry best practices and local convention including discovery, information architecture, and interaction and visual design.

Discovery Phase

First, the discovery phase focused on improving our understanding of the domain and users. We found that our exhaustive environmental scan did well to reveal the landscape of geospatial data discovery software. Our scan went beyond the scope of traditional GIS software to include mapping interfaces used in social media, real estate, hotel booking, and other commercial innovators. We tried to understand not only the approach taken by the traditional players, but also cutting-edge design by industry leaders and startups. We found that a taxonomy emerged and we derived a matrix of geospatial and mapping search features. Software fit naturally into two categories, open-source and proprietary, and we added further classification by grouping software by its ability to provide GIS data discovery. Though these software groups have distinct uses, we were able to extract common characteristics in aiding the spatial discovery use case into

FIGURE 5.1 ────────────────────────────────────

Geospatial resource discovery use cases

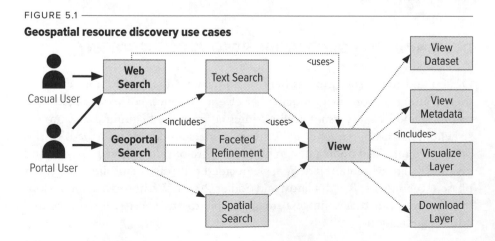

a feature matrix. This matrix consists of software on one axis and commonly implemented features on the other.

We interviewed likely users and domain experts using a prepared set of questions. We intended that these questions would provide more insight into current data discovery and future needs. We also left the interviews open-ended so that additional needs could emerge naturally from discussion (Pruitt, Adlin, and Constantine 2006; Roto, Rantavuo, and Väänänen-Vainio-Mattila 2009).

Personas

From the interview process, two classes of users emerged for our application— end users and stakeholders. Both of these user classes were critical to the success of the software, yet the users' goals were substantially different. So we refined these user needs into a prioritized list and personas. We produced six distinct personas representing anticipated users and stakeholders.

Note that as an open-source project, a principal challenge when developing these personas was maintaining focus on the discovery and access use cases. Nichols and Twidale (2003), for example, argue that open-source software has the danger of becoming overly complex since many features that seem reasonable to experts and developers are added despite dubious applicability to users. Using personas gave us a guiding reference point for functionality, and thus helped us avoid usability challenges for novice users.

Application End Users

This class of personas represents the direct users. In an academic setting, it is important for a software service to be usable by both beginners and advanced users, and as such, the spectrum of skill level is represented in our end-user personas as characterized by the following example biographies.

- *Brian Diaz*, professor of history. Diaz is an experienced scholar who is busy juggling research, teaching, and professional commitments. He would like to add more historic maps and geospatial components to his research, but finds that GIS software and applications are not that user-friendly and he doesn't have time to relearn a new discipline.
- *Andrea Payne*, PhD candidate in environmental sciences. Payne is an experienced GIS user who worked as a GIS analyst for several years before pursuing her PhD. She is used to scouring the Web to find data she needs for her research. Her experience with user-focused GIS software has been frustrating, and she met the idea of another portal application with skepticism.

‣ *Sandip Nagarkar*, sophomore in planning/urban studies. Nagarkar is a tech-savvy sophomore looking to do more work in GIS but doesn't know where to start. He expects the tools he uses to make his work easier, not harder. An early adopter, Nagarkar is eager to learn new things and adapt new technology to his workflow.

Project Stakeholders

This class of personas focuses on how the application would be deployed and operate within an institution.

‣ *Beverly Arnold*, earth sciences librarian. Arnold has been working with geospatial data for most of her career. With the advent of new online tools, she is excited about the possibility of enhancing accessibility to the large collection that the university has access to. One concern of Arnold is that this new application be focused on geospatial assets and not the same as the library's other tools.

‣ *Brandon Chavez*, GIS instructor and lab manager. Chavez's job consists of managing the GIS lab, training and providing consultations to students, and providing the campus community with access to geospatial data. By putting the GIS data resources online in an easy-to-use application, more people will gain access to available data and Chavez can concentrate on other areas of his job.

‣ *Debra Gordon*, library web engineer. Gordon has been working as a software engineer in the university library for several years. She is excited about the possibility of a new application dedicated to the vast geospatial assets the university holds. Her knowledge of open-source software and specific GIS needs is useful to the project.

At this point in the process, we began modeling metadata requirements and the application's data model, or schema. Keeping the personas in the forefront, we put their needs first and limited the required metadata fields for discovery.[2] Then we developed visual design mockups and a working prototype, which not only tested functionality but provided for community feedback and stakeholder buy-in. The prototype, specifically, also helped to further inform metadata requirements and schema design.

Throughout the design process we engaged and collaborated with the broader community. We were able to gather information from a diverse body of informants, which enhanced the overall project design. Notably, we provided design artifacts to the community which yielded feedback not previously uncovered.

User Experience Design

As per our design process, the user experience (UX) design (Nielsen 1994) is the next step. Our focus was to provide a good user experience to the student, researcher, and scholar in discovery, evaluation, and access to geospatial data, and this drove our development efforts.

1. *Geospatial focused users want to search spatially.* An overarching theme from user interviews was the need to search spatially for geospatial resources, that is, to use a map interface to navigate results. Basic spatial search has been common in geoportal applications (Chapman and Essic 2011), but a more refined, UX-centric approach to spatial search is now widely adopted in industry. Perhaps most notable, Google Maps' search interface provides users the ability to navigate an interactive map with search results dynamically updating as the map is moved. This "dynamic spatial search" has become commonplace in online search applications, implemented in reservation booking (e.g., Airbnb, Hipmunk), social media (e.g., Foursquare, Pinterest), and user review (e.g., Yelp) websites. Because of their wide adoption, users have come to expect this type of interface for their search tasks.

   A key challenge in designing a dynamic spatial search interface is providing a user with the appropriate amount of screen space for spatial interaction and display of results. We took a split screen approach to this problem, providing a list view of results and an interactive map side by side. List results show a limited amount of metadata by default, but expand when a user clicks on them, resulting in more metadata information displayed (figure 5.2).

   We needed to provide a clear relation between the list search results and the map interface. The relation provides affordance and feedback for use of the combined page areas. For example, the dynamic updating of search results based on map movement may be confusing to some users. To reduce confusion, we offer an explicit toggle control on the map which lets users turn off dynamic spatial search (figure 5.2, upper right). The label for this same control also informs users that their search results will update whenever they move the map. Perhaps the first relationship that users will notice is that when they hover the cursor over a search result in the list, the map displays the extent of that result. This bounding box visualization immediately shows the connection between both the mapping interface and search results. These elements tie together the spatial search experience and enhance the usability of the map and search results list.

FIGURE 5.2 ──────────────────────────────

GeoBlacklight search results

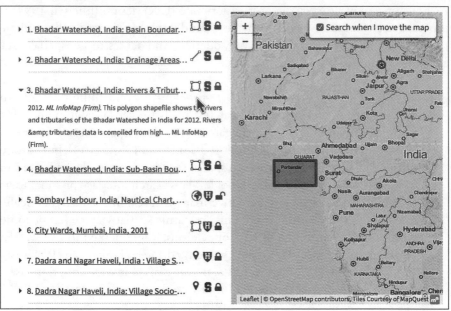

2. *Prioritize discovery objectives.* We found that both geospatial analysis software and geoportal software tried to incorporate the other into their respective interfaces. For example, analysis software provides simple discovery interfaces, and geoportal software provides complex multilayered interfaces. For discovery applications this conflation detracts from the intended goals of finding and accessing data resources. The majority of users already have other software for visualization and analysis of the data. So, we argue that providing additional analysis tools inside the discovery interface leads to user distraction and unused functionality bloating the software. By understanding and adhering to discovery as the primary motivation of the user, we enhance usability by increasing user efficiency (Nielsen 1994). In practice, opposing these dispensable feature requests can be challenging, especially when they come from an influential stakeholder. Again, having a clear understanding of the personas helps guide the user experience towards discovery objectives.

3. *Give feedback on federated service availability.* The integration of external federated services, a set of disparate services that appear unified via the user experience, is difficult because external services are sometimes not reliable. During the rapid prototyping phase of design we found that we would

need to check the ongoing availability of federated services and provide that availability feedback to the user. Otherwise, network issues, stale metadata, and service availability would impact a user's experience and confidence for accessing discovered data resources (Wolff and Parker 2014).

Once our development reached a stable state, we began usability testing our UX design. First, we sent our UX design to several domain experts for review. A more in-depth usability study protocol was planned based on initial feedback from these experts. The usability study included seven participants with a diverse range of experience with GIS software. Study sessions consisted of a recorded audio and screen capture of test participants performing a set list of tasks. We immediately found usability issues, from software bugs to unclear metadata labels. On the whole, the usability testing process improved the overall product tremendously and was indispensable as a development tool.

EarthWorks

EarthWorks is our discovery service for geospatial resources at Stanford University. It builds upon the GeoBlacklight platform, an open-source, multi-institutional software project started at Stanford University Libraries in 2013, and provides discovery services across a federated multi-institutional repository of geospatial resources. This effort is an open collaborative project aiming to build on the successes of the Blacklight discovery platform (http://projectblacklight.org) and the multi-institutional OpenGeoportal federated metadata sharing communities.

GeoBlacklight

GeoBlacklight extends Blacklight's two core search capabilities, free-text search and faceted refinement, by adding a third type of search—dynamic spatial search. "Combining free-text search and faceted refinement is powerful: it allows users to create semi-structured queries and thus access structured and unstructured content" (Tunkelang 2009). This combination facilitates the process of finding search results, narrowing the field, and quickly determining if relevant data are available.

In the implementation, the natural language text search enables full-text searching over a configurable set of metadata fields, such as title, description, author, and so on, using a Solr (http://lucene.apache.org/solr) search index. Advanced features such as spelling correction and autocomplete also aid the free-text search for a user. The search text input form is located prominently on the home page and search result pages (figure 5.3, upper half). Also, GeoBlacklight, through Blacklight's functionality, allows users to use configurable facets

FIGURE 5.3 ───

GeoBlacklight home page

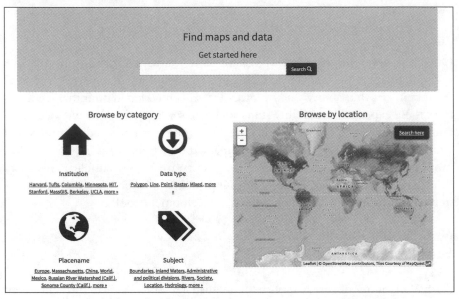

as both an entry point into a search (figure 5.3, lower left) or a refinement of a previous search (figure 5.2). We used usability testing and focus groups to help determine additional useful facets. For example, EarthWorks adds a facet for the current availability of a resource to be downloaded.

Spatial search is, in effect, a type of faceted query, but is presented in a distinct interface allowing for enhanced usability. Dynamic updating of search results allows users to explore a map to find new data resources spatially. Specifically, the spatial search returns all items that intersect the search area in the map view, and then ranks items higher if they are contained entirely within the search area.[3]

A key part of discovery is evaluating geospatial data and its utility to the user. This evaluation happens in a phased approach in GeoBlacklight—first on the search results page, and secondly on the item page. On the search results page, limited metadata for matching resources are displayed for evaluation by a searcher. GeoBlacklight uses a consistent iconography throughout the application to display provenance, access restrictions, and data type for resources (figure 5.4). By hovering the cursor over a resource in a results page, the user can see the spatial extent of the intended resource (figure 5.2, shaded box on map). By clicking on the area around the resource, users can see a metadata panel reveal itself with more information.

FIGURE 5.4 ───

GeoBlacklight iconography for facets

An individual record item page displays additional metadata than the search results page. GeoBlacklight makes the displayed fields configurable and flexible enough to enable a linked, bookmarkable search from field values. The item record page also offers an interactive preview of the resource in a map view pane, which is enabled through Web Mapping Service (WMS) or International Image Interoperability Framework (IIIF) web services. Users can also inspect the attribute table of WMS services by clicking on the map. Additional metadata (e.g., Metadata Object Description Schema [MODS], FGDC, ISO 19139) can be provided in the GeoBlacklight schema and is also viewable from this page. This multidimensional approach to data resource evaluation is intended to aid the user in their discovery tasks.

Finally, discovery via metadata is important, but without being able to download and access data resources it is frustrating for users. So GeoBlacklight offers a variety of ways for users to access discovered data.[4] For resources where a direct download link is available, GeoBlacklight presents a preferred download link to that file. Additional downloads can be generated using Web Feature Services (WFS) and WMS-provided URLs.[5] These generated data are then cached to enable faster downloads for subsequent users. Finally, users have access to the direct WMS and WFS URL links that are required by analytic GIS desktop software.

Stanford Spatial Data Infrastructure

Geoportals rely on a spatial data infrastructure for delivery and repository services, and GeoBlacklight is no exception. Spatial data infrastructures have a rich history from their emergence in the 1980s (Goodchild, Fu, and Rich 2007; Groot and McLaughlin 2000; Maguire and Longley 2005; Masser 1999; Onsrud 2007; Williamson, Rajabifard, and Feeney 2003; Wright and Wang 2011; Yang et al. 2010). They span global, international, national, and institutional scales.

FIGURE 5.5 ———

Stanford Spatial Data Infrastructure

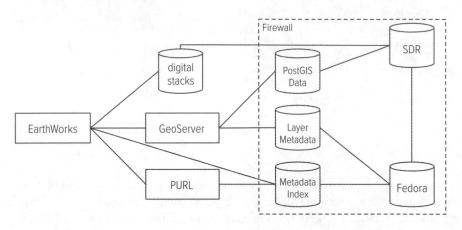

The Stanford Spatial Data Infrastructure (SSDI) is an institutional-scale infrastructure that provides discovery, delivery, and preservation for both licensed and open geospatial resources (figure 5.5). The Stanford Digital Repository (SDR; Cramer and Kott 2010; Shaon and Woolf 2011) provides the preservation services for all metadata and data. We use Fedora (http://fedora-commons.org) to maintain a working copy of all our metadata. Our "digital stacks" provide access to working copies of data files. Our PURL application provides "Persistent URL" metadata and file access for all content in the SDR. The spatial data web services, such as WMS and WFS, are provided by GeoServer (http://geoserver .org). EarthWorks provides the discovery services for all geospatial resources within our catalog, and harvests geospatial resource metadata from other institutions.

The SSDI includes GeoMonitor (http://github.com/geoblacklight/ geomonitor), a WMS availability service application. Federated WMS and WFS are used in GeoBlacklight to provide generated downloads and feature inspection. If these services were not available, or responded slowly, users usually blamed the discovery application, which is not at fault. GeoMonitor checks GeoBlacklight-indexed WMS services on a configurable schedule. It then can provide real-time updates to the discovery index. GeoBlacklight can then present a user with different views based on the availability of a layer's external services. This approach to external service availability avoids presenting a download action to a user where the download will fail or is known to be faulty.

CONCLUSION

Our goal is to build more than software; we want to build a community of open-source development and metadata-sharing practice, enabling geospatial discovery across institutions. By conducting usability research, building on robust existing open-source software components, and developing a framework for monitoring inter-institutional data availability, we are establishing the beginnings of a community of practice and a set of common tools. Maintaining software is expensive, and by planning for communal maintenance early we hope to ensure long-term sustainability. Metadata creation is also expensive, and by creating systems to collaborate and share catalog records we can shorten the significant backlog of undescribed data that is not yet easily discoverable.

Although our efforts around GeoBlacklight and EarthWorks have focused on data discovery and access, we are also focusing on the long-term management and preservation of geospatial data, an area that is often overlooked in efforts to make data available online. To this end, we are founding members of the Hydra Geospatial Data Interest Group (https://wiki.duraspace.org/display/hydra/Hydra+Geospatial+Interest+Group), and we are encouraged to see a growing interest among other institutions that also recognize the need for digital preservation strategies for their geospatial data collections.

By creating a community of practice, we can also plan for inter-institutional collection development. For example, vast quantities of GIS data being produced by public agencies and nongovernmental organizations are valuable, but effectively ephemeral. Although they might be available online via a geoportal or agency website, they are not preserved in the long term in a digital repository, and they have a tendency to disappear. Although the amount of data in question is too large for any single institution to commit to preserving, by forming collection-developing policies and cooperative agreements, together many institutions could be helping to preserve this important data. The end result would be not only better geospatial data discovery, but also future access and long-term preservation, enabling longitudinal research that is currently intractable.

Future directions in our work will focus on self-deposit for GIS research data produced by faculty members and university students. Mandates from research funding institutions increasingly require data management plans, and the Stanford Digital Repository allows scholars an easy way to comply with these requirements. By adding the SSDI and EarthWorks on top of the SDR, we not only provide scholars with a long-term home for their research, we give them compelling new ways of interacting with their data, such as through online visualizations and mapping tools like CartoDB.

We envision a world where geospatial data is managed and preserved, easily discoverable, and easily reusable in a variety of contexts. By building systems and communities of practice to support this goal, we will enable new possibilities for research.

Notes

1. Yue, P., J. Gong, L. Di, and L. He. 2012. "Automatic Geospatial Metadata Generation for Earth Science Virtual Data Products." *GeoInformatica* 16, no. 1: 1–29. For example finding aids, see https://library.stanford.edu/research/stanford-geospatial-center/data.
2. Solidifying user needs and use cases helped shape the GeoBlacklight schema. See http://github.com/geoblacklight/geoblacklight-schema.
3. Modifications to this algorithm are under way to include advanced spatial functionality introduced in Solr v4.10.
4. External service references provided in GeoBlacklight dct_references_s' field enable access to these resources. See http://github.com/geoblacklight/geoblacklight-schema.
5. GeoBlacklight currently generates Shapefile, GeoJSON, and KMZ for vector data and GeoTiff file formats for raster data.

References

Ahonen-Rainio, P. 2006. "Metadata for Geographic Information." *Journal of Map & Geography Libraries* 2, no. 1: 37–66.

Batcheller, J. K. 2008. "Automating Geospatial Metadata Generation—An Integrated Data Management and Documentation Approach." *Computers & Geosciences* 34, no. 4: 387–98.

Bidney, M. 2010. "Can Geographic Coordinates in the Catalog Record Be Useful?" *Journal of Map & Geography Libraries* 6, no. 2: 140–50.

Chapman, J., and J. Essic. 2011. "Juggling Points and Polygons: GIS Researchers' Metadata and Search Needs." *Journal of Library Metadata* 11, no. 1: 1–18.

Cramer, T., and K. Kott. 2010. "Designing and Implementing Second Generation Digital Preservation Services: A Scalable Model for the Stanford Digital Repository." *D-Lib Magazine* 16, nos. 9–10 [Internet].

De Longueville, B. 2010. "Community-Based Geoportals: The Next Generation? Concepts and Methods for the Geospatial Web 2.0." *Computers, Environment and Urban Systems* 34, no. 4: 299–308.

Durante, K., and D. Hardy. 2015. "Discovery, Management, and Preservation of Geospatial Data Using Hydra." *Journal of Map & Geography Libraries* 11, no. 2: 123–54.

Erwin, T., and J. Sweetkind-Singer. 2009. "The National Geospatial Digital Archive: A Collaborative Project to Archive Geospatial Data." *Journal of Map & Geography Libraries* 6, no. 1: 6–25.

Goodchild, M. F. 2004. "The Alexandria Digital Library Project: Review, Assessment, and Prospects." *D-Lib Magazine* 10, no. 5 [Internet].

Goodchild, M. F., P. S. Adler, B. P. Buttenfield, R. E. Kahn, A. J. Krygiel, and H. J. Onsrud. 1999. *Distributed Geolibraries.* National Academies.

Goodchild, M. F., P. Fu, and P. Rich. 2007. "Sharing Geographic Information: An Assessment of the Geospatial One-Stop." *Annals of the American Association of Geographers* 94, no. 2: 250–66.

Groot, R., and J. McLaughlin, eds. 2000. *Geospatial Data Infrastructure: Concepts, Cases, and Good Practice.* New York: Oxford University Press.

Hardy, D., and K. Durante. 2014. "A Metadata Schema for Geospatial Resource Discovery Use Cases. *code4lib Journal* 25 [Internet].

Hearst, M. A. 2009. *Search User Interfaces.* Cambridge, UK: Cambridge University Press.

Maguire, D., and P. Longley. 2005. "The Emergence of Geoportals and Their Role in Spatial Data Infrastructures." *Computers, Environment and Urban Systems* 29, no. 1: 3–14.

Masser, I. 1999. "All Shapes and Sizes: The First Generation of National Spatial Data Infrastructures." *International Journal of Geographical Information Science* 13, no. 1: 67–84.

Nichols, D., and M. Twidale. 2003. "The Usability of Open Source Software." *First Monday* 8, no. 1.

Nielsen, J. 1994. *Usability Engineering.* Amsterdam: Elsevier.

Onsrud, H., ed. 2007. *Research and Theory in Advancing Spatial Data Infrastructure Concepts.* Redlands, CA: Esri.

Poore, B. S., and E. B. Wolf. 2013. "Metadata Squared: Enhancing Its Usability for Volunteered Geographic Information and the GeoWeb." In *Crowdsourcing Geographic Knowledge,* ed. D. Sui, S. Elwood, and M. F. Goodchild, 43–61. Netherlands: Springer.

Pruitt, J. S., T. Adlin, and L. Constantine. 2006. *The Persona Lifecycle.* Amsterdam: Elsevier.

Reed, P. J. 2014. "Fixing GIS Data Discovery." Presented at FOSS4G Conference, September 8–10, Portland, OR.

Reed, P. J., D. Hardy, and B. Sadler. 2014. "GeoBlacklight Concept Design Documents" (technical report). Stanford University Libraries.

Roth, R. E. 2013. "Interactive Maps: What We Know and What We Need to Know." *Journal of Spatial Information Science* 6: 59–115.

Roto, V., H. Rantavuo, and K. Väänänen-Vainio-Mattila. 2009. "Evaluating User Experience of Early Product Concepts." In *Proceedings of Designing Pleasurable Products and Interfaces* 9: 199–208.

Shaon, A., and A. Woolf. 2011. "Long-Term Preservation for Spatial Data Infrastructures: A Metadata Framework and Geo-Portal Implementation. *D-Lib Magazine* 17, nos. 9–10 [Internet].

Tolosana-Calasanz, R., J. A. Álvarez-Robles, J. Lacasta, J. Nogueras-Iso, P. R. Muro-Medrano, and F. J. Zarazaga-Soria. 2006. "On the Problem of Identifying the Quality of Geographic Metadata." In *Research and Advanced Technology for Digital Libraries,* Lecture Notes in Computer Science (4172): 232–43. Berlin: Springer.

Tunkelang, D. 2009. "Faceted Search." *Synthesis Lectures on Information Concepts, Retrieval, and Services* 1, no. 1: 1–80.

Williamson, I. P., A. Rajabifard, and M. F. Feeney, eds. 2003. *Developing Spatial Data Infrastructures: From Concept to Reality.* London: Taylor and Francis.

Wolff, R., and K. Parker. 2014. "Usability testing: OpenGeoPortal 2.0" (technical report, paper 9). PLACE Project, University of New Hampshire Library.

Wright, D. J., and S. Wang. 2011. "The Emergence of Spatial Cyberinfrastructure." *Proceedings of the National Academy of Sciences* 108, no. 14: 5488–91.

Yang, C., R. Raskin, M. F. Goodchild, and M. Gahegan. 2010. "Geospatial Cyberinfrastructure: Past, Present, and Future." *Computers, Environment and Urban Systems* 34, no. 4: 264–77.

Yue, P., J. Gong, L. Di, and L. He. 2012. "Automatic Geospatial Metadata Generation for Earth Science Virtual Data Products." *GeoInformatica* 16, no. 1: 1–29.

CHAPTER SIX

DISCOVERY ON A SHOESTRING

Implementing a Full-Functioned Discovery Tool with Free Software and No-Extra-Charge Metadata Sources

JULIA BAUDER

The staff at the Grinnell College Libraries found ourselves torn when commercial discovery services became available. We, like many academic librarians, were attracted by the simplicity of being able to direct students to a single search box, although we also had pedagogical concerns about having a single search box that was too all-encompassing. While a general article search might be appropriate for students in lower-level classes, we wanted to ensure that students still learned how to use the powerful advanced search features of the databases designed for searching the literature of their chosen disciplines. Moreover, with so many pressing collections needs and our limited budget, we had a hard time justifying purchasing an expensive product that did not add content our users desire to our collection.

We resolved this dilemma by using VuFind, an open-source discovery layer developed at Villanova University, to create our own free single-search-box discovery layer. Our discovery layer, which we have locally branded as 3Search, combines metadata from local sources (our ILS and institutional repository), from no-extra-charge vendor application programming interfaces (APIs) that come bundled with subscriptions to EBSCOhost article databases and OCLC cataloging services, and, soon, from locally indexed article-level records that we can acquire for free from JSTOR.

In this chapter, we will discuss our discovery layer setup, the advantages of implementing our own open-source discovery layer, and the pitfalls we encountered in using only no-extra-charge metadata sources to populate our search system.

THE ENVIRONMENT

Grinnell College is a small, highly selective liberal arts college located in Grinnell, Iowa, that enrolls just over 1,600 undergraduate students. The library staff—eight librarians and seventeen other staff members—is larger than usual for an institution of this size, although still much smaller than the library staffs at the sorts of research universities that typically do a great deal of in-house open-source development. Four of the Grinnell College Libraries' employees—two librarians and two staff members—have substantial job duties related to technology, and three of them are coders.

The libraries have been ambitious in our technology initiatives, despite our small technology staff. We run a few off-the-shelf, proprietary systems, most notably our ILS (Sierra, from Innovative Interfaces), our electronic journal management and link-resolving software (360 Core and 360 Link, respectively, from Serials Solutions), and our interlibrary loan software (ILLiad, hosted by OCLC). However, most of the interfaces through which patrons access our collections are open-source applications that are locally hosted and fully under our control. These include our subject guides (which run on SubjectsPlus), our institutional repository (Islandora, which provides a Drupal interface over a Fedora repository), our digital publishing platforms (Open Journal Systems and Open Conference Systems), our digital exhibition platform (Omeka), and our archival finding aids (Archon), in addition to our VuFind-based discovery layer.

THE SOFTWARE

Our discovery layer is a lightly modified version of VuFind, open-source software developed at Villanova University. VuFind allows users to search and interact with both locally indexed metadata (such as MARC records exported from an ILS or Dublin Core records harvested from an institutional repository via OAI-PMH) and metadata that is available through APIs, typically those produced by a database vendor. For any given search, users can choose to query only metadata from a single source, such as the library catalog or a specific vendor, or they can cross-search all of the metadata sources at once. No matter which they choose, the interface that they use is as consistent as possible. Some features may only be available when searching certain metadata sources; for example, not all vendor APIs support facets, so faceted searching is not always available. Similarly, different metadata sources may make different fields available for advanced searches. However, the basic format of the results lists and record display pages, as well as functions such as tagging items, adding them to a "favorites" list, sending records via text or e-mail, or exporting records to citation management software such as Refworks or Endnote, are the same across all types of metadata.

VuFind is itself built on many other open-source applications. The user interface for VuFind is constructed with the Zend Framework, an open-source PHP framework. The indexing engine that VuFind uses for searching locally indexed metadata is Apache Solr, open-source software that has often been applied to search large collections in the library world; it also underlies Blacklight and Hydra, popular Ruby-based systems for searching library catalog records and repositories, respectively. Solr is also widely used in the larger web community, where it is deployed to provide search capabilities everywhere from whitehouse.gov to eHarmony. MARC records are indexed into VuFind's Solr index using SolrMarc, an open-source Java-based application developed by the library community that is a key component of both VuFind and Blacklight. Although VuFind's user community is relatively small compared to the user communities for many of these underlying third-party applications, users of VuFind benefit from bugs found and improvements made by those much larger communities when upgraded versions of the improved third party code are incorporated into VuFind.

VuFind is designed to be easily modifiable by the libraries that run it. For example, VuFind is quite flexible in terms of the data sources with which it interacts. As of version 2.4, VuFind shipped with drivers that allowed it to pull item status and other real-time information from sixteen different integrated library systems, with support for getting this information via standard protocols such as NCIP2 (the NISO Circulation Interchange Protocol) or DAIA (the Document Availability Information API) as well. VuFind version 2.4 also came with connectors for seven different database or discovery vendor APIs, including WorldCat, Summon, Primo Central, and two different APIs from EBSCOhost, the EBSCO Discovery Service and the EBSCOhost Integration Toolkit. However, if one's library wants to make a data source available via VuFind, and there is not currently a connector for it, the process for creating such a connector is well documented and can be completed without modifying core VuFind code.[1]

By default, when users search multiple data sources in VuFind, the results from each source are presented in a separate column in the results. VuFind currently does not support interfiling Solr results and API results, or interfiling results from multiple different APIs. This type of interfiling, like federated search, is fraught with problems: it's nearly impossible to de-duplicate records that might appear in both sources, and combining relevance rankings from multiple sources that calculate relevance in different, sometimes proprietary, ways is exceptionally challenging. Even a seemingly simple task like creating a unified list of records in alphabetical or date order is considerably more difficult and resource-intensive than it might appear on the surface.

Depending on one's perspective, this could be a major drawback to running one's own discovery layer. Both "bento-box" results displays, which keep results from different sources in their own separate containers on the screen, and unified displays that interfile results from all different types of sources, have their advantages, and different libraries have made different decisions over which display is most appropriate for their users. For the most part, those who have chosen bento-box displays have less need to grapple with the difficulties of implementing interfiled results than proponents of unified displays. However, even though we generally tend towards the bento box philosophy at the Grinnell College Libraries, we still have found ourselves struggling with this particular limitation of open-source, no-extra-charge discovery layers.

OUR INITIAL IMPLEMENTATION

When we originally launched 3Search in January 2014, it searched metadata from four different sources:

‣ MARC records exported nightly from our ILS, III Sierra, and indexed locally in Solr. This process is fully automated, using some small PHP scripts and cron jobs. In the wee hours of every morning, one PHP script queries our ILS's database, retrieves a list of identifiers for bibliographic records that staff created or modified in the ILS the previous day, and then uses Z39.50 to retrieve the full MARC records for these items and write those records into a file. Another cron job then triggers VuFind's indexing script to index that file of records into Solr. A similar process is subsequently used to retrieve the identifiers for bibliographic records that were suppressed in the ILS the previous day and to delete those records from VuFind's Solr index.

‣ Dublin Core records harvested via OAI from our institutional repository, Islandora, and indexed in the same Solr index as our MARC records. This process is also fully automated, using PHP scripts that ship with VuFind, and is also triggered by cron jobs. Since these records are in the same index as the MARC records from our ILS, they appear in the same "Grinnell's Collections" column in the 3Search results.

‣ Bibliographic records from WorldCat, searched via the WorldCat Search API. The Grinnell College Libraries have free access to this API because we subscribe to OCLC's cataloging services.

‣ Article metadata from twenty-four EBSCOhost databases, searched via the EBSCOhost Integration Toolkit API. Access to this API is included in our subscription to those EBSCOhost databases.

The WorldCat and EBSCOhost results appear in their own columns on the results screen, labeled "WorldCat" and "EBSCOhost Databases," respectively, for a total of three columns with, roughly, three different types of results: local collections, books, and articles; hence, 3Search. (See figure 6.1.)

Getting this implementation launched involved substantial coding on our part. At the time we began seriously exploring using VuFind as our primary discovery option, it did not ship with code that allowed users to search EBSCOhost databases via the EBSCOhost Integration Toolkit API, nor with an ILS driver for Innovative Interfaces' Sierra, which was still in beta at the

FIGURE 6.1 ———————————————————————————————————

An example of a search results screen in 3Search

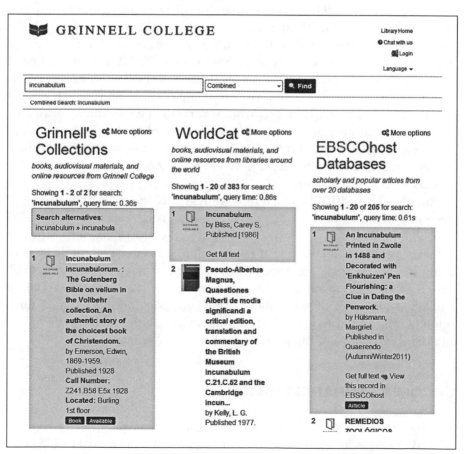

time. (The Grinnell College Libraries were one of the earliest adopters of Sierra, in part because we were excited about the possibilities that its new, more open architecture would create for us to integrate it with other software.) We wrote both an ILS driver for Sierra and a connector for the EBSCOhost Integration Toolkit, and contributed that code back to the VuFind community. If you download a current version of VuFind now, you will find both of these capabilities included.

ASSESSING 3Search

In the summer of 2014, an undergraduate "technology intern" in the libraries worked with us to perform usability testing on 3Search, focusing both on the standard functions of VuFind (e.g., searching, saving and exporting records, faceting) and on a visualization feature that we also added.[2] This testing showed that faculty, staff, and students generally did not encounter difficulties when using 3Search. The major source of problems during the testing was an issue that surfaced in 3Search on a day when several tests were scheduled: a third-party bot had crawled the WorldCat section of 3Search the previous night, pushing us over our daily usage limit for the WorldCat Search API and causing all WorldCat searches to fail for the rest of the day. This meant users who were tested that day were unable to complete tasks on the usability test that required being able to access WorldCat results. (We've since instituted a log-in procedure that prevents users who are not physically on our campus from searching WorldCat via 3Search unless they log in with valid Grinnell College credentials, which has prevented us from going over our daily World-Cat Search API limit again.)

Anecdotally, we have also seen through reference questions we've received since implementing 3Search that some of our users have some degree of difficulty in interpreting the distinctions between results in different columns. Electronic books in the WorldCat results column that our users are unable to access because we don't subscribe to that particular e-book service seem to be a particular source of confusion. A few users have also been perplexed about which record to click on when they see the same book title appear in all three columns, which happens in cases where we own a book, the book is in WorldCat, and there are reviews of the book in the EBSCOhost results.

UPCOMING ENHANCEMENTS

Shortly after we launched 3Search, we began getting questions about why JSTOR articles were not included. On investigation, we discovered that JSTOR can also be searched via an API, which is freely accessible to JSTOR subscribers after signing JSTOR's Metasearch Rider. JSTOR will also provide subscribing institutions with copies of XML-formatted metadata records for all articles in their subscribed collections, with weekly or monthly updates, again after signing a rider. Since some aspects of the JSTOR API are incompatible with the assumptions encoded in VuFind, we decided to pursue local indexing of JSTOR records.

That project proved much more technically challenging than we expected, although for an unexpected reason. Code-wise, the integration was much less labor-intensive: we only had to write an XSLT file to translate the records we received from JSTOR into a format that could be indexed into Solr using the standard VuFind schema, plus a few small scripts to download and extract the records. This is considerably less code than we had to create to write a connector for the EBSCOhost Integration Toolkit API. However, the sheer number of metadata records to be indexed presented a variety of challenges.

Our first batch of JSTOR records came as 2604 ZIP files with a total size on disk of 7.3 gigabytes (GB). After downloading and unzipping everything—processes that took several days by themselves—we had 7,497,458 files, each containing metadata for one article, with a total size on disk of approximately 37 GB. (Luckily for us, we had only purchased 10 of JSTOR's 32 collections, or we could have had even more records than that!) Trying to work with this massive collection of records was the Grinnell College Libraries' first foray into dealing with truly "big data." For comparison, a full dump of the MARC records from our ILS is only a bit over 1 million records and less than 2 GB on disk; the process of doing a complete reindex of these records in VuFind, from start to finish—generating between 20 and 24 files of approximately 50,000 MARC records each within our ILS, exporting those files, uploading them to the VuFind server, and indexing them into Solr—can be completed in a single working day.

As we tried to work with the JSTOR records, we ran into technical difficulties stemming from the size of the data that we didn't even know were possible. For example, we discovered that the limiting factor in the number of small files that can be saved to a single partition on a Linux server is the number of index nodes ("inodes") assigned to the partition, which, we learned, is set at the time of formatting and cannot subsequently be changed. We discovered this when we tried to upload all 7.5 million JSTOR metadata records and found ourselves baffled, a third of the way into the process, by "no space left on device" error messages, even though the partition was clearly less than half full. (In the end, we decided to upload and index the records in chunks, deleting the uploaded records after they had been indexed to free space to upload the next chunk, rather than creating a new partition with sufficient inodes to upload all of the records at once.)

WHICH OF THESE THINGS IS NOT LIKE THE OTHERS?

Introducing JSTOR into 3Search also surfaced previously hidden questions of how to separate the various types of results into different columns containing logically similar results. Up until that point, we had followed the path of least resistance, which had a superficial logic. The records from our ILS and our institutional repository were presented in a column labeled "Grinnell's Collections" and described in the user interface as "books, audiovisual materials, and online resources from Grinnell College." That was how we had always explained the results from our local catalog to our students: as the things that we owned. Separating WorldCat results from EBSCOhost results also seemed logical, since the WorldCat records and the EBSCOhost records were for different kinds of things. These columns were described to users as "books, audiovisual materials, and online resources from libraries around the world" and "scholarly and popular articles from over 20 databases," respectively.

However, when we began considering locally indexing JSTOR records, the hidden cracks in our superficial logic became apparent. It seemed clear that the JSTOR article records didn't logically belong in the "Grinnell's Collections" column, even though we had purchased the collections. We also have records for many things in our catalog that we do not, in fact, own, such as records for physical items available for demand-driven acquisitions, and we selectively load some records from the Center for Research Libraries in our ILS, even though our students still need to go through an interlibrary loan process to get those items. Questions of how to present those items to our users also arose as we worked through adding JSTOR to 3Search. Did we want to continue indexing records from the Center for Research Libraries into the "Grinnell's Collections" index, or did we want to index and present those records separately in the results?

For the time being we have decided to leave the "Grinnell's Collections" column in the results as it has been, to index the JSTOR records into a separate Solr index from the "Grinnell's Collections" index, and to work on interfiling the JSTOR records with the EBSCOhost records in an "Articles" column in the results. As of the time of writing, we still have to figure out how exactly this interfiling will work, and how to overcome all of the challenges discussed above, such as how to accurately sort the interfiled results, that come with it.

We will also offer users the option of interacting with the JSTOR records and the EBSCOhost records separately, in order to provide additional functionality that cannot be provided in the combined "Articles" results. This additional functionality may include more sort options than are available in the combined results, depending on whether we can make all of the possible sort options work in the interfiled results. It may also include options to choose to search only specific databases via EBSCOhost (an option that we did not code into the first version of the EBSCOhost Integration Toolkit API connector for VuFind, but one which is available via that API).

We are also interested in the possibility of providing novel search features against the JSTOR records, as we did with our visualization feature for our catalog records.[3] Automated document clustering—using an algorithm to separate records into clusters of documents on the same sub-topic, based on the text of the abstracts—is one possibility that we're interested in exploring for the JSTOR records. Novel features like these can often only be created when working with locally indexed records, since vendor APIs often do not return the information needed to create such features. (Why would they? These APIs, quite sensibly, are written to support the most common-use cases for the underlying metadata, not to return all of the information a developer might need to do something novel with the records.)

CONCLUSION

Running our own open-source, no-extra-charge discovery tool has had its challenges, but on balance we think the benefits have been worth it. We have received many of the advantages of having a discovery layer—a single search box to which to direct students and a consistent user interface across multiple metadata sources, so we can spend less time teaching students how to use the interface and more time teaching them higher-order information literacy skills—without having to pay the high monetary cost of a commercial discovery service. Although this single search box does not search all of our licensed content, it includes enough broad, general databases (especially once we complete the planned JSTOR integration) to provide a good starting point for many students' research, especially students in lower-level classes. Given our information literacy pedagogy, we would still prefer to direct upper-level students to the indexing and abstracting databases specific to their disciplines even if we had a discovery layer that searched all of our licensed content, so the amount of content accessible via our discovery tool will, we believe, be sufficient for our needs.

We have also had the extra benefit of having complete control over our user interface, giving us the ability to experiment with ways to better meet our users' needs and allowing our technical staff to develop skills that can subsequently be put to use on other projects in the libraries.

Notes

1. The documentation for creating a new ILS driver or a new connector to an external data source is available at https://vufind.org/wiki/vufind2:building_an_ils_driver and https://vufind.org/wiki/vufind2:connecting_a_new_external_data_source, respectively.

2. The visualization feature is not discussed in this chapter; for more information about it, see Julia Bauder and Emma Lange, "Exploratory Subject Searching in Library Catalogs: Reclaiming the Vision," *Information Technology and Libraries* 34, no. 2 (2015): 92–102. doi: 10.6017/ital.v34i2.5888.

3. Ibid.

CHAPTER SEVEN

AGILE OPEN-SOURCE DISCOVERY
Blacklight with EBSCO Discovery Service

SAM POPOWICH

n 2013, after several years of an unfocused discovery strategy relying on licensed, proprietary software, the University of Alberta Libraries (UAL) developed a new, more focused discovery strategy. This strategy proposed implementing an open-source discovery solution, as well as adopting processes, methodologies, and tools from the world of agile software development.[1] Along with new IT governance processes, this signaled a major change on the part of our systems department, encompassing not only hardware and software infrastructure, but also our thinking around configuration, software design, testing, and user experience (UX). Moving in this new direction also necessitated changes in work culture, including changes in workflow, team composition, collaboration, and decision-making processes.

The discovery systems librarian position was created in September 2011. At first, the position's role was ambiguous: the discovery strategy at the time amounted to "license as many discovery systems as we can afford, and put them all on the library home page." At the time we presented the traditional OPAC as the default library search, OCLC's WorldCat Local, and EBSCO's Discovery Service (EDS). That fall, we licensed Ex Libris's Primo system, to be implemented in 2012. The presentation of three different discovery systems on the library website was not intuitive, and a separate flowchart was required to help users figure out which system they should use in a given situation.

Initially, the new discovery systems librarian role was to implement Primo, which I began to do early in 2012. 2012/2013, however, turned out to be quite disruptive. In April, the chief librarian stepped down and the provincial government, which funds most post-secondary education in Alberta, heavily cut the university's budget. By the time a new chief librarian had been found, the library had already implemented some budget reduction measures, including a voluntary severance program, reduced hours, temporary closure of some library branches, and centralization/consolidation of collections. As part of this process, the library's Information Technology Services (ITS) unit decided to cancel the unfinished Primo implementation and, in order to make the discovery services on offer more intuitive (as well as to save money), also canceled our WorldCat Local license. In addition, it was recognized that in 2013 an ARL library should not be presenting a traditional OPAC as its default search interface, so in the autumn of 2013 we replaced the OPAC with an EBSCO Discovery Service search box, presenting the traditional OPAC, along with Google Scholar, as alternative search tools.

The switch to presenting EDS as the default library search was a step in the right direction, but it still did not fulfill all our student and researcher needs. A clear strategy still needed to be developed not only to give us direction as we continued to work on discovery services, but also in order to deal with data silos that had grown organically over the years. These collections included, for example, non-upgraded bibliographic records, a database of maps, historical curricula records acquired through web archiving, and small collections belonging to research groups on campus. These silos were not candidates for inclusion in licensed discovery systems for a variety of reasons. Some of them contained data that was not structured enough (e.g., metadata without a metadata schema) or not rich enough (e.g., stub or basic MARC records). Conversely, some data, such as that contained in our digitized and born-digital collections, had both richness and structure that would be flattened and lost when mapped to the schemas available in proprietary systems. Many discovery systems only handle MARC and Dublin Core records, mapping other metadata schemas to Dublin Core when necessary, which wouldn't allow us to take advantage of our full Metadata Object Description Schema (MODS) records. I developed a new discovery strategy report (Popowich 2013) over the spring and summer of 2013, which included a road map for incorporating all our data silos in a single index and search interface, and would in the end provide a single search interface for our students, faculty, researchers, and staff. The report was approved in September 2013 by the head of the systems unit, the cochairs of the library's web architecture team, the associate university librarians on the Senior Leadership

Team, as well as the chief librarian. I therefore had a clear mandate to move forward with implementing the recommendations of the report.

In preparing the discovery report, I was strongly guided by Lorcan Dempsey's *Educause Review* article entitled "Thirteen Ways of Looking at Libraries, Discovery, and the Catalog: Scale, Workflow, Attention" (Dempsey 2012). This article provides a framework for thinking about discovery systems and services that takes into account recent changes in technology and research behavior.

Underpinning much of Dempsey's discussion is what he calls the "network level" or "network scale." On one hand, the network can be thought of as a higher-level system of a particular kind of institution (the network of libraries and record stores, for example, as opposed to any particular library or record store), but on the other hand the network is also the layer of services and artifacts that provide context to individual institutions. It is in this layer, Dempsey argues, that people work: library users today operate at the level of the network instead of at the level of their local, individual library. In practice, the network is the World Wide Web: a layer above individual institutions which both links libraries together, but also links them to other kinds of organizations and services. Dempsey writes that, in recent years,

> access and discovery have . . . scaled to the level of the network: they are web scale. If I want to know if a particular book exists I may look in Google Book Search or in Amazon, or in a social reading site, in a library aggregation like WorldCat, and so on. My options have multiplied and the breadth of interest in the catalog is diminished: it provides access only to a part of what I am potentially interested in.[2]

This concept—that discovery occurs at the network level instead of the institutional level—has profound consequences not only for discovery, but also for online library services in general (link resolving and proxying, for example). We are starting to see some of these consequences playing out in library technology, but the idea raises many interesting questions about the library as web presence or service provider. Does a single unified web presence still make sense for our users? How does network-level usage affect how we employ analytics and statistics, especially social analytics? What are the privacy implications of tracking usage at the network level? How do we compete with other network-level services while still maintaining a core focus on the needs of our constituents? Do we even need to "compete," or is there another model which might fit the library's mission and strategy more closely? Dempsey does not provide concrete answers to these questions, but does illustrate ways of thinking about the problem, some of which are perennial, and some of which are radically new. Dempsey outlines a few ways in which library discovery can adapt to the requirements of the network scale:

- Provide simple search interfaces which lead to rich result sets.
- Integrate disparate library services into a single, network-level system.
- Harness alternative metadata sources and methodologies (e.g., crowd-sourcing).
- Be present in the user's workflow, rather than requiring users to come to us.

In providing simple search interfaces that lead to rich results, a discovery system would conform to users' expectations of the network (in user experience, this is called the "principle of least astonishment" or "rule of least surprise").[3] This in turn implies conformity of interface and functionality, which is enabled by library services functioning as a single entity at the network level. (This is not to say that library discovery should be monolithic—providing single-purpose services can be an important aspect of discovery—but that data and service silos should be broken down and combined into a single technology, with a single interface, to reduce duplication and be more intuitive to users.) The idea of making our information available at the network level which underpins these suggestions signals a major shift in the thinking around library discovery: rather than providing access to owned or licensed material for "our" users, we are providing our information to the open web for "any" users. Dempsey calls this "inside-out discovery" (as opposed to more traditional "outside-in discovery"), and we will return to this idea later.

Much of Dempsey's article is concerned with how these suggestions might look in practice. I took them as starting points for an investigation into discovery options, and made a final recommendation for a discovery system that would allow us to begin to focus on the network level. In addition to the Dempsey article, the 2013 discovery report adopted some of the principles of a 2009 study by the University of Minnesota as criteria for discovery system evaluation. For example, the Minnesota study identifies five trends, drawn from user studies and statistical usage reports of existing discovery systems (Web Services Steering Committee 2009):

- Users are discovering relevant resources outside traditional library systems.
- Users expect discovery and delivery to coincide.
- Usage of mobile devices is expanding.
- Discovery increasingly happens through recommendation.
- Users are searching for more than just books and journals.

In the discovery report, I tried to think about library discovery through the lens of Dempsey's network-level requirements, the trends identified by the University of Minnesota report, and the technical capacity and skills available at UAL. The following discovery systems were evaluated: EBSCO Discovery Service (EDS), Ex Libris Primo, Serials Solutions Summon, OCLC WorldCat Local, and the

Blacklight open-source system.[4] EDS, Primo, Summon, and WorldCat were chosen because they were and continue to be used extensively by academic libraries (as opposed to BiblioCommons or Aquabrowser, for example) and they are not tied to a particular ILS vendor (such as Innovative Interfaces' Encore).[5] One of the major differences between academic discovery systems (e.g., EDS) and those used in public libraries (e.g., BiblioCommons) is that the former focus on resource discovery, and always include a knowledge base of journal articles or other bibliographic material. Public library discovery systems tend to focus on "social discovery," allowing users to see other users' comments, what others have read, and so on. Blacklight is primarily used by academic libraries, but does not include a knowledge base. The need to integrate a knowledge base is one of the issues we had to address. The final factors for evaluation were:

- ‣ Open-source or proprietary
- ‣ Local or cloud/hosted
- ‣ Maintainability (infrastructure)
- ‣ Customizability (user-interface)
- ‣ Customizability (indexing)
- ‣ Supported metadata schemas
- ‣ Active development/support
- ‣ Modern underlying technologies
- ‣ In-house skills/knowledge
- ‣ Cost

These factors had no intrinsic value, but in aggregate were weighed against in-house skill and capacity, budget constraints, and risk (e.g., with an open-source project under active development, we were likely to be able to count on community support). I included Blacklight for a number of reasons. Besides being a proponent of open-source as opposed to vendor systems for library technology, I felt that under the current budgetary circumstances, we would be remiss not to evaluate an application that was free (in dollar terms) but which could capitalize on in-house skill and knowledge. In the end, the discovery report recommended continuing to use EDS while a Blacklight implementation was developed, and eventually to include EDS as one pane of a "bento box" interface design.[6] To accomplish the integration of EDS results, we are using a Blacklight plug-in developed by EBSCO, which allows Blacklight to search EDS and present results using the EDS API.

Blacklight is an open-source discovery system that uses Apache Solr[7] to index records, and a Ruby on Rails[8] web application for the user interface. It is designed primarily for MARC bibliographic records, but can be extended to include other kinds of records and, because Solr is schema-agnostic, it can index records that use any metadata schema (albeit without retaining the structure of those records). While moving to open-source software provides a distinct set of challenges, not all of which are technological, the adoption of a new (to us) web framework (Rails) was not a primary concern, as we already had some experience with Ruby, the language that the Rails framework uses, and we were looking at Rails as a possible web framework for other projects. Until this time, our programmers had written code in Java, Perl, PHP, and Cold Fusion, and it was deemed advantageous to begin to move toward streamlining our language and infrastructure stack.

The decision to move more fully in an open-source direction, and to unify our programming language and web-framework stack, was made as part of a formalization of our IT governance processes. Faced with a reduction in staffing and a need to modernize processes and workflows, UAL's systems department was at the time adopting the Information Technology Infrastructure Library (ITIL). ITIL is a management framework which seeks to define

> the organizational structure and skill requirements of an information technol-
> ogy organisation and a set of standard operational management procedures and
> practices to allow the organisation to manage an IT operation and associated
> infrastructure.[9]

Reworking our internal processes and procedures allowed us to think about modernizing our entire software development, configuration, and deployment workflow. Adherence to strict project management principles was also new to the department. A suite of ITIL, project management, and Agile-software-development methodologies was adopted for the Blacklight implementation project. Some of these methodologies necessitated the adoption of new tools and technologies (e.g., Ansible, an automated configuration tool, similar to Puppet and Chef) but also required changes in organizational culture, in the areas of team structure, work distribution, collaboration, documentation, and others. In the end, the development consisted of myself as technical lead and codeveloper, one of our web application developers as the other codeveloper, and a system administrator. The team looked at both Scrum and DevOps models of team formation and work,[10] but as the team was so small, and none of us were assigned 100 percent to the discovery implementation, we decided to adopt as many Agile principles and methods as we could without going "full Scrum" or "full DevOps."

One of the most challenging aspects of organizational culture that we recognized fairly early on is the tension between the traditional, service, model of library work and a more project-based model. Typically, library units provide services (cataloging, reference, interlibrary loan), and library workers work on a queue, either of bibliographic material, or users at the reference desk, or interlibrary loan requests. Project work also happens, but the core work of the unit is its service function, and this takes priority. This model breaks down when faced with work that is fundamentally project-based, and which requires that staff be assigned 100 percent to the project at hand, something the traditional model can't ensure. In short, having software development project teams composed of staff members who also provide services, or thinking of multiple software development projects as services that can and should be offered simultaneously, has a negative effect on the ability of a software development team to focus and concentrate on the project at hand. The Blacklight team was supporting and developing other software projects and IT services at the same time as the implementation project. This was a challenge that was raised within the systems department, but was never fully addressed. As a result, work on the Blacklight implementation tended to move forward in fits and starts, and it was difficult to get uninterrupted staff time for working on the project, even though discovery was identified as a strategic priority for UAL.

There were, of course, technical challenges in addition to organizational ones. We planned to adopt many new tools (for example, GitHub,[11] Ansible,[12] Vagrant,[13] and Jenkins[14]) in addition to Ruby on Rails and some useful libraries (e.g. Opinionated Metadata[15] and Solrizer[16] for mapping bibliographic metadata in XML to Solr indexes). There were metadata questions to be answered, and metadata remediation to be undertaken. Metadata in various formats had to be extracted from native systems and mapped to particular index fields, and metadata without an explicit format had to be analyzed and then mapped.

Perhaps the most challenging, but rewarding, aspect of the project, however, was the adoption of a new focus on student requirements and student experience. In 2013 UAL espoused a set of strategic priorities that emphasized student experience (along with research data management and preservation) and allowed us to focus on student feedback and student needs or preferences in designing the system. The new discovery system would specifically not be a staff tool, and would only secondarily attempt to meet the needs of researchers and faculty (other discovery strategies, such as better exposure of library material on the open web, were considered as ways to improve the researcher and faculty experience).

The explicit focus on student requirements allowed us to justify coming down on the side of the student when conflicting requirements arose, say, between student need and staff need. We were able not only to avoid "feature creep" (e.g., staff-only features were not considered hard requirements), but we were able to defer some design decisions until we had done sufficient usability testing. This marked a major change in the thinking around software design and user experience at UAL, and was only possible because of a change in strategic focus and the use of open-source software. In a proprietary, vendor-driven software ecosystem, features are already built into a licensed system; in an agile, iterative, open-source world, features can be added and modified when enough information is gathered. Nothing is set in stone.

Working on implementing a discovery system from the ground up not only required dealing with technical challenges (e.g., overcoming data siloing, meeting user experience needs), but also brought us face-to-face with the larger questions of discovery and discoverability. Is the library still the best starting point for research? What is the role of Google/Google Scholar in the research workflow? Are there ways that we can better integrate our services into users' workflow, which includes Google, but is also broader than Google? Some of these questions were raised by Dempsey's "Thirteen Ways" article, but also in discussion with librarians at other institutions and other service areas. Data supported some propositions, contradicted others, and was insufficient to draw conclusions for the rest. Clearly, in addition to technical challenges and responses to broader questions, analytics needed to play a major role in our new system. The combination of extensive analytics (the UAL systems department is a heavy user of Google Analytics) and in-depth usability testing should give us not only a solid discovery system in the short term, but also point the way for future development and strategies.

Autumn 2013 to summer 2014 were taken up with project planning and infrastructure work (server reorganization, hardware purchases, planning, and provisioning development environments using Ansible and Vagrant). The core development team consisted of only three staff members, none of whom had the discovery project as their sole focus, even for defined periods of time. The core team drew upon knowledge and work being done in other areas, primarily the digital projects department, who were at that point planning to implement Hydra as a digital asset management system.[17] We were able to share some infrastructure and continuous integration work (e.g., Ansible, Vagrant, Jenkins CI) as well as to share knowledge around Ruby and Rails best practices.

Between summer 2014 and spring 2015, active development of the Blacklight system was under way. We wanted to start gathering user feedback early, but we also decided to present users with a working version of the software rather than gather feedback in a vacuum. This runs counter to some requirement-gathering methodologies, but the fact that we knew we were developing a discovery system allowed us to come up with a beta version before moving to user assessment. Prior to the launch of the beta site, we conducted a spot check on the design and basic functionality, from which we got some good initial pass/fail feedback. The next step was to speak to the newly instituted Student Library Advisory Council, both to unveil the new website and discovery system and to gather some feedback, but also to get their help in getting together student constituencies for full-scale usability testing and focus groups after the beta launch.

To sum up, the 2013–2015 discovery implementation project built on changes within the organizational culture of UAL, both in terms of strategic priorities and technical responses to financial challenges. A clear mandate for a student-centered system, the adoption of a full open-source stack, the preparedness on the part of IT librarians and staff to adopt new technologies, process, and procedures, all contributed to the implementation of a discovery system that would satisfy fiscal, experiential, and information-management requirements in a large and complex organization. The beta version of the new discovery system was launched in May 2015, and was followed by assessment and usability testing. A second round of development took place in the summer and fall, with the system going into production in January 2016.

As part of the initial launch, we have tried to communicate the flexibility of the software, in terms of both design and functionality, as emphatically as possible. This is done so that students, faculty, and staff do not feel constrained by the initial state of the application. A suite of acceptance tests, covering workflow and relevance ranking, have been developed so that we can keep track of decisions, and have a way of regression-testing the application through further iterations. Transparency was also a priority for us; the application code is freely available on GitHub, and our backlog of outstanding development issues is also hosted there.[18]

The process of choosing and implementing an open-source discovery system has certainly been challenging, but it has always been rewarding. Along with our Hydra implementation, Blacklight puts the library in a good position for open and sustainable development of digital projects that serve the needs of our core constituents. The challenges have been cultural as well as technical; information technology, public service, metadata, and cataloging staff have had to think differently about how we do the work we do. In an organization as large as UAL, such changes can be difficult, and the learning and acclimatization will take time. But the benefits in terms of increased stability and flexibility, and higher levels of trust and effectiveness can be huge. Rewards come in the form of risk- and skill-sharing, as we participate in the wider world of open-source development and implementation. Letting go of the idea that our workflows, staff, or students are somehow unique allows us to build on standard methods and processes that have been developed and tested within various communities, and which are themselves flexible, sustainable, and open to change. Longer-term rewards are expected in the ability to add collections to the discovery interface, to build scoped interfaces for particular groups or projects, and to fluidly modify the indexing and the interface as new requirements come to light. By implementing two systems from the same ecosystem (Blacklight and Hydra) we are able to deploy time and expertise more efficiently, which, in an era of budget uncertainty and belt-tightening, is an important consideration.

Notes

1. For an overview of agile, see http://en.wikipedia.org/wiki/Agile_software_development.
2. Dempsey 2012, para. 11.
3. Wikipedia, "Principle of Least Astonishment". https://en.wikipedia.org/wiki/Principle_of_least_astonishment.
4. Blacklight (http://projectblacklight.org) was initially developed at the University of Virginia in 2009. More information can be found in Sadler 2009.
5. These discovery systems were also chosen for evaluation in the *Library Technology Reports* special issue on web-scale discovery (Vaughn 2011).
6. For bento box designs, see Lown, Sierra, and Boyer 2013.
7. Apache Solr, http://lucene.apache.org/solr/.
8. Rails, http://rubyonrails.org.
9. ITIL Open Guide, www.itilbrary.org.
10. "Agile" is a broad term for ways of organizing and working on software projects, primarily associated with the open-source world. Scrum is a flavor of Agile, and DevOps is another way of thinking about the division of labor within software projects. For Agile, see http://agilemanifesto.org/; for Scrum, see https://www.scrum.org; for DevOps, see http://devops.com.
11. GitHub, http://github.com.
12. Ansible, www.ansible.com.
13. Vagrant, www.vagrantup.com.
14. Jenkins, http://jenkins-ci.org.
15. Opinionated Metadata, https://github.com/projecthydra/om.
16. Solrizer, https://github.com/projecthydra/solrizer.
17. Hydra uses Blacklight as its index and search interface: http://projecthydra.org.
18. University of Alberta Discovery Repository. http://github.com/ualbertalib/discovery.

References

Dempsey, Lorcan. 2012. "Thirteen Ways of Looking at Libraries, Discovery, and the Catalog: Scale, Workflow, Attention." *Educause Review,* December 10. www.educause.edu/ero/article/thirteen-ways-looking-libraries-discovery-and-catalog-scale-workflow-attention.

Lown, Cory, Tito Sierra, and Josh Boyer. 2013. "How Users Search the Library from a Single Search Box." *College and Research Libraries* 74, no. 3: 227–41. http://crl.acrl.org/content/74/3/227.full.pdf+html.

Popowich, Sam. "Discovery Report." 2013. http://hdl.handle.net/10402/era.41274.

Sadler, Elizabeth (Bess). 2009. "Project Blacklight: A Next Generation Library Catalog at a First Generation University." *Library Hi Tech* 27, no. 1: 57–67.

University of Minnesota Web Services Steering Committee. 2009. "Discoverability Phase 1 Final Report." http://purl.umn.edu/48258.

Vaughn, Jason. 2011. "Web Scale Discovery Services." Special issue, *Library Technology Reports* 47 no. 1.

CHAPTER EIGHT

USING BLACKLIGHT FOR ARCHIVAL DISCOVERY

ADAM WEAD AND JENNIE THOMAS

Since 2010, the Rock and Roll Hall of Fame and Museum's Library and Archives has been building an online catalog (http://catalog.rockhall .com) to ensure that archival materials, both physical and digital, are discoverable within the context of a traditional MARC-based library catalog. The central concept behind the implementation is the discoverability of archival items separate from their collections. "Items" here refers to those components described in the most detail in a finding aid, be they series, files, or individual objects. This separation enables the return of search results that include books and audio and video recordings, as well as archival collections and specific items within those collections. This approach yields other benefits, such as a better browsing experience for large finding aids and easier searching within individual collections. However, the greatest benefit is the ability to display digital objects from the behind-the-scenes asset manager within the hierarchy of their originating collections.

HISTORY

In 1983, after being contacted with a proposal for a television show called "The Rock and Roll Hall of Fame," Ahmet Ertegun, cofounder of Atlantic

Records, contacted *Rolling Stone* founder and editor Jann Wenner and other music industry moguls with the idea of establishing an institution to honor the greatest artists, producers, and record executives in popular music—and the Rock and Roll Hall of Fame Foundation was born. This in turn ushered in the annual Rock and Roll Hall of Fame Induction Ceremonies in 1986. From the museum's earliest conception, a Library and Archives for rock and roll history had been a goal: an institution to not only house and exhibit artifacts related to rock and roll history, but an institution to preserve that content and to educate and provide access to scholars and fans alike. Unfortunately, there was no room in I. M. Pei's museum pyramid design for a true Library and Archives, and the Hall of Fame searched for another solution for twelve years.

In 2007, a portion of the Cuyahoga Community College (Tri-C) Metro Campus's new Tommy LiPuma Center for Creative Arts was offered as the site for the Rock Hall's Library and Archives, located about two miles from the museum. Upon completion of construction in 2009, the museum began hiring staff, whose first tasks were to move collections from off-site and to design systems and workflows, following library and archival standards and best practices. Over a two-year period, staff not only took stock of those collections but also accessioned and processed new acquisitions; determined future staffing, processing, preservation, cataloging, and systems needs; and designed processing manuals to train future staff.

COLLECTIONS

The vision for the Library and Archives has always been to create the most comprehensive repository of materials relating to the history of rock and roll. The Library and Archives' mission is to collect and preserve materials on not only the Hall of Fame's inductees and rock and roll in general but its predecessor and related musical genres as well, and provide access to those resources to scholars, educators, students, journalists, and the general public in order to broaden awareness and understanding of rock and roll, its roots, and its impact on our society.

In January 2012 the Rock and Roll Hall of Fame and Museum's Library and Archives opened to the public, granting scholars and fans access to its collections. The Library and Archives is home to over 400 archival collections, including the personal papers of performers, photographers, rock music journalists, critics, historians, record executives, poster artists, collectors, and fans, as well as the institutional records of the Rock and Roll Hall of Fame and Museum and the Rock and Roll Hall of Fame Foundation.

The Library and Archives also houses a growing library collection that includes thousands of books, periodicals, and sound and video recordings that support the archival collections and the work of the museum.

The strength of the Rock Hall's collections, however, lies in hundreds of boxes of music business records from disc jockeys, record executives, artist managers, records labels, historic venues, recording studios, specialists in stage design and lighting, and long-running concert tours. The archival collections also contain important individual items, such as personal letters penned by Aretha Franklin and Madonna; handwritten working lyrics by Jimi Hendrix and LL Cool J; and rare concert recordings from the New York nightclub CBGB in the 1970s.

THE PROBLEM

Playing to the strengths of the archival collections presented a significant problem because unique items were often described within large collections of hundreds of items, or described within a collection that highlighted a particular donor rather than the items within. Compounding this issue was the presence of standard library holdings that could easily overwhelm search results with content that might not be related to users' search requests.

Effective discovery of content needed to combine the Library and Archives' three primary metadata formats (MARC, EAD, and PBCore) in a way that presented a uniform interface to the user. MARC records included all non-archival and non-digital holdings: traditional library formats such as books, periodicals, and audiovisual recordings. EAD records provided the descriptive standard for all archival content. The PBCore XML standard was chosen to describe digitized and born-digital content.

While numerous products existed to facilitate discovery within a MARC-based catalog, very few featured any practical solutions for such diverse sets of metadata. Most strategies involved describing archival content using MARC standards and representing the item using MARC records. This was effective for collection-level description, where a single record could serve as the discovery point for the collection, with links to finding aids, but discovery at the archival item level was not possible without creating numerous separate MARC records for each item within every collection.

The products that did offer enough customization of metadata formats were prohibitively expensive, limiting the Library and Archives to purchase a simpler ILS product that did not offer these kinds of features.

SOLUTION STRATEGY

Providing effective discovery of the Library Archives' many formats hinges on the use of different software products that form a solution bundle. The key parts of this bundle are a Solr indexing solution and a Blacklight front end that provides the user access to this index. The remaining parts of the bundle are mostly custom-built to serve as means for feeding EAD description in the Solr index.

Blacklight

Developed as an open-source, community-driven effort, Blacklight is a web application specifically designed to search and display MARC data. Although it has changed recently to use geodata and other non-MARC sources specifically for the management of digital collections, at the time the Library and Archives implemented it, it was only using MARC data.

At its core, Blacklight uses the Ruby on Rails technology platform with Ruby as the programming language and a gem, or software module, called "Rails" that is specifically engineered for the rapid development of web applications. The adage for Rails developers is "convention over configuration," meaning that the lower levels of an application's details are less important than its high-level, visible, and actionable details. Therefore, using conventions of software design and automatically generated code significantly decreases the amount of time it takes to complete a project.

The other key technology that Blacklight utilizes is Solr, an end-to-end search and indexing application written in Java. Originating back in the late 1990s from the search company Excite, the original application was purchased by the Apache Foundation and exists as an open-source product, called "Solr," as well as a paid product called "Lucene."

Solr is the critical component of Blacklight, serving as its search engine. MARC records are indexed according to a supplied configuration that defines which fields in the MARC record are to be searched, displayed, or provided as facets. Each implementation offers complete control over how this takes place. Any number of fields may be indexed in any number of ways. This requires knowledge of the Solr product, but the results are similar to what one might expect when performing a Google search.

Solr results are ranked according to relevance, just as results are from Google. Fields in the MARC record may be weighted differently to affect relevance. For example, a record with search terms in the title might be ranked higher in relevance than another record with those same terms in a note field. Other fields can be designated as non-searchable, meaning their contents might be displayed in search results, but they are not searched during a query.

The other important feature of Solr is its ability to facet. Any field may be identified as a facet field, but the most common ones in Blacklight implementations are fields such as subject headings, authors, format types, and languages. Facets drive the "discoverability" of a Blacklight application, enabling users to explore the catalog without even searching, or to refine existing searches by limiting results to a specific facet, or subset of the results, that share a common field.

Archivists' Toolkit

While the Library and Archives' MARC records are maintained using Millennium (now Sierra) at Case Western Reserve University, a system to manage archival collections was still needed. Using Lisa Spiro's January 2009 Council on Library and Information Resources (CLIR) report on archival content management software as a starting point for decision making, a number of products were demonstrated and tested.[1] At the time, the two most commonly used products were the archivist-designed Archivists' Toolkit and Archon. The final determination was made for Archivists' Toolkit, primarily based in its ease of customization and use within the constructs provided by *Describing Archives: A Content Standard (DACS)*.[2]

Archivists' Toolkit, or AT, provides all the necessary features to accession, arrange, and describe archival collections and their contents. Multiple archivists use AT simultaneously, creating complete finding aids for use by staff and patrons. Because AT lacks a public interface, the primary vehicle for disseminating its finding aids is either a PDF or HTML document, or XML following the standards of Encoded Archival Description (EAD), the de facto standard used by archives in the United States.

EAD XML is common currency among archives, and many software products and tools exist to process it and render it usable in a variety of contexts. Most common are making HTML files from EAD, or PDFs, similar to what AT does. However, it is less common to find EAD indexed in Solr. While indexing EAD XML, or for that matter any kind of XML into Solr is a trivial task, there are no accepted standards or any existing shared solutions for doing so.

solr_ead

The primary motivation for choosing Blacklight was the ability to display MARC- and EAD-related data in the same catalog. Solr, as a content-agnostic search engine, does not discern the sources of its information; however, a process was needed for indexing EAD XML into Solr to make it searchable in the same way as MARC data. This meant that similar fields in a MARC record had to be correlated to "fields" or relevant sections of the EAD. Technically speaking, these were XML nodes.

The Rails gem "solr_ead" was developed as the component that would take EAD XML and index it into Solr. It was configured in such a way that the user could identify which Solr fields would correlate with which XML nodes in the EAD. This was done using the features of XPath, a language used to query XML documents. For example, any EAD would have the title rendered in XML as:

```
<ead>
 <eadheader>
  <filedesc>
   <titlestmt>
     <titleproper>Alan Freed Collection</titleproper>
   </titlestmt>
  </filedesc>
 </eadheader>
</ead>
```

We can search for the value of titleproper using the xpath syntax:
    /ead/eadheader/filedesc/titlestmt/titleproper

This in turn can be indexed in Solr as a field simply called *title,* along with MARC records that have the contents of their 245 fields indexed into the same field *title* in Solr. Using this simple cross-walk of titles from MARC to EAD, one can search for both according to their titles.

The above approach works well with simple 1:1 correlations between a MARC item and an overall collection. AT could bypass this entire process and export a MARC record from a given collection; however, there was a substantial amount of data loss. Because EAD was designed to contain information about the entire collection, including the details of its individual items, a single MARC result from Solr was not enough to describe one collection that might contain hundreds or thousands of items.

Hydra

The Library and Archives' digital asset management platform is Hydra, a stack of technologies that utilize the Fedora repository architecture atop a Ruby on Rails framework. Because it uses many of the same components as Blacklight, it is a good choice because they share similar technologies in one server deployment.

Hydra provides a lot of flexibility for indexing XML and uses the same strategy of XPath queries enabling the mapping of fields in PBCore XML onto fields like title, creator, and others that are used in the Library and Archives' catalog. Exporting records from Hydra was customized to include descriptive metadata from PBCore as well as technical metadata gathered during the ingest of digital files. Using MediaInfo, a utility that captures information about audiovisual files, technical properties such as color scheme, bit rate, and other information were added to Hydra's assets. This data was not kept in the PBCore record but could be included in the exported Solr record because it does not adhere to a specific metadata schema and will accept any field and value it is given.

Search Results and Relevance

One of the important aspects of the Library and Archives' collections is that they contain unique, singular items. For example, a set list written by Elvis Presley or the lyrics to Jimi Hendrix's "Purple Haze" are not only single items but collections in and of themselves. Yet there are also single items of importance within a collection of hundreds of items, such as handwritten lyrics by Tom Waits in the Jeff Gold Collection. If a search was performed for Waits's lyrics, the results need to include the item but not necessarily the collection. In short, it is the item, not the collection, that needed to be the required unit of discovery.

The Library and Archives' catalog search results became such that "items" in search results could include MARC items, such as books, recordings, or journals, as well as archival collections and those items within collections. This enabled the user to explore the holdings as deep as the unique items held within them.

In order for archival items to be indexed in Solr, solr_ead had to produce multiple Solr documents for a single EAD. This effectively meant pulling apart a collection into its component parts—thousands in some cases—and indexing each piece as a separate entity. These entities were identified according to the component levels in the EAD. Each finding aid could have as many as six levels of components: collection or record group, series, subseries, files, or individual items. For example, a sample collection might be arranged like this:

Collection
  Series A
    Folder 1
      Item 1

This arrangement would produce four entities, or documents, that would be indexed into Solr: one document for the collection, and three documents for each component: series, file, and item. While solving the problem of searching for items, this created several additional problems. The first was relevance. As described earlier, Solr will return results in order of relevance, meaning that when searching collections, it was possible to see an item from a collection ranked higher in relevance than the collection in which it was housed. It was also possible to have an item's parent components, such as the series, subseries, or folders, appear in the search results as well.

To solve the problems of relevance ranking, non–item–level components were eliminated from search results and collection-level results were weighted much lower in the rankings than items. For example, a user searching for "Tom Waits lyrics" would receive a ranked list of results in which the archival item that included the lyrics itself was first, followed by the archival collection in its entirety. After experimenting with different weighting strategies, archival collections were weighted lower in the results based on format type. Assigning a simple Boolean field to an archival item identifying it as an item removed medial hierarchical levels (e.g., series, subseries, or even folder in some instances) from the search results.

XSLT for Display

Another problem with breaking apart EAD finding aids was that it destroyed the archival arrangement, a fundamental requirement for any user of archival materials. Although it was responsible for displaying all the MARC records and key elements of our finding aids, Solr was essentially a search tool. Since finding aids could be very large, transforming them into HTML using XSLT offered better performance than rendering individual parts of the finding aid via fields in Solr. Because the Rails application provided full control over the display of content, any combination of Solr fields or generated HTML could be used.

EAD finding aids were transformed into HTML in two varieties. One kind was a conversion of the entire finding aid so that the user could scroll and view the complete document. A second version, which supported the default view of all our collections, only converted the top-level portions of the document and excluded the collection-level organization. Items and their corresponding hierarchical levels were displayed within their own page using the data from Solr, making additional XSLT steps unnecessary. This also greatly improved performance. If a user found a particular item within a collection, viewing the information for the item only showed the item itself and the immediate hierarchical level that contained it. Viewing a series displayed all the items within it, up to fifty, at which point the user could continue loading more. This improved performance for viewing collections that had upwards of hundreds or thousands of items in a series.

Responsive Redesign

While the initial version of the catalog was not optimized for mobile devices, the second major release subscribed to a responsive design style that would adapt to devices of varying display sizes. These included large or small desktop computers, as well as tablets and mobile phones. Using Bootstrap as the foundation of the user interface, the Library and Archives was able to present all of the collection information to any user, regardless of the size of their display.

Our indexing strategy played a key role in evolving a responsive design. Even with very large finding aids, the essential viewing information could be reduced to a single item and its relevant containers, such as a series or folder. Traditional finding aids on the Web that display entire collections at once are not suited to the smaller displays of today's handheld devices.

In order to preserve the browsing features of a finding aid, links to other parts of the document were maintained in every view of the collection. These included links to top-level sections such as biographical information, collection history, access, and use. To maintain perspective, breadcrumb trails were provided so that users could see how many levels deep a particular item was. Also, the user was able to search within collections if they were looking for a particular item.

USER PERSPECTIVES

Serving the Needs of Archivists, Librarians, Museum Staff, and Patrons?

The Library and Archives search interface provides users with a familiar public face, that of a standard library catalog or Google search box. For patrons who, for the most part, are not typical users of archival collections, the familiarity of an interface that pulls all collection materials, be they library, archival, or digital, with one search was essential. Equally important was a search return of individual component records from archival finding aids, rather than forcing users to wade through what is, in some cases, hundreds of pages of inventory per collection.

Item-level search returns on archival collections were also helpful to the staff of the museum and the librarians for discoverability purposes, as their standards and best practices fall within item-level description. The only loss in translation occurred when "item-level" description did not include an actual single item but rather a folder of items.

For the archivists, this search interface has eased interactions with the public and staff. Each component record has a permanent URL. The bookmarking feature of the catalog allows for easy identification of what materials users are interested in, and the chosen items can be directly e-mailed to Library and

Archives staff in order request materials for a research appointment or repro-
duction request. This has also made it easier for archivists to pinpoint materials
within the collections to recommend to potential researchers. With the addition
of the breadcrumbs and the appearance of series descriptions with the archival items, there have also been fewer questions regarding just what an item is
that a user finds in the catalog. The archival item and its context is more easily
identifiable to even a user new to archival collections.

Preserving the Finding Aid Experience Online

The benefits to breaking the component parts of the finding aid were obvious
to everyone from the start. The most important aspect for the archivists being
not only adherence to *DACS* but also the retention of the context of individual
archival items within their originating collections. In general, the scope and
contents notes in finding aids provide the most depth of description, so on their
own the archival items could potentially be lacking a great deal of information.
With the Library and Archives' interface, the closest level of description to the
item is available on the screen (i.e., the series description for a file) while the
levels above are accessible via breadcrumbs. See figure 8.1.

The left-hand menu of the finding aid also provides additional means to
navigate the different sections of the finding aid, so all the archival information
for the collection is there per *DACS,* but the structure makes it less difficult for
a user to get bogged down by a document that may be hundreds of pages long
in its complete form. However, if the user desires a browseable document, there
is also an HTML version available under the View icon, a view of the EAD

FIGURE 8.1

Individual item record in a finding aid ("Appointment, address, and pass books") with the
next highest level of description listed above for context ("Series II: Personal Appointment
Books"), and all levels of description available through breadcrumbs

behind the finding aid for archivists, and a tab on the left under which users can search within a collection—in case someone gets the collection in a search results list without easily being able to discern why the collection came up in their results—or for those who need to drill down further to find out more.

Staff Involvement during Development

The development of both Blacklight and Hydra involved a close-working team that included the director of the Library and Archives, head archivist, catalog and metadata librarian, systems and digital collections librarian, and the public services librarian. Each individual brought to the table the concerns of their area of work, knowledge of their field's standards and best practices, and experience working in those fields for multiple years. One- to two-hour weekly meetings were held to discuss the design, implementation, and use of the products, with attendees bringing their favorite examples of products or components of products already in use and their vision for what these products should eventually be able to do.

Reactions/Discussions

It may help to understand how this has changed staff thinking in regard to processing, particularly description. For instance, where restricted notes previously would have been included at every level of the finding aid corresponding with the restricted items (series, subseries, file, and/or item), staff now streamline this so that the notes do not show up multiple times on the screen.

The clarity of the new interface provides for more confident delivery of the description of a collection's hierarchy. Breadcrumbs are something many institutions have been utilizing for years, but this interface allows the user to click back to view the scope and contents and any additional notes that may occur at higher levels of the collection description. It's very obvious now, as figure 8.2 shows, that the files listed here are a part of the Artist and Subject Files subseries for the series of Ralph Gleason materials in the Jeff Gold Collection, and a researcher can quickly and easily see the context of the materials. Clicking on an individual file within the list, the researcher will still see the most closely related hierarchical level, in this case "Subseries 1: Artist and Subject Files," retaining the context of the materials to the collection as a whole.

Finally, because the new discovery interface brings together the descriptions of the physical media from the finding aid and the metadata from Hydra for the corresponding digital file, it cuts down on the amount of description needed in the finding aids, because the more detailed, item-level information for each digital object or group of objects will come directly from Hydra. See figures 8.3 and 8.4.

FIGURE 8.2 ——

Subseries-level view

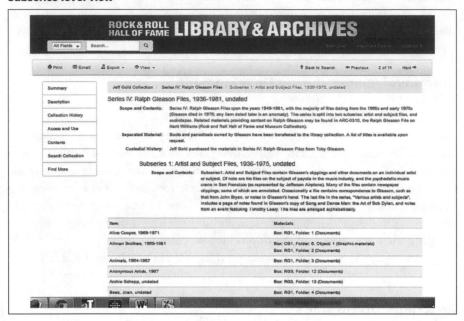

FIGURE 8.3 ——

Item-level information from EAD

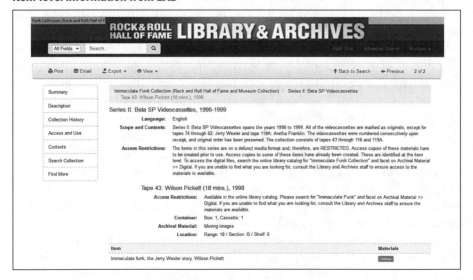

FIGURE 8.4 ───

Item-level information from combined EAD and PBCore records

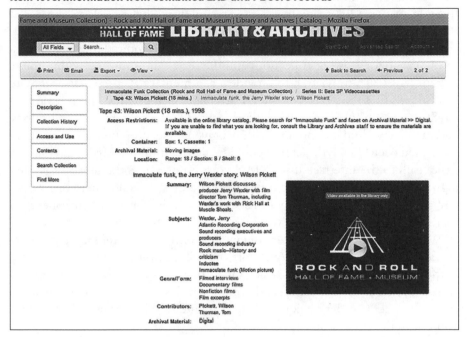

INTEGRATING DIGITAL CONTENT

Combining the content and description from our digital asset manager was the final piece in the catalog puzzle. Because items had already been teased apart from their collections in the Solr index, the process of adding digital content to collections was a matter of injecting new items into existing collections. The plan was to export Solr records from Hydra's Solr index into the Solr index of the Blacklight catalog. This would enable the discovery of digital content at the metadata level. However, the description of the digital content needed to be indexed in such a way that it would map to the Solr fields created from MARC and EAD records.

ARTK Gem for AT Integration with Rails

The Library and Archives uses Hydra to ingest, manage, and catalog both digitized and born-digital content that is part of an existing archival collection. While these collections were described and arranged using AT, Hydra had no knowledge of the collections and series created in AT. In order to export data from Hydra's Solr index to the catalog's, it was necessary to find a way to include this information. Otherwise, an exported record from Hydra could not be placed into the existing archival collection hierarchy preserved in the catalog index.

To do this, one more piece of linking software was required to enable Hydra to query AT for existing collections and the series and subseries within them. A gem (ARTK) was written to provide a rudimentary Representational State Transfer (REST) interface to the AT database. Using Rails' ability to query MySQL tables, a REST API was built that would query for existing collections, and query any child component within a given collection. Because everything happened over HTTP, this ability could be used within the Hydra interface to make calls to the interface using AJAX. Put simply, while the user was editing a given record for a digital item in Hydra, he or she could query and assign any archival collection and any of its series, subseries, or item components to that item.

When the collection and component are assigned to an item in Hydra, they are saved in the PBCore XML. At export, the collection and component included in the Solr record is sent to the catalog index. Because the newly exported record is now linked at the collection and component level to an existing collection and component in the catalog, the digital content will appear with the other content in the finding aid. See figure 8.5.

FIGURE 8.5 ———————————————————————————————————————

Assignment of digital items in Hydra to the EAD finding aid component levels

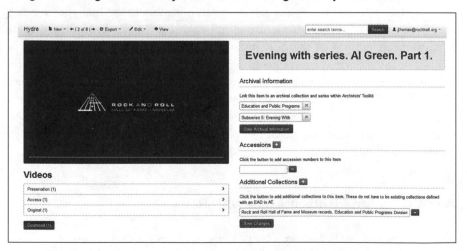

Advantages and Disadvantages

The principle advantage of this solution was gathering outside content and combining it into an existing structure. The AT database contained all collection information, yet it was closed and could not incorporate external data. This was accomplished via a third source, Solr, which served as the common index for AT and Hydra data. The disadvantage was that the amalgamated data did not persist in the same way that EAD and PBCore does; in other words, there is not a canonical source that represents the collection with all of its content, both analog and digital.

The digital content that is inserted into the finding aids as they appear in Blacklight is never pulled back into AT; it only resides in Hydra. Similarly, the collection information that is pulled into Hydra only concerns a single component record; additional collection information, such as hierarchy, is never pulled into Hydra.

LOOKING BACK, LOOKING AHEAD

Given the staff resources of the Library and Archives, it might have been a better choice to undertake one development project, such as the Hydra asset management system or the custom catalog application. However, because the two were dependent upon one another, it is impossible to know if the catalog would have been a success without Hydra. If another asset management system was in use that had basic features to export descriptive content, it is very likely that it would have worked equally well as Hydra; however, given that many digital asset managers lack PBCore support, a different metadata schema might have been required, and there a standard asset manager would not have had the ability to manage the Library and Archives' large preservation video files, generally 2–3 terabytes each.

While the final solution suited the Library and Archives' discovery needs perfectly, it did require substantial development using custom-built software applications. The software was open-source, and therefore free of charge, but there was no support mechanism other than contacting developers via e-mail and posting questions to lists. Since only one developer was working on the project, all of the knowledge was with one person. Documentation was provided throughout, but it was impossible to fully document the workings of every step in the process.

The software that the catalog utilized also developed as well, taking on new features and releases. It was necessary to update these components as they were released to ensure that the catalog stayed current with the latest software patches and security releases.

Further progress with additional features was also hindered due to the complexity of the implementation. While the staff had targeted additional features and requirements, it was not clear when those features could be implemented because other projects needed attention as well, such as additional features added to Hydra: image and audio ingestion and description, preservation management for all digital content, and records management capabilities to support digital content created across the institution; and to Blacklight: the ingest and display of museum records from the content management database TMS for the permanent artifact collection.

Driving the Library and Archives' current direction is the museum's new strategic plan, a major focus of which is providing digital access to collections. To date, collection materials have been digitized based on reference requests and through special projects funded by outside sources, the foundation, and the museum. Through these means, the Library and Archives has accumulated about eleven terabytes of digital content—250,000 images and some audio—that are currently waiting for a digital asset management system that can ingest them and allow for PBCore description, and a discovery interface to make them accessible. Including the video content managed through Hydra and stored in an LTO-5 tape library, the Library and Archives is approaching 400 terabytes of total data. That much data management requires a system with preservation capabilities, preferably OAIS-compliant, in order to provide long-term storage and access to the digital files, including support for new media, migrating defunct file formats, and authenticating data.

Another major piece of the puzzle as the Library and Archives moves forward is the need for an institutional repository for museum staff to upload documents, photographs, audio, and video that they need to share with each other. The Library and Archives would like to see this combined with an electronic records management system in order to preserve the institution's born-digital content.

Finally, the additional features that were left out of the original catalog design as lower priorities are still desired, including community engagement functionality. Popular music is something nearly everyone has a connection with, and being able to mine that excitement and knowledge to let our users transcribe handwritten documents from archival collections, tag items with additional descriptors, write reviews, see recommendations based on a search, create personal lists, view a browseable virtual shelf of books, or post to social media accounts straight from the catalog would all be necessary additions to a future set of access systems for the institution.

Notes

1. Spiro, Lisa. "Archival Management Software: A Report for the Council on Library and Information Resources." CLIR, January. Spiro, Lisa. *Archival Management Software: A Report for the Council on Library and Information Resources.* Washington, D.C.: CLIR, January 2009.
2. *Describing Archives: A Content Standard.* Chicago: Society of American Archivists, 2007. Please note that *DACS* has since been revised, once in 2013 and again in March 2015.

Reference

Society of American Archivists. 2007. *Describing Archives: A Content Standard.* Chicago: Society of American Archivists.

CHAPTER NINE

CREATING A "MAGICAL" REQUEST AND DELIVERY EXPERIENCE FOR PATRONS USING A BLACKLIGHT-BASED CATALOG

MATTHEW CONNOLLY, JENNIFER COLT,
JOANNE LEARY, AND MELISSA WALLACE

I n the summer of 2012, the Cornell University Library (CUL) launched a major initiative to overhaul its search and discovery interface. At the time, CUL offered WorldCat Local as its primary catalog and Voyager as a secondary option. Most searches against library resources originated at the main CUL website, while lists of results appeared in a variety of native interfaces. As part of the initiative, the newly formed Discovery & Access Implementation Team was to develop a new CUL website and a Blacklight-based catalog. In addition, the team was to create a new discovery layer between the website and Blacklight, designed to combine and display search results from different sources.

The open-source Blacklight project code allows for extensive customization. In addition to modifying the user interface and fine-tuning the Solr index serving as a data source behind the catalog, the team customized advanced search functionality; searches for authorities, call numbers, and databases; and item requests. Improvement of the library's requests system was an early project goal. The system developed by the Implementation Team and that this chapter describes was intended to streamline the process of getting a user from viewing an item record in Blacklight to holding or viewing the item itself. We wanted that process to be so simple that we half-jokingly referred to it as "magic" requests.

CUL'S REQUEST ENVIRONMENT

When we undertook this project, our goal was not to reduce the growing complexity of our collections and their delivery, but rather to make the complexity invisible to the user. To achieve this, we had to map out the existing request scenarios and develop algorithms that would present the best option to the user—the one delivery method that would convey the material to them in the shortest possible time. Ideally, other options would be presented as well, ranked by delivery time.

Types of Requests

Voyager provides three internal functions for requesting physical items held at Cornell. The rules for placing the requests (what types of materials may be requested and by whom) are defined in the Circulation Matrix, discussed in the next section.

The three *internal* types of requests are:

▸ Holds (can be placed on items that are checked out; due date is not changed)
▸ Recalls (can be placed on items that are checked out; due date is shortened)
▸ Library-to-Library Delivery (can be placed on items that are available in the stacks and eligible to be delivered to another library for pickup)

In addition to the internal requests, there are three external systems that allow for requesting physical items or scans of items that may, or may not, be held at Cornell.

The three *external* types of requests are:

▸ Borrow Direct (a consortium of libraries from which we can request books that are not available from Cornell)
▸ Document Delivery (provides scans of articles or book chapters held at Cornell)
▸ Interlibrary Loan (provides materials or scans of materials that are not held by Cornell nor available through Borrow Direct)

Circulation Matrix

The rules for circulating and requesting in Voyager are coded into the Circulation Matrix, which is based on three variables:

▸ Circulation Policy Group (18 groups or libraries)
▸ Patron Group (22 groups)
▸ Item Type (40 types)

For any given borrower/library/item type combination, the matrix determines whether the loan can proceed, what the loan period will be, whether the item can be requested through each of the internal request options, how many notices will be sent, and many other details.

There are 15,840 possible combinations for our library system, but not every combination is encoded in the matrix (a bit less than half of them are). To cover situations not encoded in the matrix, a default rule is assigned; each library chooses its own default rule definitions.

Library profiles, in addition to the matrix, define blanket policies about borrowing limits and blocks, and define shelving or processing locations. A custom calendar is referenced for calculating due dates and fines. Calendars are updated once a year and reflect each library's hours of operation and any special blackout dates on which charged items will not fall due.

Placing a Request in Voyager (Classic Catalog)

To place a request in Voyager, the user logs into the system, then searches for and selects an item. User credentials determine which internal request options are available for an item, but Voyager does not indicate the fastest option. Moreover, external options are not presented at all during the request process; the user must already be aware of Borrow Direct, Document Delivery, and Interlibrary Loan, and know which (if any) are appropriate for the desired item. Frequently, Borrow Direct and Document Delivery are faster options than Recall or even Library-to-Library delivery. These options do not appear in the list of request alternatives, and it is entirely up to the user to know about them.

In general, turnaround time for Borrow Direct is much faster than for Recalls (3–5 days versus up to 14 days for recall). Borrow Direct also has a higher fill rate. Turnaround time for Document Delivery and Library-to-Library Delivery is 1–2 days; but in the case of needing an article from a volume, rather than the entire volume, Document Delivery is far more convenient.

ARCHITECTURE OF A MAGIC REQUEST

The new CUL catalog is based on the open-source Blacklight project (projectblacklight.org). Blacklight is written in Ruby on Rails, a popular web development framework. Although we could have added the request system's code directly into our customized Blacklight project, we opted instead to implement it as a separate Rails engine. An engine, in Rails parlance, is a project within a project: a self-contained application that extends the functionality of the application it's embedded inside. This means that the Blacklight catalog can work quite happily without the presence of the Requests engine, but a Requests engine can be added to an existing Blacklight instance and—in theory—immediately offer magic requests.

Users first encounter the Requests System Engine (RSE) when they click a "Request" button on an item record page in Blacklight. This marks the crossing point from the main Blacklight project into the RSE. As soon as the button is clicked, the user is passed through an authentication page to make sure that he or she is a valid Cornell University member or guest. Next, the system retrieves the user's Cornell ID and the Solr document associated with the requested record. From the Solr document, the RSE obtains all of the holdings and item records linked to the requested bibliographic record. The Solr document also indicates whether or not a record is considered to have multivolume holdings (as determined in Solr by examining several fields in the original MARC record). If it is, then the user is asked to select a particular volume to request before going any farther.

The RSE then takes the holdings and item records, or the subset of those records for a particular volume, and analyzes each one of them to determine key pieces of information:

- ‣ Is the item *available?* (What is the item's current status?)
- ‣ What is the item's *loan type?* This can be a regular loan, day loan, or "minute" loan (a loan period of hours rather than days or weeks).
- ‣ What delivery methods are available for the item?

Possible delivery methods vary with the item's loan type and availability, as well as with the user's affiliation (Cornell member or guest). As outlined in the previous section, CUL offers six different delivery methods that have to be considered on a case-by-case basis.

Once the available delivery methods have been calculated for each item, the RSE sorts the methods by delivery speed. The fastest delivery method is presented to the user as the optimum choice. However, the request is not actually executed until the user confirms that choice. If, for whatever reason, the user doesn't want to use the suggested method, the other available methods are also displayed as secondary choices that can be selected (see figure 9.1). Once the user confirms a delivery method, the actual request is sent to the native system responsible for the request type: Voyager for Library-to-Library delivery, recall, and hold; Borrow Direct; ILLiad for Interlibrary Loan; and so on. If all else fails, users are directed to "ask a librarian" about an item's availability.

FIGURE 9.1 ──

The request options offered to a Cornell-affiliated user for Erik Larson's *Dead Wake*.
The fastest delivery choice, Borrow Direct, is prominent as an action button.
Secondary delivery options appear listed below it.

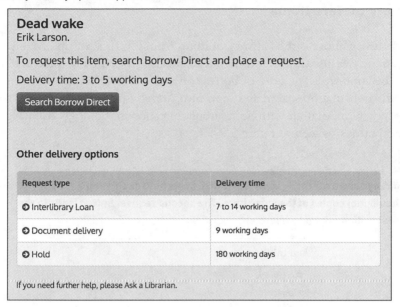

External Connections

Fulfilling a request always involves a handoff from the RSE to an external system. Handoffs are handled as follows:

- Voyager requests are placed through Voyager's APIs by constructing a specially formatted request URL.
- Interlibrary loan requests are handled by the ILLiad system, which does not offer the same type of transparent requests as Voyager. The Requests system passes users into the ILLiad request submission form, which they must fill out themselves and submit. However, the RSE can use an OpenURL to pre-populate some of the ILLiad form fields with item metadata.
- Borrow Direct, until recently, did not offer APIs. We initially worked around this issue by using our own instance of Index Data's Pazpar2 metasearch engine to determine item availability at Borrow Direct partner libraries. However, this approach frequently failed to return accurate results. With the newly released APIs, we are able to quickly and easily determine whether an item is available or not. For the moment, the handoff to Borrow Direct to fulfill a request is still clumsy; users are taken to the Borrow Direct search interface to locate

and request their items. However, the APIs also give us the ability to place requests from within the RSE, which we intend to add in a future release.

Delivery of Rare Items

Not discussed above is the delivery of items from CUL's Rare and Manuscript Collections. Because these items are noncirculating, they are not included in the RSE's decision tree. The request button on a rare item takes the user through an RSE confirmation screen and then into Atlas Systems' Aeon reading room delivery system. An item with both circulating and rare holdings will have two request buttons, as seen in figure 9.2.

FIGURE 9.2 ——

The holdings and availability view when CUL owns both circulating and rare (noncirculating) copies of the same item. The second request button leads to the Aeon reservation request system.

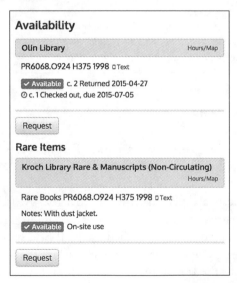

Theory and Practice

Our first pass at creating a magic request system was relatively simple. Based on a user's Cornell affiliation and an item's availability and circulation type, we constructed a fairly straightforward logic tree to determine which types of delivery could be offered to the requester. Unsurprisingly, the reality of requesting items at CUL turned out to be far more complex than we had originally accounted for. Over time, we have had to modify the logic in our code to account for new or revised circulation policies, changes to the external delivery systems we work with, and numerous edge cases that we failed to take into account at the beginning. Those changes, coupled with our inexperience with Ruby on Rails programming at the beginning of the catalog project, means that the RSE code base is in need of a complete overhaul to improve its efficiency and maintainability.

USER INTERFACE

Strategy for User Interface Design

Despite the complicated structure underlying the loan types, borrowing rules, and technical architecture of the RSE, the primary goal of the user interface was to make this complex process appear simple and seamless to the end user. To achieve this we focused on several areas of the user interface:

- ‣ The availability information displayed with the item record
- ‣ The call to action
- ‣ The subsequent screens for each request method

The Availability Information on the Item Record

On the item record, we simplified the holdings information so that a user could determine whether they could (a) go to a library in person to get the item (off the shelf, from reserves, etc.), or (b) request it via some other method (Borrow Direct, Interlibrary Loan, Library-to-Library delivery, hold, etc.). In addition to the item location, a simple icon indicates whether or not an item is available. We added a prominent "Request" button just below the availability information to point users toward the next step in requesting the item. Figure 9.3 shows an example.

FIGURE 9.3 ───

The availability box showing item status

FIGURE 9.4 ——

Three different "request" links in the Classic Catalog

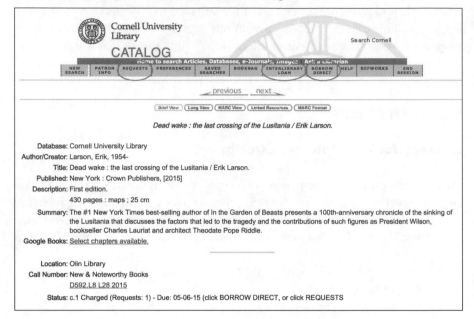

We use a set of three icons to denote availability: a green check mark for items currently available; a red clock for items currently checked out or unavailable; and a yellow question mark, which rarely appears, for items with unknown status.

The Call to Action

In the Classic Catalog, if a user wanted to request an item, they had to click one of three links, all of which were located far from the availability information (see figure 9.4). The user would need to click on a link labeled:

▸ "Requests" for Recall, Hold, or Library-to-Library Delivery
▸ "Borrow Direct" for Borrow Direct requests
▸ "Interlibrary Loan" for Interlibrary Loan or Document Delivery requests

In the new interface, we put the "Request" button in a more logical place: right below the availability information. Additionally, instead of making the user parse out the meaning of "Borrow Direct," "Interlibrary Loan," "Document Delivery," "Library-to-Library Delivery," "Recall," or "Hold," we simply labeled the button "Request," regardless of method. The suggested method of delivery is displayed on the following screen.

Request Method Screens

Because the delivery options are provided by different services and software, different request screens are displayed after a user presses the Request button, depending on what delivery method has been chosen. Intermediary screens are provided to lessen the abrupt change when leaving the catalog and entering a new system.

Descriptive button labels indicate to the user what to expect from the system they are entering. As described earlier, the RSE is presently unable to request a Borrow Direct item within our own interface because we have not fully implemented the Borrow Direct API. The label "Search Borrow Direct" indicates that we couldn't directly request an item in Borrow Direct from our catalog, but that the user needs to go to that system and start a new search.

Recall in figure 9.1, the status of *Dead Wake,* by Erik Larson, is shown as checked out but available via Borrow Direct, Interlibrary Loan, Document

FIGURE 9.5 ——

Dead Wake, **with Interlibrary Loan as the selected delivery method**

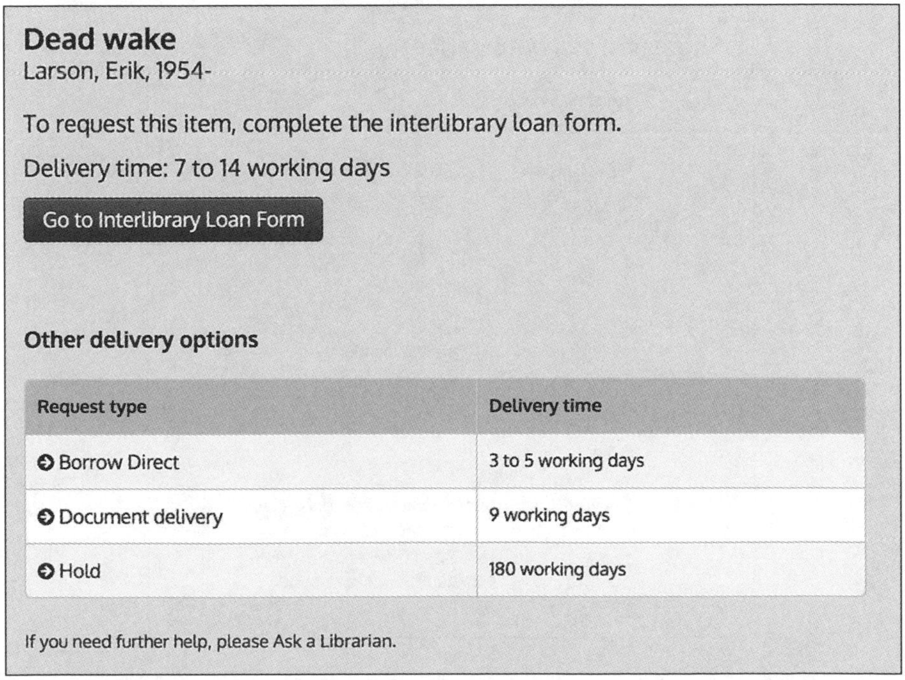

Dead wake
Larson, Erik, 1954-

To request this item, complete the interlibrary loan form.

Delivery time: 7 to 14 working days

Go to Interlibrary Loan Form

Other delivery options

Request type	Delivery time
❯ Borrow Direct	3 to 5 working days
❯ Document delivery	9 working days
❯ Hold	180 working days

If you need further help, please Ask a Librarian.

Delivery, and Hold. The RSE has determined the book is not available for recall because it is a shorter-term loan item.

Likewise, for Interlibrary Loan, we use the label "Go to Interlibrary Loan Form" to indicate that the user must fill out a request form within the interlibrary loan system (see figure 9.5).

The button text for the Rare request screens indicates not only that the user must complete another request, but also that the item will be delivered to the reading room.

Accommodating the Complexity of Different Item Types

In addition to the complexity of the delivery systems, the items themselves are often complicated. Multivolume items require an additional screen where the volume can be selected, because our system only allows for the delivery of one volume at a time, and the volume must be chosen in order to determine the request method. The selected volume is then displayed on the request form, where it can be changed (see figure 9.6). Selecting a new volume will cause the system to reevaluate the recommended delivery type.

FIGURE 9.6 ————————————————————————————————

The request screen for a multivolume work, with volume select list

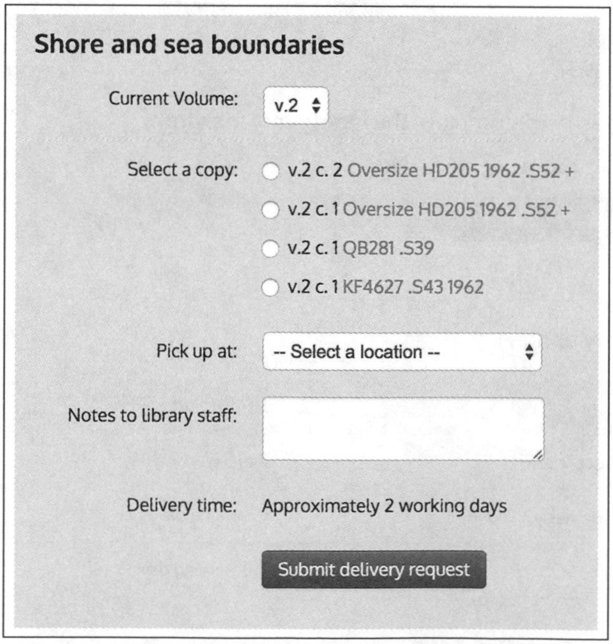

Shore and sea boundaries

Current Volume: v.2

Select a copy:
- v.2 c. 2 Oversize HD205 1962 .S52 +
- v.2 c. 1 Oversize HD205 1962 .S52 +
- v.2 c. 1 QB281 .S39
- v.2 c. 1 KF4627 .S43 1962

Pick up at: -- Select a location --

Notes to library staff:

Delivery time: Approximately 2 working days

Submit delivery request

We made sure to display non-Romanized versions of titles and authors in the RSE views in addition to English or Romanized titles.

RESULTS IN PRACTICE

We received feedback about the new Requests system through usability testing and reports from library staff and users during the development, beta, and production stages.

Usability Testing

We performed both formal and informal usability tests on the new catalog throughout the development process. We received some useful early feedback regarding availability status and the requests process. Examples of requests-related findings include:

▸ *Users were confused by the choice of icons to indicate the availability status of an item.* Early in the development phase, we tested users' ability to understand what our chosen availability icons meant. In the original icon set, we had a checkmark, clock, and letter "i" for "info." We thought the initial meaning of these icons would be clear and accessible for all users. We added the colors green (check mark), red (clock), and blue ("i") as an additional cue for users without color blindness issues. Based on this testing, we removed the info icon because users didn't know what it meant. Users had a reasonable idea of what the check mark and clock icons meant in terms of item status, so we kept those, and in place of the info icon, we added a yellow question mark for when the status of an item is unknown.

▸ *Forms on request screens were confusing.* While we attempted to simplify the various request screens, specific aspects of them still remained perplexing. Example feedback included:

    — "The request screen is a bit confusing; I didn't understand the Borrow Direct alert message. The estimate times for the different delivery options are not clear."

    — "For request screen, make it easier to fill out the date the item is no longer needed. Use radio buttons and plain language."

    — "On the request screen, 'date not needed' should only be for Holds, and not Recalls."

FIGURE 9.7 ——

A link to "Libraries Worldwide" for print copies is provided for certain online-only items

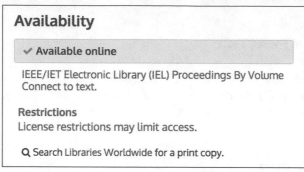

This initial testing allowed us to eliminate a few of the early bugs and simplify the readability of the request forms. It also gave us confidence that we were headed in the right direction with the user experience for this new functionality.

Feedback from Staff and Users

In July 2014 we launched a beta release of the new catalog and received a large amount of feedback from both library staff and users about the RSE and availability display. It was clear from this feedback that the complexity of the request logic allowed some bugs to remain. Some of the primary issues included:

▸ *Not enough ways to get to Borrow Direct or Interlibrary Loan.* Users and staff reported that they were unable to search Borrow Direct for items that they knew would be findable there. They also reported that for certain electronic-only items, it was unclear how a user could request a print copy instead. To solve these problems, we added links to Borrow Direct and Interlibrary Loan in the catalog header, allowing direct access to those services, and we added a "Looking for more?" box with links to related search results in WorldCat Local. Linking to WorldCat Local from Blacklight allows users to view and request items that are not in Cornell's collection, a feature users had been accustomed to when WorldCat Local was the library's primary catalog. In addition, we added a link to the World-Cat Local formats and editions page for each e-book, which provided a connection between online items and their print versions (see figure 9.7).

▸ *Display other request options instead of collapsing them.* When we first designed the interface, we didn't want to overwhelm users with the different request methods. We focused on displaying the fastest method of delivery and hid the others in a collapsible menu labeled "Other options," which a user could click to select a different method. However, after launching the catalog in beta, and hearing some feedback about how users were confused when looking for other delivery options, we decided to display the "Other delivery options" table at all times. We found that showing the table didn't add clutter to the interface, and it helped teach users about the other available delivery options.

Request Bugs

In some instances, users would attempt to request an item and were presented with an error screen. The exact reasons for the error varied, but it was often due to an edge case in the logic tree that we had not previously encountered. These can usually be corrected in the Requests system code. We use AppSignal (https://appsignal.com), a service that monitors Ruby web apps for problems, to detect when unexpected errors occur. If a user encounters a bug that generates an error, AppSignal automatically e-mails the RSE developers and creates an issue in our bug-tracking system. Users of the catalog and request system, especially librarians within CUL, also report issues to us directly using a feedback form available throughout the catalog.

METRICS

We attempted to determine whether the RSE made a difference in the number of requests placed and filled in each category. Although we were able to look at counts and turnaround times and compare those metrics to similar time segments from previous years, it became clear that we could not draw conclusions about the effect of the new system because of confounding factors:

- ‣ The Voyager (Classic Catalog) interface was (and still is) in production, allowing users to request items through that interface as well as through the new catalog. We cannot separate the requests by origin, so we are not able to link metrics specifically to new catalog requests.
- ‣ Requests (and all circulation statistics in general) have been trending downward for years, and most precipitously in the past three years. It is difficult to determine with any confidence whether the new catalog interface had any effect on the trend, either positive or negative. Observed changes may be due to evolving user expectations and demographics and the increasing availability of online resources.

CONCLUSION

Rethinking how requests would be fulfilled in Cornell University Library's new catalog has been a learning experience on many levels: gaining familiarity with Ruby on Rails, designing an interface that would make the system as easy as possible for users, grasping the complexity of the existing requests system, and understanding the tradeoffs necessary to balance simplicity for users with the arcana of library systems. Often, library projects similar to ours place more emphasis on the discovery side of "discovery and access"; the magic requests project was intended to create an access system that would match our overhauled discovery layer. This is not a trivial problem. Although the CUL Requests system is a major improvement over what it replaces, there is still considerable room for further refinement.

Our first attempt to make the complexities of delivery transparent to users, the Requests System Engine, is by necessity a set of technical and policy-based compromises. A completely transparent system would have no need to present the user with additional data or forms after a single "Request" button is clicked. As automated library systems and APIs become more popular and sophisticated, we may one day be able to make our system truly magical—but we're not there yet.

If discovery systems could assume that request and delivery were a simple and successful process, they could be built so that a user's cognitive burden was lessened when doing research or trying to access materials. While an extensive display of holdings- and item-level metadata may be necessary in some cases to distinguish materials that are similar but not identical, in many cases the user does not need or want so much detail. Likewise, in a majority of delivery requests, the specifics of where an item is coming from or how it is being delivered is unnecessary information for the user; he or she simply wants to get an item *from the library,* not from Voyager or an annex building or interlibrary loan. If a discovery system were able to deliver on the promise of reliable magic delivery in such a way as to instill confidence in its users that they would receive the items they want in a timely manner, then libraries could begin to break down one more barrier that hinders today's users, so accustomed to a one-click-purchase, simple search environment, from placing their full trust in a library's search box.

PART III

INTERFACES

CHAPTER TEN

THE BENTO BOX DESIGN PATTERN

JASON THOMALE, WILLIAM HICKS, AND MARK PHILLIPS

B ento. The word describes a type of meal packed into a compartmentalized container, usually associated with Japanese boxed lunches. It elicits flavor, color, whimsy, and convenience (see figure 10.1).

The academic library community has adopted this word to describe a type of search user interface (UI) evocative of the boxed lunch, where results from

FIGURE 10.1 ———————————————————————————————
Japanese bento box

FIGURE 10.2 ——

University of North Texas bento box search interface

different systems are grouped by category and appear on the screen in separate boxes (see figure 10.2). For libraries that employ it, the bento box UI fulfills the role of primary resource discovery mechanism and thus features prominently on their websites.

As a portal–like UI for presenting multiple streams of search results at once, the bento box UI occupies a strange niche in the library discovery ecosystem. On one hand, bento box design is entirely grassroots-oriented. Explicit vendor support for such interfaces is almost nonexistent. Little library literature exists discussing it as an identifiable phenomenon, and little true research has been done on its effectiveness, making it seem not worth studying within the library profession. Perhaps, due to its grassroots nature, it's seen as yet another library hack—a workaround for perceived failures in vendor-provided interfaces—but not a viable solution to a more general problem.

On the other hand, it *is* catching on rapidly (and in prominent places). As of March 2015, libraries at universities including Stanford, University of Michigan, University of Virginia, North Carolina State, Columbia, Johns Hopkins, University of Illinois at Urbana-Champaign, Cornell, University of North Carolina Chapel Hill, Duke, George Washington University, and the University of North Texas had invested time and money creating their own bento box UIs to use as their primary search interface.

FIGURE 10.3 ——

Google SERP with bento-like components

Furthermore, design elements that are unmistakably bento-like have been cropping up more often *outside* of libraries, especially within the search engine results pages (SERPs) for the major web search engines. For instance, consider the SERP from Google search shown in figure 10.3.

In this chapter, we posit that bento box design is worth examining, not so much as a library hack, but as an interaction design pattern. This provides a useful framework for discussing the evolution of library discovery—including bento box design itself—and for exploring interrelationships between library discovery and web discovery.

ABOUT INTERACTION DESIGN PATTERNS

Design patterns are a way of describing generalized components that work to address particular problems within a particular context.[1] Architect Christopher Alexander is credited with first articulating the concept in the late 1970s in his books *A Timeless Way of Building* and *A Pattern Language*. Though design patterns began as an architectural concept, software engineering latched onto them in the mid-1990s, and, a few years later, the field of human-computer interaction also began to adopt them.[2]

According to Alexander:

> Each pattern describes a problem which occurs over and over again in our
> environment, and then describes the core of the solution to that problem, in
> such a way that you can use this solution a million times over, without ever
> doing it the same way twice.[3]

Central to a design pattern are, first, the problems that pattern is trying to solve
and, second, the environment or context in which it exists. The pattern itself
is a solution that is both generalized and specifically applicable to the given
problem, though it may need to be interpreted when implemented to fit the
particular application at hand. Additionally, design patterns (and hence the
problem domains they address) may be defined at different levels—from broad
("large") to narrow ("small").[4]

Placing bento box design within this framework means considering explicitly
the design problem it solves within its broader environment. So what *is* the
context for bento box design? To answer this, we must wrestle with a perhaps
uncomfortable question: are *library discovery* and *web discovery* different contexts
or not?

CONTEXTS FOR BENTO BOX DESIGN

Discovery

At the broadest level, we describe the context that bento box design addresses
as *discovery,* a recent label for an old concept: enabling people to pick out what
they need from an otherwise unmanageable mass of information. It may be
hard to think about in anything but modern terms—after all, with the advent
of the Internet and the Web and the proliferation of mobile devices and social
media, we are living through an unprecedented information explosion. But
the basic problem long predates the Web—and even modern libraries, for that
matter. We are far from the first civilization in history to deal with feelings of
acute information overload in the face of advancing technology. Historian Ann
Blair's *Too Much to Know* recounts how overabundance of information and the
need to manage that information has been a fact of intellectual life in many
information-producing cultures dating back to antiquity.[5]

Information management and discovery in theory are not difficult. Techniques
used for managing information to facilitate discovery in essence do not change.
Blair calls these the "four S's of text management": storing, sorting, selecting,
and summarizing.[6] In the same vein, author James Gleick writes that strategies
for managing information "boil down to two: filter and search."[7]

Practically, however, the contextual details that surround the information we manage make all the difference. How much information? How is it stored? How do we expect people to use it? What tools do we have at our disposal? How does it change over time? What are the cultural, political, social, and economic circumstances around its creation and publication?

The contextual details surrounding the information that libraries manage are complex, mainly because libraries have a long history and, as large institutions, inertia. The Web, in its underlying simplicity, has highlighted and perhaps exacerbated that complexity, even as it has become completely entwined with our discovery methods. Now the Web embodies both the primary set of technologies we use to facilitate discovery of our content and yet at the same time also a mass of content that *we don't manage* that is fundamentally different than what we manage.

And this dual nature of library discovery—being *on* the Web but not *of* the Web, so to speak—is key to understanding more specifically the problems facing modern library discovery solutions that bento box design attempts to address.

EVOLUTION OF THE MODERN LIBRARY DISCOVERY PROBLEM DOMAIN

Libraries versus Automation

What we've seen happen over the past decades as libraries have wrestled with the Web both reflects and has roots in what happened last century. In the mid-1940s, a sudden explosion in published scientific research following World War II triggered an information crisis in the scientific and intellectual community. Traditional modes of information dissemination, which included libraries, struggled to organize everything and make it accessible.[8] Fremont Rider in 1944 identified and elucidated several problems related to "the astonishing growth of our great research libraries" in his influential *The Scholar and the Future of the Research Library*.[9] Writing as a librarian, he viewed the main problem as one of economics: extrapolating based on the rate of growth American research libraries had enjoyed since their inception showed a situation that was quickly becoming economically unsustainable. But shortcomings in traditional methods of managing that information were part of the problem. Rider writes, "We seem to be fast coming to the day when, unless it is afforded the most expert sort of bibliographical service possible, civilization may die of suffocation, choked in its own plethora of print."[10]

In 1945, Vannevar Bush's seminal article "As We May Think" trumpeted the scientist perspective on this nascent crisis—one which was not at all favorable to libraries. Bush writes:

The summation of human experience is being expanded at a prodigious rate, and
the means we use for threading through the consequent maze to the momentar-
ily important item is the same as was used in the days of square-rigged ships.[11]

During the ensuing decades, as the sense of crisis grew, what science historian
Mark D. Bowles has termed the "information wars" erupted—a culture clash
between "documentalists" (scientists) and librarians (humanists). Documentalists
embraced emerging computer technology and saw it as a tool to help manage
the onslaught of information through automation, while librarians "frequently
recoiled in fear from the prospects of automation."[12] According to Bowles,
librarians' fear stemmed not from the prospect of automation per se, but rather
from those who wielded it. At the heart of the information wars was a power
struggle—a struggle for librarians to maintain their professional identity in the
face of an outside group that seemed to want to wrest it from them.

Librarianship's eventual absorption of the documentalists may have been inev-
itable. In the 1960s, '70s, and '80s library automation picked up steam. Searchable
abstract and indexing databases and online catalogs of MARC records emerged.
Information retrieval and information science, both rooted in documentalism,
became part of library schools' curriculum—today, we have schools of library
and information science (or even just information schools). But despite this
seeming merger, librarians' professional identity crisis was never really resolved;
Bowles's scientist/humanist duality remains an integral part of our professional
experience.[13]

Inertia and Fragmentation

The twentieth-century information crisis and subsequent information wars
seem to have repeated with the arrival of the Web. Circumstances and technologies external to libraries have caused a dramatic increase in the amount of
information that's published and available; library discovery technologies that
were once cutting edge don't translate; and library discovery again lags behind
a sudden onslaught of information. Whereas perhaps it was once libraries versus
automation, now it becomes libraries versus the Web.

A library quality that underlies all of these events is inertia. Changing how
we store and organize information is difficult because we have a lot of resources
tied up in existing organization methods and technologies. Vannevar Bush in
1945 complained about libraries' antiquated methods of information organization; James Thompson in 1982 railed against "the unusable library" and the
card catalog; Roy Tennant proclaimed in 2002 that "MARC Must Die."[14] Overcoming inertia is, in part, a matter of figuring out how to migrate our existing

information to new formats to make it compatible with newer technologies. Cultural, economic, and political realities often add to this inertia. Content providers and publishers are slow to adapt. Even as we successfully migrate existing information, remnants of the source formats and technologies remain tied up in the data, and our data becomes fragmented. And fragmentation has become a defining characteristic of library content.

LOCAL VERSUS LICENSED MATERIALS

Fragmentation has occurred along one fault line that's especially important for library discovery: material that we own and manage locally versus material that external vendors license to us. Locally owned material includes physical items we purchase, such as books, CDs, and DVDs, along with electronic content produced at our institution, such as digitized archival materials, institutional repository materials, and the information on our website. Licensed material includes much of what now tends to fall under the umbrella of electronic resources, such as databases of content (mostly from journals) managed by external publishers and content providers.

The gulf between local and licensed content is huge. We have no control over licensed content. The amount of content we license tends to dwarf the content we manage locally. In an academic context, licensed content tends to be what's most valuable to our end users. (In fact, the content we license tends to correspond with the content that academics were primarily concerned about during the twentieth-century information crisis, namely academic and scientific journal output.) And there's been little incentive for each publisher to ensure its content and metadata are interoperable with content from other publishers, which contributes to fragmentation between licensed resources.

THE CRUX OF THE LIBRARY DISCOVERY PROBLEM

Although libraries and the library profession have mostly embraced computers, automation, and now the Web, our discovery systems remain difficult to use. The fragmentation of our content has led to fragmentation of our systems. In this environment, library users must visit different systems' respective interfaces to find and use different sets of resources—some of which we control and some of which we don't. And because the distinction between them has as much basis in library and academic history, culture, economics, and politics as it does in anything meaningful to users, figuring out which system is best to use for what purpose is challenging.

Comparatively, using web search is dead simple. A search engine index contains one huge set of resources; you enter a query and get one list of results, ranked by which are most relevant. This simplicity is a big draw for using the Web, and, in fact, user studies conducted over the past 10 to 15 years have shown undeniably that most of our users prefer using web search over library discovery tools.[15] As a result, libraries have understandably looked at web search as a model to emulate.

But how does one take the needs web search meets and create discovery tools that meet similar needs in the library context?

SOLUTIONS FOR MODERN LIBRARY DISCOVERY

One seemingly simple way to do this might be to optimize library content for web search and rely on search engines for discovery. We're already putting most of our resources on the Web, so making them discoverable then becomes a search engine optimization (SEO) task. Such a solution is attractive because it eliminates the need to compete with search engines for users' attention and it pushes our material out in the venues where our users are most likely to find and use it. This is certainly a goal worth working toward, and indeed may be the best way to ensure our materials are findable within the discovery environments our users actually use.[16] But this strategy makes it difficult to accommodate the huge portion of licensed materials existing behind paywalls. Even if these materials are discoverable on the open Web (or via tools like Google Scholar), they generally aren't *obtainable* without accessing them through the library's infrastructure, for example, using their link resolver. In that case, discovery becomes intertwined with obtainability: ensuring that people can discover what they can access through the library and that it's apparent how they can access it.

Another solution, then, is to try to funnel users to our discovery tools and make those function as much like web search as possible: defragment our systems and our data, or at least try to make the discovery experience seem less fragmented to our users, and adopt design patterns germane to web search, such as the single results list (e.g., from a typical search engine results page, or SERP). And this is where the majority of effort in modern library discovery system development has focused.

FEDERATED SEARCH

One way to deal with a fragmented search environment is to search multiple targets at the same time. In the early and mid-2000s many libraries around the world worked to implement large-scale federated search systems that would do exactly that—take a user's query and execute it simultaneously on a number of remote databases. The system would begin to receive search results asynchronously and either display them as received or create a merged results set from the various targets.

While federated search was perhaps a valid strategy to try to overcome *local* library system fragmentation, the large-scale implementations had problems handling the scale of *licensed*-resource fragmentation—one library might subscribe to hundreds of databases, but searching more than a handful at a time was (and is) technically unfeasible. Even searching a small number led to usability problems: confusion about what exactly was being searched, queries taking too long to run, poor relevance ranking, and results not being presented in a way that makes sense.[17] On top of that, for libraries, maintaining the knowledge bases required to facilitate federated searching was challenging; if a search target changed the way it was serving up records or the interfaces that it allowed users to search, it might cause problems in retrieving results from that target.[18]

WEB-SCALE DISCOVERY

Another approach to solving fragmentation is to mimic web search more directly: create one large index of resources that behaves more like a typical web search engine. Putting as much library data as possible into that one index allows users to query the index and quickly retrieve a large set of matching results.

Companies like Serials Solutions with their Summon product and EBSCO with their EBSCO Discovery Service pioneered this approach during the late 2000s, ushering in the era of web-scale discovery. They began working with library content providers to amass large numbers of resources in unified indexes containing millions of unique items. Libraries interested in offering the "single search" solution their users wanted were quick to work with these vendors. In addition to the licensed and open access content aggregated as part of these products' "global" indexes, institutions began to include their library catalogs, digital collections, and archival finding aids in these systems as well. Libraries were now able to offer their users a true single-search solution that searched a large index containing millions of resources and presented a single list of relevance-ranked results.

The big win with web-scale discovery is that it addresses the licensed-resource fragmentation problem better than anything else has and, perhaps, could (without a fundamental change in content providers' business models). But does the single-search solution it offers libraries address users' needs adequately enough to consider it *the* solution to the library discovery problem?

If we think of library discovery and web discovery as two different design contexts addressing two separate problem domains, and if we examine the problems web search has actually solved within its particular domain, it becomes clear that, although web-scale discovery may emulate the *superficialities* of web search, it can't (and doesn't) effectively address key problems the way web search has.

In the 1998 paper that first presented the prototype Google search engine, Sergey Brin and Lawrence Page discuss what problems they were trying to solve with their new search engine. The main problem was keeping up with the sheer scale of the Web—not just scaling up technology, but also ensuring quality search results as the Web grew. Search engines at the time faced the exact same problem that libraries faced during the information crisis in the twentieth century: too much information was being created and the methods being used to organize it and make it discoverable were becoming less effective. Any given search query could match millions of documents, and users were not willing to look beyond "the first few tens of results."[19] For Brin and Page, what ultimately enabled them to solve that problem was their PageRank algorithm, which relies on the structure of web content to calculate better relevance ranking and boost search precision. In short, that the content on the open Web exists as a network of freely accessible, hyperlinked documents is what has allowed Google and search engines using similar ranking mechanisms to thrive.

Web-scale discovery systems mimic web search by re-creating the single search index, the search interface, and the single search results list, but their Achilles' heel is that they have not been able to produce relevance-ranking algorithms that work as effectively.[20] This is because the fundamental feature of the Web that library discovery can't replicate is the *content*. Decades—centuries—worth of inertia have baked fragmentation right into our systems and data; even when dumped into one index, there's no way to make library content behave the way that web content behaves without actually turning it into web content. Thus, the very qualities that make PageRank work for web content and make relevance ranking for web search work effectively are missing from library content.

One aspect of search relevance that seems particularly important in academic libraries is content type. Some evidence from user testing suggests that mixing certain content types—especially books and articles—in library search results is problematic, and other evidence suggests that the distinctions we make between types of library content do make sense to users and even match with the tasks and expectations they have while using our systems.[21] Intuitively, this makes some sense. Students might have assignments that require them to find and cite three books and six scholarly journal articles. They may want to find DVDs or video games that the library lends to entertain them during downtime. Faculty and researchers in science and engineering often focus on journal articles that facilitate their work within their particular specialization; they may gravitate toward one or a few particular databases relevant to their field, and they may teach their students to do the same. Faculty in music might be more interested in finding recordings and scores than journal articles and books.

But a system can't surface the most relevant content types for a particular user query if it doesn't know what those *are*. If users don't narrow their searches using an advanced search option or a facet, results in a single list-style SERP could seem wholly irrelevant due to the dominance of an irrelevant content type. And forcing users to use advanced search options and facets to obtain the most relevant results destroys the illusion of a web search–like experience.

BENTO BOX DESIGN

If a single list-style SERP design pattern tends to work poorly when brought into a library discovery context because library content types are too heterogeneous, might a *multi*-list design pattern, with results categorized by content type, work better?

North Carolina State University (NCSU) began experimenting with this idea when they built their "Quick Search" system, which was initially released in August 2005. Screenshots from early versions show that the UI looked like a web search results screen enriched with content from additional sources. The primary result type was library web pages, but Frequently Asked Questions, related subjects, and links to other library searches were included in sections above and to the right of search results. As Quick Search evolved, it began incorporating additional result types, such as items from their library catalog and journals from their electronic resource management system.[22]

In August 2010 NCSU released a redesign of Quick Search that featured what we might now call the quintessential "bento box" design, incorporating

FIGURE 10.4 —————————————————————————————————

Screenshot from Villanova University

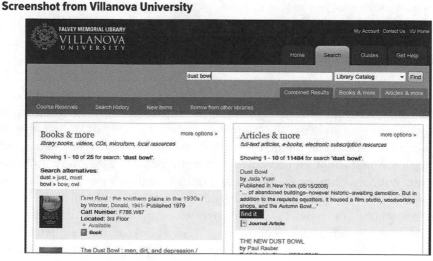

Used courtesy Villanova University and the NCSU Libraries.

results from articles, the library catalog, journals, databases, and the library website in a compact three-column layout that presented the majority of results above the fold.[23] In fact, Tito Sierra, one of the developers of Quick Search, coined the term *bento box*, with the first published use referring specifically to this version of their UI.[24]

Despite its clear influence on the design concept, NCSU is not the sole originator of the bento box design. The University of Michigan unveiled a distinctly bento-like search results design as part of a library website redesign in August 2009, and Villanova University released a two-box design (featuring only articles and catalog results) in late 2010, shown in figure 10.4.[25] In the years immediately following, many libraries released their own implementations—some bearing more resemblance to NCSU's and Michigan's and others to Villanova's.

Although design specifics may vary from implementation to implementation, they share many of the same qualities. Generally, bento box applications function similarly to federated search systems: they submit a user's search to multiple systems at once and bring together results into a single display dynamically. They take advantage of the fact that library systems are fragmented roughly along content-type lines—for example, the library catalog might provide books and media results, and a web-scale discovery system might provide articles results. These systems tend not to have the usability problems associated with federated search because they search fewer targets that are more locally controlled. They also preserve the relevance ranking from each target system, avoid the need to de-duplicate results from multiple systems, and typically provide a way into each system to get more results. Providing a taste of the first few results from each system gives users a broader overview of what types of resources the library might have related to a given query than they'd get from a single relevance-ranked list of results.

BENTO BOX DESIGN AS INTERACTION DESIGN PATTERN

At the beginning of this chapter we stated that design patterns can exist at a broad level or a narrow level, and we posed the question about whether the bento box design pattern addresses the context of library discovery or web discovery. We've shown how library discovery and web discovery are different and that the bento box design pattern is particularly suited to the library discovery problem domain. But do we find bento box displays outside of the library context? Is this a design pattern that's used within the wider and (significantly) more publicly visible world of commercial search, enterprise, or public site search engines? Is it informed by other aspects of interface design? If so, are there implications for libraries? The simple answer is of course, yes. Aspects of the design can be detected within web portals like "My Yahoo" and (the now-defunct) iGoogle, both online web applications, but it can also be seen in physical media as well such as military and commemorative shadow boxes, Asian-inspired curio-cabinets, and of course our interface's namesake.

In answering these questions more deeply, let's first step back for a moment and think about the design pattern itself as it pertains to a broader context.

When we evoke an Asian-inspired lunch box to describe our SERP, we attempt to construct a visual metaphor for the interface that translates a perhaps foreign and novel design into a familiar, somewhat universalized pattern. The bento lunch box performs an analogous function to our emergent interface, which presents the individual with a crafted selection of items, often compartmentalized by type, form, genre, or function. Notably, sections of the container are discretely organized and sized in such a way as to emphasize the relative importance of one box and its contents to others. Library stakeholders, acting in this metaphor as partner or parent, understand the needs of their patrons—and the strengths of their own collections—and can package this material into a convenient container allowing the user to evaluate its contents based on the needs of the day.

Like all metaphors, however, the parallels eventually break down. Rather than interacting with and consuming the entire container, the searcher picks and chooses a small subset of returned elements that are of most value to them and moves on to a third party after their initial sampling.

FIGURE 10.5

Screenshot of Windows 8

While the bento box SERP can be viewed as a design pattern employed by libraries to address library users' needs, we should note that it exists within an evolutionary chain of interfaces and design metaphors in which we are immersed. One need only look at Microsoft's Windows 8 (see figure 10.5) or any number of "dashboard-like" interfaces on the Web to find that displaying data in an array of variably sized boxes is well suited to the screens we interact with on a daily basis.

LISTS, LISTS, EVERYWHERE

Consider then, the single-result list design pattern. Search has long been dominated by interfaces where a linear set of items is presented in a single vertical column. Even the addition of secondary columns containing faceted navigation or paid advertisements largely conforms to this pattern.

However, this "list-as-signifier," while a familiar and expressive form, becomes increasingly problematic as its content grows beyond the point of reasonable evaluation or when one seeks to intersperse groups of related materials. The former is clearly illustrated by the SEO industry's continued attempts to boost client websites to the top organic result. The latter is illustrated by typical image and product searches, which, in the best-known variants, employ a grid-based display. By limiting white space and optimizing screen real estate, these displays perform a utilitarian function, but they also intimate visual metaphors many users in the real world can identify, such as art galleries and products lining physical store shelves.

Increasingly, commercial providers like Google and Microsoft have been enhancing their primary SERP beyond a single homogeneous results list to one that integrates more contextual information about a query. Here the single-list pattern breaks down, and these interfaces begin bearing some similarities to the bento box approach.

BLOCKS OF KNOWLEDGE AND UNIFIED DISCOVERY

When we look at a Google SERP in a desktop browser at the beginning of 2015, as shown in figure 10.6, we find the familiar list of organic and paid results. Depending on the query, we may also encounter regions of the screen populated via some kind of knowledge object, such as those displaying harvested "site links," grids of images, maps, local businesses, reviews, notable figures, weather, and an array of tangential related facts and figures. Microsoft's Bing provides a similar SERP, with suggestions for related search queries, recent social network activity, links into popular third-party providers, and many other similar options.

While integrating more contextual information into a SERP is currently limited to a handful of search providers, similar displays can be seen in a variety of other places. Unlike most library bento box applications, however, these systems tend to query a more centralized and controlled data set—and, in some cases, they rethink the contents of the search result entirely. For example, the Internet Movie Database segments search results into clearly defined regions of the screen, with sections devoted to titles, names, keywords, and companies, while providing a simple scope selector for further refinement by a number of system-defined categories. Similarly, a query to Apple's iTunes Store yields a screen divided into a number of discrete regions that might include horizontal image grids of books, music, courses, genres, series, or apps, alternating with vertical listings of individual tracks, podcasts, episodes, performers, and so on. As with the previous example, other link-based navigation and search suggestions are provided in a secondary column.

FIGURE 10.6

Screenshot of Google

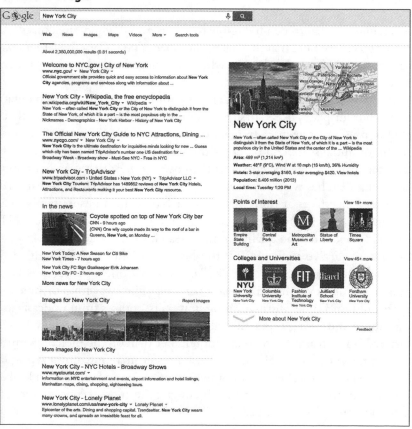

When users submit a query to Home Depot's website, they usually receive a grid-based result set. But for searches that match product categories, users are redirected into a bento-like display, where different sections highlight project ideas, installation services, videos, new products, or facets leading to more specific queries. This latter pattern is particularly noteworthy; Jakob Nielsen, who decries the general ability of people to formulate decent search terms, notes positive outcomes with Costco's product search, which behaves similarly to Home Depot's.[26] Though perhaps "cheating," redirection into a category-based display demonstrates a variant solution to the same type of problem that libraries face when trying to make heterogeneous content types discoverable within a single-index, single-search system. Rather than dump a user into a monolithic list or hope that the user will further interact with facets in a secondary column, the developers have curated a result display based on contextual clues and available data.

A DESIGN PATTERN THAT WORKS

A search interface has to be intelligible to the user, and when one considers the examples given, we note that they take a number of cues from the larger lexicon of patterns available to developers, which are increasingly based on studies of users' experiences and behaviors.

In nearly every case cited above, and within many library implementations of bento box displays, users' first interaction is with a simple input that has limited or no scope selectors. In practice, this pattern reduces cognitive load at the point of initial search and accepts the reality that "users are more likely to change the search scope in retrospect than during their first search attempt."[27] This finding matches with our own from a comprehensive three-year analysis of discovery interfaces at the University of North Texas: users rarely change default options before their initial search, even though such changes could have a profound impact on the quality of their search experience.[28]

Once users arrive at the SERP, the bento box interface presents data in contextualized groupings, or "chunks," of information. Whether it is Google segmenting local movie showtimes for a particular film away from organic results *about* that film or iTunes distinguishing university courses from podcasts in different groups and listing types, this allows users to employ a strategy based on pattern recognition and contextualization rather than on the mental gymnastics needed to recall the original query on each result in a long, unforgiving list.[29]

Indeed, when researchers within the field of SEO marketing have looked at Google's evolution from its 2005 SERP design to its most recent iteration, they have found a shift from a longer, almost singular focus by users on the "golden triangle" at the top of the page to a quicker, wider sweep of the elements on the screen.[30]

Not surprisingly, then, the bento box display conforms well to much of the interface design wisdom and SEO practice that has emerged over the last few years. Maynes and Everdell note that many users focus on only the first few results within the results list. Bento box interfaces, due in large part to the space limitations imposed by the display, typically only render a handful of items within each region. For users, this means results are succinct, manageable, and easier to evaluate. Users can weigh their original query results by facets like form, type, or function, but they aren't required to do so by blindly clicking through to a secondary screen. This can have benefits for both experienced searchers and novices, as it promotes some degree of serendipity.

Content strategists, and even Google's own new "Material Design"

FIGURE 10.7 ————————————

Screenshot of Google Material Design's Card-based display

This card collection contains cards with varied content types and layouts.

interface guidelines, implore providers to present content in short, easily digestible segments and to demarcate sections through the use of headings and logical blocks of related function.[31] The bento box display often succinctly describes the contents of a section through the use of scannable headings, and, much like Material Design's "Card" metaphor, groups items into collections that highlight differences between groups (see figure 10.7).

Finally, as an added bonus, since library bento box displays are normally developed locally, they allow for greater control of HTML structure. In practice this means that bento box searches can have customized source ordering, responsive or adaptive designs, and the inclusion of accessibility helpers such as ARIA that are not always available in vendor-controlled systems.

The bento box design pattern is therefore, above all, highly usable. It affords users the ability to focus on only the most relevant items within the interface, to further explore the source and offerings of any single group, or to reformulate a query given the strengths and weaknesses of the existing results.

CONCLUSION

In the end, after having examined contexts and problem domains of both library discovery and web discovery, we can perhaps conclude that these two contexts are simultaneously different *and* the same. Indeed, much of the content libraries are trying to make discoverable via the Web is incompatible with open web content: it's legacy data representing real-world objects that are difficult to encode as web pages and may have licensing and other issues attached to them. But trying to make these types of resources discoverable is a more universal problem than we might think. *All* organizations that have to make legacy data or physical products findable on the Web wrestle with similar issues. As the Web evolves, even search engines are tinkering with displaying information that contextualizes or more directly addresses users' queries rather than simply returning a list of web pages that match: "things not strings," as the blog posting announcing Google's Knowledge Graph states.[32]

What libraries call bento box design, then, is a generalized interaction design pattern that we find outside as well as inside libraries. It offers libraries the chance to present our content to end users in a way that is both simple in its design and yet allows us to reimagine what it means to present *relevant* results within a library context. If the past is truly indicative of the future, information resources will continue to be created at an increasing rate, and we all will continue to struggle providing discovery services that help our users thrive amidst the deluge. Finding new ways to improve relevance for users within various problem domains will likely be vital.

However, libraries should understand that no discovery system or design pattern offers an easy fix to the underlying fragmentation of our data. That problem has been with us for a long time, and the only solution is actually to *improve our data:* to adopt data formats that are compatible with the technologies we use to make them discoverable, that interoperate well with nonlibrary data, and that are open enough to allow discovery outside of libraries.

Notes

1. Luke Wroblewski, Martijn van Welie, and Bill Scott, "Design Patterns: Part 1," *LukeW: Ideation + Design,* 2006, www.lukew.com/ff/entry.asp?348.
2. Jenifer Tidwell, *Common Ground: A Pattern Language for Human-Computer Interface Design,* 1999, www.mit.edu/~jtidwell/interaction_patterns.html.
3. Christopher Alexander, *A Pattern Language* (New York: Oxford University Press, 1977), x, https://archive.org/details/APatternLanguage.
4. Ibid., xii.
5. Ann M. Blair, *Too Much to Know* (New Haven, CT: Yale University Press, 2010), 1.

6. Ibid., 3.

7. James Gleick, *The Information: A History, a Theory, a Flood* (New York: Pantheon Books, 2011), 409.

8. Mark D. Bowles, "The Information Wars: Two Cultures and the Conflict in Information Retrieval, 1945–1999," in *Proceedings of the 1998 Conference on the History and Heritage of Science Information Systems,* ed. Mary Ellen Bowden, Trudi Bellardo Hahn, and Robert V. Williams (Medford, NJ: Information Today for the American Society for Information Science and the Chemical Heritage Foundation, 1999), 156–58, http://webdoc.gwdg .de/ebook/s/2001/chf/www.chemheritage.org/historicalservices/asis_documents/ asis98_bowles.pdf.

9. Freemont Rider, *The Scholar and the Future of the Research Library* (New York: Hadham, 1944), ix.

10. Ibid., 14.

11. Vannevar Bush, "As We May Think," *The Atlantic Monthly* 176 (1945), www.theatlantic .com/magazine/archive/1945/07/as-we-may-think/303881/.

12. Bowles, "The Information Wars," 162.

13. As evidenced by differences in culture between, for example, reference librarians, catalogers, metadata practitioners, programmers, and so on.

14. Bush, "As We May Think"; James Thompson, *The End of Libraries* (London: Clive Bingley, 1982), 7–16; Roy Tennant, "MARC Must Die," *Library Journal* 127, no. 17 (2002), http://lj.libraryjournal.com/2002/10/ljarchives/marc-must-die/#_.

15. Citing all relevant studies would be an exercise in exhaustion. As early as 2005, Jillian R. Griffiths and Peter Brophy conducted a study concluding that "students prefer to locate information or resources via a search engine above all other options, and Google is the search engine of choice." Griffiths and Brophy, "Student Searching Behavior and the Web: Use of Academic Resources and Google," *Library Trends* 53, no. 4 (2005): 550, http://hdl.handle.net/2142/1749. Their study cites an even earlier 2001 study by Dianne Cmor and Karen Lippold, which suggests that students "use the Web for everything" (Griffiths and Brophy, 541). Many later studies have reported the same findings.

16. Lorcan Dempsey, "Discovery and Disclosure," *Lorcan Dempsey's Weblog: On Libraries, Services, and Networks,* 2006, http://orweblog.oclc.org/archives/001084.html.

17. John Boyd et al., "The One-Box Challenge: Providing a Federated Search That Benefits the Research Process," *Serials Review* 32, no. 4 (2006): 248–49, 251–53, doi:10.1016/ j.serrev.2006.08.005.

18. Ibid., 253.

19. Sergey Brin and Lawrence Page, "The Anatomy of a Large-Scale Hypertextual Web Search Engine," in *Seventh International World-Wide Web Conference (WWW 1998).* (Brisbane, Australia, 1998), 1.3.1, http://ilpubs.stanford.edu:8090/361/.

20. Elizabeth Namei and Christal A. Young, "Measuring Our Relevancy: Comparing Results in a Web-Scale Discovery Tool, Google, & Google Scholar," in *Creating Sustainable Community: The Proceedings of the ACRL 2015 Conference, March 25–28, Portland,*

Oregon, ed. Dawn M. Mueller (Chicago: Association of College and Research Libraries, 2015), 523–24, www.ala.org/acrl/sites/ala.org.acrl/files/content/conferences/confsand preconfs/2015/Namei_Young.pdf.

21. For example, Sue Fahey, Shannon Gordon, and Crystal Rose, "Seeing Double at Memorial University: Two WorldCat Local Usability Studies," *Partnership: the Canadian Journal of Library and Information Practice and Research* 6, no. 2 (2011): 3–4, 9, https://journal.lib .uoguelph.ca/index.php/perj/article/view/1552; Dana McKay, "Gotta Keep 'Em Separated: Why the Single Search Box May Not Be Right for Libraries," in *CHINZ '11: Proceedings of the 12th Annual Conference of the New Zealand Chapter of the ACM Special Interest Group on Computer-Human Interaction* (New York: ACM, 2011), 109–12, http://dl.acm.org/citation.cfm?id=2000772; Julie Meloni to Blacklight mailing list, August 3, 2011, https://groups.google.com/forum/#!msg/blacklight-development/ letW_2625xY/POjyXq2bn4UJ; Jonathan Rochkind, "Article Search Improvement Strategy," *Bibliographic Wilderness,* 2012, https://bibwild.wordpress.com/2012/10/02/ article-search-improvement-strategy/; Troy A. Swanson and Jeremy Green, "Why We Are Not Google: Lessons from a Library Web Site Usability Study," *The Journal of Academic Librarianship* 37, no. 3 (2011): 226–27, doi:10.1016/j.acalib.2011.02.014; Jason Thomale, *Resource Discovery System Usage Report, 02–01–2012 to 08–25–2014,* 2014, http://digital .library.unt.edu/ark:/67531/metadc499075/.

22. Tito Sierra, "A Single Search Box Interface to the NCSU Libraries, Two Years Later," presentation, Digital Library Federation Spring Forum 2007, Pasadena, CA, March 12, 2007; e-mails from Steven Morris, one of the creators of Quick Search, to the author, July 21 and 27, 2015.

23. Cory Lown, Tito Sierra, and Josh Boyer, "How Users Search the Library from a Single Search Box," *College & Research Libraries* 74, no. 3 (2013): 233, http://crl.acrl.org/ content/74/3/227.full.pdf.

24. Rochkind, "Article Search Improvement Strategy"; Lorcan Dempsey, "Thirteen Ways of Looking at Libraries, Discovery, and the Catalog: Scale, Workflow, Attention," *EDU-CAUSE Review Online,* 2012, www.educause.edu/ero/article/thirteen-ways-looking -libraries-discovery-and-catalog-scale-workflow-attention; e-mail from Tito Sierra to the author, August 2, 2015. According to Sierra, the first published used of the term *bento box* occurred in the article he coauthored with Cory Lown and Josh Boyer, "How Users Search the Library from a Single Search Box," written in 2011.

25. Ken Varnum, "The New University of Michigan Library Web Site," *Library Tech Talk: Technology Innovations and Project Updates from the U-M Library I. T. Division,* 2009, www.lib.umich.edu/blogs/library-tech-talk/new-university-michigan-library-web-site; e-mails from Andrew Nagy and Demian Katz, the developers of Villanova's search interface, to the author, June 9 and 10, 2015.

26. Jakob Nielsen, "Converting Search into Navigation," *Nielsen Norman Group: Evidence-Based User Experience Research, Training, and Consulting,* 2013, www.nngroup.com/articles/ search-navigation/.

27. Katie Sherwin, "Scoped Search: Dangerous, But Sometimes Useful," *Nielsen Norman Group: Evidence-Based User Experience Research, Training, and Consulting,* 2015, www .nngroup.com/articles/scoped-search/.

28. Thomale, *Resource Discovery Systems Usage,* 7–11.

29. Raluca Budiu, "Search Is Not Enough: Synergy between Navigation and Search," *Nielsen Norman Group: Evidence-Based User Experience Research, Training, and Consulting,* 2014, www.nngroup.com/articles/search-not-enough/.

30. Rebecca Maynes and Ian Everdell, "The Evolution of Google's Search Results Pages & Effects on User Behavior," *Mediative,* 2014, http://pages.mediative.com/SERP-Research.

31. "Material Design," *Google Design Guidelines,* www.google.com/design/spec.

32. Singhal, Amit, "Introducing the Knowledge Graph: Things, Not Strings," *Official Google Blog,* 2012, http://googleblog.blogspot.com/2012/05/introducing-knowledge-graph -things-not.html.

References

Alexander, Christopher. 1977. *A Pattern Language.* New York: Oxford University Press. https:// archive.org/details/APatternLanguage.

Blair, Ann M. 2010. *Too Much to Know.* New Haven, CT: Yale University Press.

Bowles, Mark D. 1999. "The Information Wars: Two Cultures and the Conflict in Information Retrieval, 1945–1999." In *Proceedings of the 1998 Conference on the History and Heritage of Science Information Systems,* 156–66, ed. Mary Ellen Bowden, Trudi Bellardo Hahn, and Robert V. Williams. Medford, NJ: Information Today for the American Society for Information Science and the Chemical Heritage Foundation. http://webdoc.gwdg.de/ebook/s/2001/ chf/www.chemheritage.org/historicalservices/asis_documents/asis98_bowles.pdf.

Boyd, John, Penny Pugh, Marian Hampton, Pat Morrison, and Frank Cervone. 2006. "The One-Box Challenge: Providing a Federated Search That Benefits the Research Process." *Serials Review* 32, no. 4: 247–54. doi:10.1016/j.serrev.2006.08.005.

Brin, Sergey, and Lawrence Page. 1998. "The Anatomy of a Large-Scale Hypertextual Web Search Engine." In *Seventh International World-Wide Web Conference (WWW 1998).* Brisbane, Australia. http://ilpubs.stanford.edu:8090/361/.

Budiu, Raluca. "Search Is Not Enough: Synergy Between Navigation and Search." 2014. *Nielsen Norman Group: Evidence-Based User Experience Research, Training, and Consulting.* www.nngroup.com/articles/search-not-enough/.

Bush, Vannevar. "As We May Think." 1945. *The Atlantic Monthly* 176: 101–8. www.theatlantic .com/magazine/archive/1945/07/as-we-may-think/303881/.

Dempsey, Lorcan. "Discovery and Disclosure." 2006. *Lorcan Dempsey's Weblog: On Libraries, Services, and Networks.* http://orweblog.oclc.org/archives/001084.html.

———. 2012. "Thirteen Ways of Looking at Libraries, Discovery, and the Catalog: Scale, Workflow, Attention." *EDUCAUSE Review Online.* www.educause.edu/ero/article/ thirteen-ways-looking-libraries-discovery-and-catalog-scale-workflow-attention.

Fahey, Sue, Shannon Gordon, and Crystal Rose. 2011. "Seeing Double at Memorial University: Two WorldCat Local Usability Studies." *Partnership: The Canadian Journal of Library and Information Practice and Research* 6, no. 2: 1–14. https://journal.lib.uoguelph.ca/index.php/perj/article/view/1552.

Gleick, James. 2011. *The Information: A History, a Theory, a Flood.* New York: Pantheon Books.

Google Design Guidelines. "Material Design." www.google.com/design/spec.

Griffiths, Jillian R., and Peter Brophy. 2005. "Student Searching Behavior and the Web: Use of Academic Resources and Google." *Library Trends* 53, no. 4: 539–54. http://hdl.handle.net/2142/1749.

Lown, Cory, Tito Sierra, and Josh Boyer. 2013. "How Users Search the Library from a Single Search Box." *College & Research Libraries* 74, no. 3: 227–41. http://crl.acrl.org/content/74/3/227.full.pdf.

Maynes, Rebecca, and Ian Everdell. 2014. "The Evolution of Google's Search Results Pages & Effects on User Behavior." *Mediative.* http://pages.mediative.com/SERP-Research.

McKay, Dana. 2011. "Gotta Keep 'Em Separated: Why the Single Search Box May Not Be Right for Libraries." In *CHINZ '11: Proceedings of the 12th Annual Conference of the New Zealand Chapter of the ACM Special Interest Group on Computer-Human Interaction*, 109–12. New York: ACM. http://dl.acm.org/citation.cfm?id=2000772.

Namei, Elizabeth, and Christal A. Young. 2015. "Measuring Our Relevancy: Comparing Results in a Web-Scale Discovery Tool, Google, & Google Scholar." In *Creating Sustainable Community: The Proceedings of the ACRL 2015 Conference, March 25–28, Portland, Oregon*, 522–35, ed. Dawn M. Mueller. Chicago: Association of College and Research Libraries. www.ala.org/acrl/sites/ala.org.acrl/files/content/conferences/confsandpreconfs/2015/Namei_Young.pdf.

Nielsen, Jakob. 2013. "Converting Search into Navigation." *Nielsen Norman Group: Evidence-Based User Experience Research, Training, and Consulting.* www.nngroup.com/articles/search-navigation/.

Rider, Freemont. 1944. *The Scholar and the Future of the Research Library.* New York: Hadham.

Rochkind, Jonathan. 2012. "Article Search Improvement Strategy." *Bibliographic Wilderness.* https://bibwild.wordpress.com/2012/10/02/article-search-improvement-strategy/.

Sherwin, Katie. 2015. "Scoped Search: Dangerous, But Sometimes Useful." *Nielsen Norman Group: Evidence-Based User Experience Research, Training, and Consulting.* www.nngroup.com/articles/scoped-search/.

Sierra, Tito. 2007. "A Single Search Box Interface to the NCSU Libraries, Two Years Later." Presentation at the Digital Library Federation Spring Forum 2007, Pasadena, CA, March 12.

Singhal, Amit. 2012. "Introducing the Knowledge Graph: Things, Not Strings." *Official Google Blog.* http://googleblog.blogspot.com/2012/05/introducing-knowledge-graph-things-not.html.

Swanson, Troy A., and Jeremy Green. 2011. "Why We Are Not Google: Lessons from a Library Web Site Usability Study." *The Journal of Academic Librarianship* 37, no. 3: 222–29. doi:10.1016/j.acalib.2011.02.014.

Tennant, Roy. 2002. "MARC Must Die." *Library Journal* 127, no. 17: 26–28. http://lj.library journal.com/2002/10/ljarchives/marc-must-die/#_.

Thomale, Jason. 2014. *Resource Discovery System Usage Report, 02–01–2012 to 08–25–2014.* http://digital.library.unt.edu/ark:/67531/metadc499075/.

Thompson, James. 1982. *The End of Libraries.* London: Clive Bingley.

Tidwell, Jenifer. 1999. *Common Ground: A Pattern Language for Human-Computer Interface Design.* www.mit.edu/~jtidwell/interaction_patterns.html.

Varnum, Ken. 2009. "The New University of Michigan Library Web Site." *Library Tech Talk: Technology Innovations and Project Updates from the U-M Library I.T. Division.* www.lib .umich.edu/blogs/library-tech-talk/new-university-michigan-library-web-site.

Wroblewski, Luke, Martjin van Welie, and Bill Scott. 2006. "Design Patterns: Part 1." *LukeW: Ideation + Design.* www.lukew.com/ff/entry.asp?348.

CHAPTER ELEVEN

ONE-TO-MANY

Building a Single-Search Interface for Disparate Resources

COLE HUDSON AND GRAHAM HUKILL

L ibraries provide access to a complex array of resources, but it comes as little surprise that many struggle with this task. The ubiquity of Google in modern research has placed libraries in the position of trying to emulate or set themselves apart from the search engine, regardless of how appropriate it is to compare libraries to Google. There are numerous ways in which libraries can improve the search and discovery experience for patrons, and for many, this improvement currently comes in the form of custom-built or commercial discovery systems—which aggregate disparate library content into a single results display. But, regardless of discovery systems' potential, as Lown, Sierra, and Boyer (2013) conclude, libraries should learn and balance user expectations with the actual capabilities of library information systems. In an effort to find this balance, our work led us to a singular goal: providing a single-search interface for our complex array of library resources. What resulted was a discovery tool we named QuickSearch.

Developed in-house, QuickSearch is a single point of interaction, "bento style" search portal, displaying search results from disparate resources in discrete boxes. These resources come from numerous independent, back-end systems, including search results from the library catalog, Serials Solutions Summon Service, research guides, journals, our institutional repository, digital collections, databases, and a site search of the entire university website. The term *bento* comes from Japanese cuisine where different parts of a meal are compartmentalized in aesthetically pleasing ways; this ultimately is the aesthetic goal of compartmentalizing search results from disparate resources on the results page.

In this chapter we are not advocating for specific programming languages or technologies; instead, we aim to share our underlying design principles and philosophy in developing QuickSearch. As we see discovery moving toward constantly shifting silos of data that must be aggregated for users, we tried to imagine an architecture that accommodates this reality.

Vendors (e.g., Serial Solutions, EBSCO) offer products that aggregate library resources, but as we shall see, these products are, by nature, incomplete and incomprehensive. We are unable to rely on vendors for a single point of search, yet we are also unable to create our own single resource index. The discovery landscape is changing too quickly, and our staff is too small for a monolithic approach. Instead, we have chosen to address data silos individually and loosely couple them together under a single banner: QuickSearch—software that our small team of developers can update and maintain. This approach seems to be well received by users and has already resulted in increased access to resources.

This chapter will first outline QuickSearch's key features (see figure 11.1), discuss explored and realized approaches, and conclude with an appraisal of the impact QuickSearch has had on user behavior patterns.

FIGURE 11.1 ——

Screenshot of QuickSearch displaying results for "biology" search

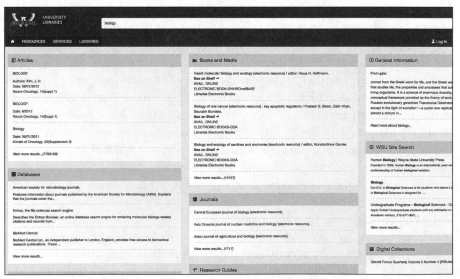

POTENTIAL APPROACHES AND WHY THEY DIDN'T WORK

To meet our goal of providing a comprehensive, intuitive search tool across all library resources, from a single interface, we first explored a range of different possible approaches. This section will discuss these, noting why they were not a good fit for us, in an effort to contextualize the development of QuickSearch and explain how it addressed problems with these other approaches. (See table 11.1.)

TABLE 11.1 ———

Overview of explored approaches

Approach	Problem	QuickSearch's Solution
Web-Scale Discovery Services	Do not contain all library resources	WSDS results are valuable, incorporated as "Articles" box
Single Index of Library Resources	Difficult to rank, difficult to maintain	Currently avoids ranking
Monolithic Software Approach	Brittle, hard to update, too much maintenance	Simply designed, low barrier to construction, easy to update, resilient to catastrophic failure

WEB-SCALE DISCOVERY SERVICES

Providing a single point of interaction for search is increasingly a focus of vendors, as they realize how valuable this would be to libraries and their users. Companies such as EBSCO, Ex Libris, OCLC, and ProQuest all have products that index multiple resource types, including databases that they operate and provide access to, abstracts from other vendors' databases, and even MARC records for books and media from a library's catalog. These platforms are often referred to as "web-scale discovery services" (WSDS). The number of distinct items in these platforms is staggering—our own ProQuest "Summon" platform returns 632,286,219 results for a blanket search. Yet still, some library resources are not included, making them effectively invisible to our users.

　　Web-scale discovery services include resources from a variety of sources. They are well suited for searching individual articles because they include articles from a wide variety of journals and databases, in addition to MARC records they pull from library catalogs and other resources. But in spite of the increasingly wide net that web-scale discovery services cast over a library's resources, vast swaths are often missed: institutional repositories, digital collections, databases, research guides, information on the university or library website, and so on. These omissions can happen for a variety of reasons, three of which we will explore further below.

One reason resources might be absent from a WSDS is that they don't fit neatly into the model the service is using for indexing and searching resources. As advanced and sophisticated as they get, web-scale discovery services still rely on quasi-traditional approaches to modeling library resources: titles, authors, dates, publishers, and so forth. For example, they are ill prepared to accommodate a university's website search results where complex, algorithmic ranking of pages is useful, if not essential. Library research guides are another example of resources that do not fit neatly into that model. Web-scale discovery services are successful only insofar as the resources we seek can be described and searched in a meaningful way through their interface.

Second, it is possible the resources are inaccessible to the WSDS, or too small and unique to be indexed by a large, vendor-created WSDS. For example, at Wayne State University we have a growing institutional repository (Digital-Commons@WayneState) and online digital collections, neither of which are indexed by our Summon platform. These are valuable library resources, but are missed completely.

Thirdly, even within resource types that a WSDS is able to index and search, there might be gaps when resources are not included due to "reluctant vendor participation/partnerships or to choices of resource inclusion made by libraries" (Ellero 2013). In effect, the coverage of a WSDS is a moving target, which does not always support comprehensive, repeatable searching.

The point here is not to provide an in-depth analysis of web-scale discovery services, which other articles have expertly done (e.g., Ellero 2013), but instead to show that despite their vast reach, there are library resources they currently cannot, and perhaps will not, index for search.

SINGLE INDEX: APPLES AND ORANGES

Another approach to providing a single-search interface for library patrons is to put metadata records from disparate sources into a single index, and provide a search interface from that single point. Cosmetically and conceptually it is quite similar to Google, in that all resources would come from a central index, interleaved into a single list of results. This approach looks elegant on paper, but is fraught with its own problems. A particularly thorny one is that

> library data just doesn't have the same characteristics as Web data. It just doesn't. Though . . . lots of folks working on Web Scale Discovery have made big strides, nobody has "solved" relevance ranking for full library discovery the way Google solved it for the Web. (Thomale 2015)

This quote from Jason Thomale during his talk at Code4Lib Annual in 2015 (also see chapter 10, "The Bento Box Design Pattern," by Thomale, Philipps, and Hicks) very nicely sums up the problem of creating a single index, comprised of multiple resource types, to search and provide results: the resource types that are included are simply too different, and ranking them as search results is an effort in futility. Search algorithms that power a single database or resource type are complex at best, but ranking multiple resource types increases that complexity exponentially.

With the goal of a single-search box interface, a bento-style approach sidesteps some problems with this approach, namely it does not purport to rank variant resource types. Instead, it provides these resources on equal footing, leveraging the ranking algorithms internal to each resource's individual search interface.

MONOLITHIC SOFTWARE APPLICATION: LESS CODE, MORE UNIFORMITY

A third approach is to design a system in which resources share common pathways and code. Each "box" on the page has to ask its associated database for data in a particular fashion. Each database returns this data in a particular form. Given five to ten boxes, the complexity of code needed to handle these differences can grow quite dramatically. The way to prevent this would be to pass everything through a common processing pipe that would handle requesting and returning data to the "boxes" on the page. This approach would allow for less overall code and more uniform features between the boxes. If every box uses the same processing pipe, potentially when an update to one box is applied, it would apply to all. This approach, however, is not without its pitfalls.

The main issue with this kind of approach can be best expressed in its need for dedicated staff to manage the system. In a 2001 IBM white paper, Paul Horn states that the greatest obstacle facing the IT industry is complexity. "In fact, the growing complexity of the I/T infrastructure threatens to undermine the very benefits information technology aims to provide." This problem is one of scale, because soon, he warns, there would not be enough IT professionals to handle the rise in complex, interconnected systems (Horn 2001). Dystopic vision aside, Horn does touch upon a key issue that applies to any organization regardless of size—the increased human cost of ever more complex systems. Horn's premonitions are relevant to our work with QuickSearch. Maintaining a more complex and better-integrated system would be cost-prohibitive in terms of dedicated staff time. We have no full-time front or back-end web developers.

The main development team consists of librarians and system administrators, for which application development is only a part of their job duties. If we followed a monolithic development approach, one in which we wrote DRY (Don't Repeat Yourself) code, this would naturally lead to something such as a common processing pipe for all resource types, but the costs of maintaining this approach would increase.

Another issue to contend with is that the resources which power Quick-Search undergo changes and upgrades at different rates either because of (1) internal decisions to change how we interact with a resource, or (2) changes to resources outside of our control (such as Serial Solutions' Summon service or Springshare's LibGuides API). When the resources share a common processing pipe, any changes we make to one resource would have to not disrupt the functionality of other resources. This, in turn, increases the amount of testing needed to ensure that all the resources still retrieve and display results correctly. With enough people and very established application development workflows, interconnected systems can be run smoothly. With our small team, this was a major roadblock to adopting this overall approach.

QUICKSEARCH: OUR APPROACH, OUR SOLUTION

Given our goal of a single-search interface across all library resources, we developed QuickSearch with the shortcomings of other approaches firmly in mind, focusing on a low-barrier, manageable approach we hoped would hit all of our requirements.

The design principle is straightforward: QuickSearch is a representative specimen of the bento box-style search interface, where results from different sources are returned to visually discrete boxes on the results page. One page, one search box, results from as many library resource types as possible.

DESIGN PRINCIPLE: EVERY BOX FOR ITSELF

As opposed to the monolithic approach discussed above, we opted for an architecture with a much lower barrier to entry. Figure 11.2 is an overview of the QuickSearch architecture.

Our strategy going into development—when the number of resources types (boxes) was still fluctuating—was to have each "box" on the search results page have its own "pipe" back to the original source that provided results relevant to the current search. The advantages to this approach have been numerous.

FIGURE 11.2 ──

Architecture of QuickSearch

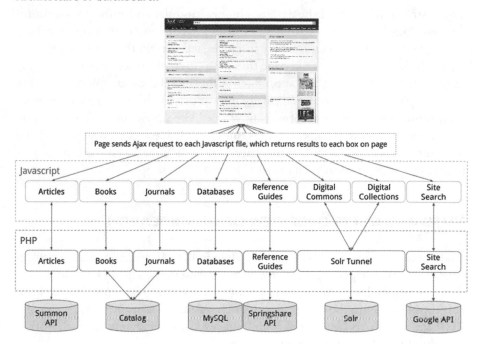

LOW BARRIER TO CREATION

Even during the process of identifying and configuring data sources that would populate the search results, we could start building "pipes" for known resource types and could begin prototyping the page. In a monolithic–based approach, it might have been cumbersome to wait on unknowns like this, such that we could fold them into more terse and purposeful code.

EASY TO COMPREHEND

Just follow the arrows! Most librarians who work with electronic resources will be familiar with the databases at the bottom of the figure (some are vendors, some are databases with indexed resources). Except for a couple of unique cases where different "boxes" share "pipes," there is a near 1:1:1 ratio from Java-Script-populated "box," to PHP "tunnel," to database on the back end.

WELL SUITED FOR A SMALL TEAM

The distributed nature of the design—highly modular and autonomous routes for each "box"—made it easy to develop with a small number of people working on the front and back ends. In many instances, we split up the work by resource type, where each person would code the "pipe" for a given resource from beginning to end. They would be responsible for the actual database queries, moving up through PHP, JavaScript, and finally into displaying results. In a larger, more monolithic system, this kind of workflow would be nearly impossible. The only constraint we had was that box results must be reliable and consistent with the resource's native results set; the mechanics of each "pipe" were determined by the nature of the resource database.

NUTS AND BOLTS OVERVIEW OF QUICKSEARCH

Aside from the traditional markup and styling in HTML and CSS, the application consists of JavaScript- and PHP-mediated interactions with HTTP-accessible data end points. JavaScript renders resource data onto a user's page, while PHP communicates with the data resource. Each resource has its own JavaScript and PHP scripts which handle querying and response separately from the other available QuickSearch resources.

When a patron first uses the QuickSearch tool, their query term(s) are captured via JavaScript. AJAX (Asynchronous JavaScript and XML) calls, each connected to a separate box on the page, then pass along the data for processing by the server. Server-side scripts written in PHP take care of formatting and sending query terms to their corresponding database. When the database responds back with the patron's requested resources, the PHP script processes and sends the data back up the pipeline. Finally, the data is passed back to the QuickSearch web page where it is inserted into the database's corresponding box. Due to the built-in asynchronicity of the AJAX calls, which handle the patron's input and the database's corresponding output, each set of data is returned only when it is ready and the resource's failure and speed (or lack thereof) has no impact upon the other resource boxes or their ability to load data from their own data sources.

IMPACT AND ENGAGEMENT

QuickSearch was launched November 6, 2013, as an additional search option among a cluster of search interfaces. Though it provided an umbrella search that covered resources from other search interfaces, it was not until August 2014, when we launched a redesign of the website, that we did away with the search interface cluster approach and featured QuickSearch as the primary search interface from the library home page.

Since that time, inroads for search and discovery have changed dramatically. What used to be unique and isolated search interfaces have become a single point of interaction. The result has been largely positive. Users have demonstrated active and sustained engagement on the search page; resources that were previously unsearchable and inaccessible from the library website are now discoverable; and we received a healthy dose of "No News Is Good News" feedback from users.

INCREASED ACCESS TO RESOURCES

A driving force for the creation of QuickSearch was to provide discoverability to resources that were previously unsearchable from the library website. Nevertheless, many of the resources now searched by QuickSearch were, in fact, previously searchable from the library website via a tabbed search interface on the library home page: Articles ("Everything"), Books and Media ("Catalog"), Databases ("Article Databases"), Journals ("Online Journals"), and even Site Search.

Though all of these resource types were searchable, tab usage was inconsistent, and search was certainly not possible across all resource types at once. The effect hurt serendipitous discovery across resource types, and required a duplication of effort on the user's part, constantly repeating searches in different interfaces, navigating the challenge and peculiarities of each.

With the launch of QuickSearch, a new tab was created allowing users to search across these resources with one search (see figure 11.3).

FIGURE 11.3 ————————————————————————————

Pre-redesign website tabbed search interfaces with QuickSearch included

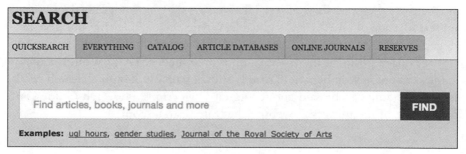

FIGURE 11.4 ───

Current website without tabbed search interfaces, featuring QuickSearch as the sole search box in header

Even with the addition of QuickSearch, tab usage was still inconsistent and confusing, and patrons still had the option to search specific resource types via their isolated search interface. With the redesign in August 2014, we moved away from the tabbed search cluster, and for the first time, started pushing all library search and discovery traffic from our new standard header (see figure 11.4) through QuickSearch.

As user searching began routing through QuickSearch only, many library resources that were previously hidden from search and discovery on the main library website were, for the first time, exposed to all searches, for all users. This includes our Institutional Repository (DC@WSU), our Digital Collections (WSUDOR), Library Research Guides, and a more sophisticated Site Search of the entire wayne.edu domain.

This exposure has resulted in increased use and awareness of these resources. Since QuickSearch launched in August 2014, through March 2015, it has directed users to resources previously unsearchable from the library website:

- 800 + visits to digital collections
- 3,800 + visits to library research guides
- 3,500 + visits to DC@WSU

Those visits to DC@WSU, as an example, are particularly encouraging. DC@WSU is a Software-as-a-Service (SaaS) from Bepress, with a website and search interface entirely removed from the library infrastructure. Usage of this resource was limited to the traffic we could direct there, often just for known items such as electronic theses or dissertations. These near 4,000 visits not only demonstrate increased usage of DC@WSU's valuable, Wayne State scholarship, but have produced increased awareness around DC@WSU and its mission as the university's institutional repository. Increased campus awareness of DC@WSU is a major, somewhat unforeseen benefit of simply showing up on the QuickSearch results page. The same can be said about Digital Collections, Research Guides, and other parts of the university website that Site Search scours.

USER ENGAGEMENT BY THE NUMBERS

Just shy of 300,000 visits (where a "visit" is defined as a new user visiting the page, or a returning user after thirty minutes or more) at the time of this writing, QuickSearch represents a substantial portion of all traffic to the library website, which had approximately 1,600,000 visits in this same time period. But even more interesting than simple visits to the page is user behavior once there.

To collect statistics on QuickSearch, we use an open-source website analytics platform, Piwik (http://piwik.org/). We tracked visits to the page, searches on the page, and clicks to actual resources. While "outlinks" (in Piwik nomenclature) may contain clicks to the header menu items, we believe the vast majority of those clicks are to QuickSearch search results. We have recently started quantifying only QuickSearch clicks; this will allow us greater granularity in future analysis. From this tracking, a couple interesting insights emerge.

First, use of QuickSearch was minimal until it was featured as the primary library search interface; even though it was offered as a tab on the search interface cluster, and at one point even the default one, it was not widely used. Traffic increased sharply around the beginning of the fall semester after the redesign. For our team, this slow rollout was a good time to identify and fix bugs, while traffic was slow. Having other librarians test the system by performing searches and noting irregularities was instrumental during that time.

Second, and perhaps the most interesting insight to emerge from the numbers, is the behavior of users on the page. Reviewing the analytics have identified a rough 1:2:4 ratio of visits: searches: resource use.

Piwik's web logs serve as a cross-check. We can look at anonymized individual user visits to see the activity in search terms and links out. While these do not perfectly model the 1–2–4 ratio we see in the graphs, they serve as sketches of common user behavior that leads to the patterns we observe among users overall.

QuickSearch demonstrates a high level of user engagement. By contrast, even a website such as our LibGuides platform—with plenty of dynamic content—has a much closer 1:1:1 ratio of visits, activity, and outlinks.

We believe we can assert that users are engaged with the website, performing and refining queries, and perhaps most importantly, are being exposed to a large and diverse array of library resources. While we cannot make inferences about the relevance of search results for our users at this time, we are happy with this level of engagement. Understanding user engagement with QuickSearch in a more comprehensive way is a next step as we continue to develop and refine this tool.

"NO NEWS IS GOOD NEWS"

In thinking about the impact QuickSearch has had on discovery for our patrons, we spoke with our user experience librarian who has been operating a survey since the launch of QuickSearch and the website redesign. The survey was provided to users as a banner across the top of QuickSearch. While we initially lamented only 45–50 survey responses regarding QuickSearch, this librarian astutely pointed out that considering more than 300,000 QuickSearch searches, only 45–50 responses, and the somewhat unfortunate reality that most feedback is negative when it does come back, one might chalk up a small response rate to "No news is good news," and assume it quietly became a successful and functional search interface for users. If things were not working well, we most likely would have heard about it.

Further user data supports this as well. Figure 11.5 represents returning visitors to QuickSearch. Over the course of a semester, the number of returning visitors increases. While QuickSearch is our primary search interface now, other more targeted search interfaces do still exist, even featured prominently as "QuickLinks" on the front page, yet users continue to return to QuickSearch to perform their searches.

Given these markers, and some anecdotal testing and feedback from users, we feel confident that QuickSearch has integrated itself as the primary search interface for our users, with a high degree of use and engagement, providing discoverability and access to a wider array of library resources than ever before, from one location.

FIGURE 11.5 ─────────────────────────────────────

Returning users to QuickSearch (visits triggered by user searches)

CONCLUSION

In building QuickSearch, we are confident that we met our goal of providing a service that unites our disparate resources. It is sustainable for our development team, and we see the continued and sustained use by our patrons as positive. However, regardless of the tool's current success, we realize that user expectations about resources and their presentation will evolve. Even now, we are evaluating radical changes to QuickSearch's interface. Regardless of how it evolves, we are confident the design principles that underlie QuickSearch—modular components, ease of development for a small team, and flexibility towards resource types—will remain constant as we move our discovery efforts forward.

ACKNOWLEDGMENTS

Building QuickSearch was a collaborative effort within the library. Development would not have been possible without the feedback and input of our librarians and staff. Particular credit and thanks to Rachael Clark, Joseph Gajda, Niranjan Jadhav, Axa Mei Liauw, Joshua Neds-Fox, Elliot Polak, Vinay Potluri, and Negib Sherif.

References

Ellero, Nadine P. 2013. "Integration or Disintegration: Where Is Discovery Headed?" *Journal of Library Metadata* 13, no. 4: 311–29.

Horn, Paul. 2001. *Autonomic Computing: IBM's Perspective on the State of Information Technology.* Armonk, NY: IBM.

Lown, Cory, Tito Sierra, and Josh Boyer. 2013. "How Users Search the Library from a Single Search Box." *College and Research Libraries* 74, no. 3: 227–41.

Thomale, Jason. 2015. "You Gotta Keep 'em Separated: The Case for Bento Box Discovery Interfaces." Lecture presented at the Code4Lib conference, Portland, Oregon, on February 11, 2015.

CHAPTER TWELVE

INTEGRATING DISCOVERY TO IMPROVE THE USER EXPERIENCE

SONYA BETZ AND IAN ROBERTON

n October 2011, a small group of librarians and technical staff, the members of MacEwan University Library's newly formed Web and Emerging Technologies Advisory Committee, held an off–campus retreat for a full day of brainstorming and problem-solving. Central to the day's discussion was the problem of discovery. MacEwan University, a medium–sized undergraduate university in Edmonton, Canada, dedicates significant resources to developing its library collections to support the research and study of its students and faculty. In 2011, having recently gone through an institutional transformation from a community college to a fully accredited undergraduate university, MacEwan University Library was in a phase of active collection building, and its resources had grown dramatically in the preceding five years. However, despite having unprecedented access to more materials, particularly in electronic formats, students' survey responses indicated that their satisfaction with our collections had been steadily decreasing since 2008 (NRG Research Group 2010). The Advisory Committee discussed this paradox in depth: the library was spending more than ever on collecting resources in easily accessible formats; it was an early adopter of EBSCO Discovery Service, a tool that was supposed to make those resources simple to find; and MacEwan also had an extremely active information literacy program that introduced thousands of students a year to the basics of finding resource in the library. Our expectation was that these activities would lead to a measurable increase in student satisfaction with our collections, but surprisingly the opposite was happening. Why?

MacEwan's *LibQual 2011* survey provided some context; it revealed significant levels of dissatisfaction when users were asked whether we met their expectations for a "website that enables users to locate information on their own, easy-to-use access tools that allow users to find things on their own and making information easily accessible for independent use" (MacEwan University Library 2011). Many comments reflected a frustration with not being able to locate and access full-text e-journals. Although MacEwan was purchasing or subscribing to the materials students were searching for, finding and using those materials seemed to be problematic for many of them.

TWO BARRIERS TO DISCOVERY

As with most libraries, the primary access point to MacEwan's collections, both physical and virtual, was the website. All of the tools and resources purchased and subscribed to were collected and linked to through the website. The library spent considerable time and energy crafting the structure, organization, and design of this space, and developing content for pages about its people, services, and collections. We created widgets to launch users into the vendor-supplied discovery tool, library guides, integrated library system, and many other services. And, like most libraries, our accountability for our online environment ended at our virtual exit doors: the moment a student moved into a vendor's online space, we could no longer claim responsibility for the student's user experience. Unfortunately for our students, this philosophy has led to a confusing and disconnected user experience, and to the two main issues that were fundamentally at the root of our students' problems with discovery.

The first fundamental problem we could clearly identify was the disjointed and inconsistent experience of library discovery. Published research around user experience and web-scale discovery tends to focus on the usability of the tools themselves, and the benefits of discovery layers in replacing earlier combinations of federated database searching, or individual database and catalog searching. For example, Asher, Duke, and Wilson (2012), Comeaux (2012), and Gross and Sheridan (2011), all examine the usability of particular discovery products, and while identifying some obstacles to usability, generally indicate that web-scale discovery layers lead to improvements in the overall search experience.

However, unlike the controlled environment of a usability test, holistic library discovery is messy and unguided. A typical discovery experience is provided by many different vendor-supplied products working together, and students must use multiple interfaces from the beginning of their search to the point where they successfully locate a book or article. The discovery environment at MacEwan University, prior to the 2014 launch of our new site, was an excellent example of this disjointed experience. For example, a student began her search for a book on the MacEwan Library's home page, where we displayed a search box widget for our discovery tool, EBSCO Discovery Service (EDS). Once the student entered search terms, she was launched into the EDS interface to view search results. If the student found the book for which she was searching, and clicked the "place hold" button, she was transported to the ILS, Sirsi Symphony. Here she needed to log in to the ILS, using credentials that were different from her MacEwan University log-in and password. Only after she had navigated this confusing gauntlet of three separate user interfaces, and an unfamiliar log-in, was she able to place a hold on a book. Students searching for articles may have had to interact with four interfaces: the library's website, EDS, a link resolver (SFX), and the publisher platform hosting the content. Each interface presented different navigation, different vocabulary, different look and feel, and different interactions with elements like buttons and images. Consistency, long recognized as one of the most important criteria of usability, allows users to easily navigate an online space because the elements are predictable and coherent (Nielsen and Loranger 2006; Ozok and Salvendy 2001; Shneiderman and Plaisant 2010). The uncoordinated, multi-interface environment of discovery wreaks havoc on students' expectations for consistency. A link labeled "PDF" in one interface may be called "Download Article" in another. The link back to a library's home page may move from the right side to the left, or be buried in an image. Each vendor interface requires the student to relearn the rules, and not surprisingly, our observations and student feedback suggested that students were finding discovery overly complex and difficult.

A second issue that we identified was the growing importance of mobile devices to our students. In 2011, 33 percent of Canadian cell phone users owned a smartphone, but the adoption of smartphones among cell phone owners 18 to 24 years old was more than double the national average, at 72 percent (Quorus Consulting Group 2012). We fully expected those numbers to continue to climb, and indeed 2015 statistics have confirmed this trend (comScore 2015), but our mobile site in 2011 was basic, at best, and as soon as students linked out of our site to external resources or search tools, they were at the mercy of vendors who provided mobile access inconsistently if at all. Even in 2011, there had been much ink spilled in the professional library literature over the necessity and value of providing access to all devices (Bridges, Rempel, and Griggs 2010; Cummings, Merrill, and Borrelli 2010; Lippincott 2010; Paterson and Low 2011; Seeholzer and Salem 2010). Not only was there general agreement in the literature that mobile access to library services was becoming increasingly important, but at a local level we were also seeing increases in mobile traffic to the library's website being tracked by Google Analytics.

As a consequence of these initial discussions in late 2011, we developed a strategic plan that prioritized improving the students' search experience by solving these two issues. Over the following three years we worked on a number of initiatives that explore the concepts of mobile first delivery, and more importantly, integration of our vendor-supplied services into a single user interface.

FIRST STEP TO INTEGRATION: THE MACEWAN LIB IOS APP

Considering how many vendor interfaces we rely on, it was a daunting task to conceptualize how best to integrate them into our online environment. As a first step, we decided to start with a small, well-defined project that could address some of our concerns with mobile access, provide a proof-of-concept product, and help us begin to tackle the design challenges that small screens produce. Our top priorities were to integrate our discovery tool, the EBSCO Discovery Service and our ILS, Sirsi Symphony, into a single unified interface. By early 2012, both EBSCO and Sirsi were providing APIs or web services that would allow us to interact with the products without relying on their vendor interfaces.

We submitted a proposal to an internal MacEwan Student Technology Fee grant to secure funding to develop an iOS app. We recognized the many constraints that exist in developing a platform-specific app, but these concerns were outweighed by the benefits for our situation. An iOS-specific app would allow us to design for a limited number of screen sizes and a single operating system. We could also produce one single, defined product. At the time, apps were gaining significant traction, and of the mobile visits to our site, over 70 percent were coming from an iOS device. Most importantly to our development team, the restricted scope of this project would provide us with opportunities to become familiar with the different technologies, and allow us to solve problems in a lower-risk environment. We viewed this project as a learning experience, and an important step towards our ultimate goal of integrating our discovery environment with a responsive library website. Our proposal was successful in securing funding and we worked with a local Edmonton company to develop the MacEwan Lib app that was launched in October 2012.

The MacEwan Lib app was a simple concept, but it continues to be an uncommon approach in library mobile app development. Rather than creating an app that links out to our discovery tool, catalog, and other external services, we used a combination of vendor- and custom-developed application programming interfaces (APIs) and web services to integrate discovery and user account functions into the app itself. The result is a much more seamless user experience with a single user interface.

When users first open the app they're asked to authenticate with their Mac-Ewan credentials. A simple local application checks a user against Sirsi Symphony, EDS, and other university services. Once users are authenticated, the MacEwan Lib app can store the credentials on their device, so they only need to log in again if their password changes or they choose to log out.

The MacEwan Lib app uses Sirsi Web Services to manage holds, track users' checked out and overdue items, display user fees, and renew items. It uses the EDS API to search the catalog as well as MacEwan's licensed database content. Together, these services offer incredibly powerful and flexible design options for the user interface. For example, a user can conduct a search directly within the app. Search limits are expandable from the bottom of the page (see figure 12.1). If a user finds a book that she would like to place on hold, she can tap a hold button directly within the search results (see figure 12.2). The MacEwan Lib app places the request in the background with Symphony Web Services, and the user only needs to confirm her pickup location (see figures 12.3–12.5.) To check on the status of the hold, or to renew items she has already checked

FIGURE 12.1 ————————————————
MacEwan Lib search screen

FIGURE 12.2 ————————————————
MacEwan Lib search results screen

FIGURE 12.3 ————————————————

MacEwan Lib item record screen

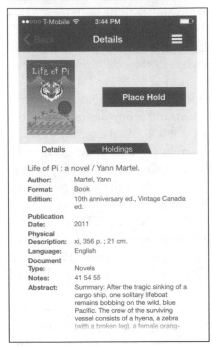

FIGURE 12.4 ————————————————

MacEwan Lib hold location screen

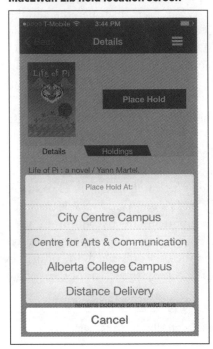

out, she can view her account within the app. Other library information, such as hours, contact details, and branch locations, are contained in a local database, and the app makes use of built-in iOS functionality to add value such as maps and directions to branches and simple dialing of phone numbers. PDF articles can be saved to the device for reading off-line or shared using familiar tools. Because the MacEwan Lib app consolidates all of these services, the user only interacts with a single user interface that is custom designed for the device he or she is using. The user experience is dramatically improved.

Response to the app from students and staff at MacEwan was extremely positive. The student newspaper ran two feature stories (Bell 2013; Pennyfeather 2013), the app was shortlisted for a Digital Alberta Award—Best in Mobile Applications, and won the MacEwan University Award for Innovation in 2013. Actual engagement with the app is more difficult to assess. Although it has been downloaded by over 3,400 users to date, who have run more than 41,300 individual sessions, 1,295 of those users only interacted with the app on the day they downloaded it. However, there is a significant number of users who return to the app and use it frequently. A total of 25.8 percent of users are still interacting with the app a month after they've downloaded it, and we record an average of 18.56 active users every day, with peaks that coincide with the academic schedule.

FIGURE 12.5 —————————————————

MacEwan Lib hold confirmation screen

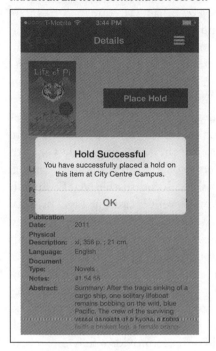

We conducted in-person user tests with students and identified improvements to our design. We also integrated a new service, Ares eReserves, by building a local API to communicate with Ares and connecting it to our app. Now users could easily see items on reserve for their courses in the main menu of the app without logging in to a separate service. We released a new version with this feature in fall 2013.

The MacEwan Lib app was an excellent proof-of-concept project. It provided us with a useful testing ground for exploring the concept of integration in a low-risk environment. We could solve problems like authentication and slow load times without large-scale changes to the rest of our web environment. We were also able to experiment broadly with designing the interface for a mobile discovery experience that worked well for our students. The confines of designing for a restricted number of screen sizes and operating systems allowed us to focus on the details and provided useful boundaries on the scope and scale of what we could do.

However, it was clear from the outset that the app would only be a first step in developing a fully integrated online experience. An iOS app has significant limitations. While ideal for providing a working proof-of-concept, the app is only accessible to those with an iPhone or iPad. Although the majority of our students using mobile devices were on these platforms, a sizeable number were not, and many had no smartphone at all. Almost immediately post-launch we began to field questions from students and faculty asking when an Android version would be available. In addition to problems of access, creating an app also creates a new user experience problem in that there was now very little consistency across platforms. Users coming to our website would have a very different experience from those using the app, creating a similar issue to the one we were seeking to solve. Finally, maintenance and updates for iOS apps can be challenging. Every time we want to make a change to the code, a new version needs to be uploaded to the iTunes App store and made available to users. Users may or may not update the app on their device, making critical fixes difficult to distribute.

THE VIRTUAL SERVICES INTEGRATION PROJECT

Responsive web design (RWD), first described by Ethan Marcotte in 2010, offers solutions for issues of multi-device access and consistency across platforms. The popularity of this approach has increased dramatically in recent years, and many libraries have successfully integrated RWD strategies into their online environments. Kim (2013) and Glassman and Shen (2014) provide useful overviews of the many benefits to libraries of a responsive approach, as does Reidsma in his recent LITA guide to responsive web design (2014). Rempel and Bridges (2013) identify responsive design as a solution that allows mobile site users more flexibility than a pared-down mobile version of their website, while Gayhart, Khalid, and Belray (2014) describe the University of Toronto's responsive catalog.

We decided to scale up the concepts we explored in the MacEwan Lib app within a responsive web design that would consolidate our high-priority services and provide an integrated discovery environment accessible from any device with an Internet connection. We began preliminary planning on this project, named the Virtual Services Integration Project (VSIP), in summer 2013. The new online environment launched in January 2015. In addition to being a totally redesigned and restructured website, this new environment includes discovery and user account functions and a responsive web design framework.

The working concept for VSIP includes a number of different components, all of which need to work together seamlessly in order to provide a fully integrated, user-friendly experience. Building on the knowledge gained during the development of the MacEwan Lib app, we used a combination of vendor-supplied APIs and web services along with locally developed applications to integrate discovery and account functions within a content management system.

Similar to the structure of the MacEwan Lib app, we are using the EBSCO Discovery Service API to power our discovery functions and Sirsi Symphony Web Services to manage account functions. However, rather than connect these services directly to the user interface and content management system, we built local APIs to act as an intermediary layer. Although our custom APIs mirror some of the existing functionality of the EDS API and Sirsi Web Services, they are a critical component of our integrated environment. Our locally developed APIs allow us to separate the display of information in the user interface from the queries being passed to third-party services. They also provide a standardized format to display items retrieved from different services, provide a single point of contact for external services, unify elements like session numbers and database IDs, and give us a measure of flexibility and independence in the event we change providers for major products like our ILS or discovery service.

The three most important APIs we constructed were simply named "Search," "Borrower," and "eReserves." The Search API places calls to the EDS API (for example, a search term and location limit) and returns results in a standard format. The Search API also places calls to Sirsi Symphony Web Services to retrieve item-specific information, such as a call number, availability, and status. The Borrower API manages user account functions. This API connects Sirsi Web Services to our user interface, manages authentication of individual users, and places calls to Sirsi Symphony to make and cancel holds, renew checked-out items, display fines, and complete other account functions. The eReserves API manages the connection between the user interface and our electronic reserves service, Ares. We use this API to send user information to Ares and return relevant courses and item information.

The user interface is built primarily in Drupal through a combination of custom and contributed modules. Drupal's flexibility, modularity, and extensibility were a good match with the level of experimentation and adaptation we needed for this project. Finally, we wrapped up the responsive elements of the design in a theme based on the Zurb Foundation framework.

INTEGRATION AND THE USER EXPERIENCE

Throughout the development process, user input has been an invaluable component of determining design and functionality. Early in the planning stages of the project, we ran student focus groups to probe student needs and expectations, met with faculty to help us understand their work processes, and held workshops with library staff to help pin down key components based on their front-line experience. We approached this project as a holistic redevelopment of the entire web environment, rather than the creation of a stand-alone discovery tool, and our user testing strategy reflected this philosophy.

Post-launch user testing has been critical to ensuring the success of the new web environment and is an ongoing exercise with rapidly shifting priorities. One of the measures of success we identified was ensuring users could complete six top tasks in the new site: find a book, find an article, locate a database, place a hold on an item, determine the library's hours, and locate citation help. We conducted user testing with two methodologies to generate rich, qualitative data. We used Krug's "Thinking Out Loud" protocol (2006) to run a series of testing sessions where participants were asked to communicate their thought processes as they worked through tasks. We also used "Guerrilla" usability testing (Nielsen 1994) to examine specific aspects of functionality, or when testing a specific design improvement.

After the testing, we analyzed the data and classified the usability issues. We were pleased to see that the majority of testing participants were able to accomplish the defined tasks. For example, finding a book and placing a hold, a significant obstacle in our previous web environment, presented little difficulty to participants. This improvement can be attributed to a clear call to action—the Place Hold button—appearing in the results list, and the seamless integration we created between the discovery layer and ILS (see figures 12.6–12.9).

However, there were definite problems associated with our discovery design. The facet limiters on the results page were not very visible, and students misunderstood their function because of ambiguous labels. Some participants had difficulty discerning different formats due to the similarity of representative icons. The MacEwan University Library is a member of a consortium of academic libraries with a shared catalog, and participants also had difficulty differentiating between items that were available at MacEwan and items that were available at our partner libraries.

Improving these problem areas is an ongoing exercise, carried out in small development pushes that tackle prioritized issues first. However, because we have complete control over the interface, we have a tremendous amount of flexibility in our capacity to create solutions that meet the needs of our users. For example, in an early effort to easily visually identify material from our local collections, MacEwan items were shown in the results list with a subfield that displayed the call number. Items that were from a consortial partner library

FIGURE 12.6 ————————————————————————————————

VSIP search screen on iPad

FIGURE 12.7 ————————————————————————————————

VSIP item record with hold button

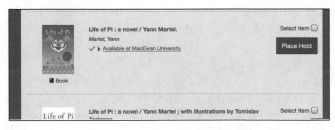

FIGURE 12.8 —————————————————————————————————————

VSIP hold location screen

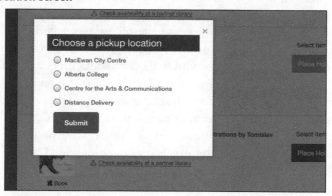

FIGURE 12.9 —————————————————————————————————————

VSIP hold confirmation screen

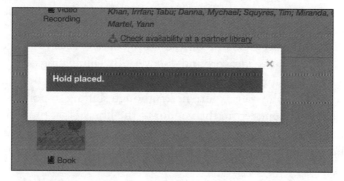

would appear in the search results without a call number. Our testing participants were confused by this distinction, so we clarified the design by creating three different labels: "Available at MacEwan," "Unavailable at MacEwan," "Available at a partner library." The text is now clearly identified as a clickable link, uses color-coded icons to provide visual emphasis, and expands to display the call number and status of the item. These changes led to substantial improvements when examined with guerilla usability testing.

CONCLUSION AND CHALLENGES

Despite positive initial feedback, it's still too early to understand fully how successful we have been in improving the discovery experience by integrating our online services through our web environment. We have solved our primary goals of creating mobile access to all devices, by working with a responsive web design framework, and we've integrated our discovery service and ILS seamlessly within that space. However, as a result, we've created some significant issues. For example, we must consider how to provide access to functions that are embedded within vendors' products. EDS provides users with the ability to select, save, and share lists of items, along with formatted citations. To duplicate these features in our environment requires assessment and prioritization, and a commitment to expending resources to re-create services that we are already paying for through our subscriptions. Although there's a strong case to be made for our ability to improve on the user experience provided by the vendor, in times of economic constraint, this position may not be defensible. At issue too is the quickly shifting nature of library discovery. With the growing prominence of linked open data, this project may prove prescient, allowing us to adapt more easily the output of our APIs to make our collection metadata accessible more widely. On the other hand, without careful planning for the future, and adequate resources to ensure continued support for this initiative, we may find ourselves quickly outdated.

Regardless of the eventual outcome, this project has proven an excellent testing ground for innovative ideas around discovery. By eliminating our dependence on vendor interfaces for our discovery service and ILS, we have been able to take complete control of the user experience. Although shifting responsibility for the design of that experience from the vendor to the library is at times frightening, it is also ultimately empowering. Rather than be faced with the frustration at our inability to influence the design of vendor interfaces, we now have the ability to change what isn't working for our students. Ultimately, this project represents not just a new approach to discovery, but a strong commitment to prioritizing the student experience.

References

Asher, Andrew D., Lynda M. Duke, and Suzanne Wilson. 2012. "Paths of Discovery: Comparing the Search Effectiveness of EBSCO Discovery Service, Summon, Google Scholar, and Conventional Library Resources." *College & Research Libraries* 74, no. 5: 464–88. doi: 10.5860/crl-374.

Bell, Justin. 2013. "MacEwan Library Gets iPhone App." *The Griff*, January 27. http://thegriff .ca/2013/01/library-gets-iphone-app/.

Bridges, Laurie, Hannah Gascho Rempel, and Kimberly Griggs. 2010. "Making the Case for a Fully Mobile Library Web Site: From Floor Maps to the Catalog." *Reference Services Review* 38, no. 2: 309–20. doi: 10.1108/00907321011045061.

Comeaux, David J. 2012. "Usability Testing of a Web-Scale Discovery System at an Academic Library." *College & Undergraduate Libraries* 19, nos. 2–4: 189–206. doi: 10.1080/10691316 .2012.695671.

comScore. 2015. *Digital Future in Focus: Canada 2015.* Canadian Wireless Telecommunications Association. http://cwta.ca/wordpress/wp-content/uploads/2015/06/Digital-Future -in-Focus-2015-CANADA.pdf.

Cummings, Joel, Alex Merrill, and Steve Borrelli. 2010. "The Use of Handheld Mobile Devices: Their Impact and Implications for Library Services." *Library Hi Tech* 28, no. 1: 22–40. doi: 10.1108/07378831011026670.

Gayhart, Lisa, Bilal Khalid, and Gordon Belray. 2014. "The Road to Responsive: University of Toronto Libraries' Journey to a New Library Catalogue Interface." *Code4Lib Journal* 23. http://journal.code4lib.org/articles/9195.

Glassman, Nancy R., and Phil Shen. 2014. "One Site Fits All: Responsive Web Design." *Journal of Electronic Resources in Medical Libraries* 11, no. 2: 78–90. doi: 10.1080/ 15424065.2014.908347.

Gross, Julia, and Lutie Sheridan. 2011. "Web Scale Discovery: The User Experience." *New Library World* 112, nos. 5/6: 236–47. doi: 10.1108/03074801111136275.

Kim, Bohyun. 2013. "Responsive Web Design, Discoverability, and Mobile Challenge." *Library Technology Reports* 49, no. 6: 29–30.

Krug, Steve. 2006. *Don't Make Me Think! A Common Sense Approach to Web Usability.* 2nd edition. Berkeley, CA: New Riders.

Lippincott, Joan K. 2010. "A Mobile Future for Academic Libraries." *Reference Services Review* 38, no. 2: 205–13. doi: 10.1108/00907321011044981.

MacEwan University Library. 2011. *LibQual 2011 Executive Summary.*

Marcotte, Ethan. 2010. "Responsive Web Design." *A List Apart* 306. http://alistapart.com/ article/responsive-web-design.

Nielsen, Jakob. 1994. "Guerrilla HCI: Using Discount Usability Engineering to Penetrate the Intimidation Barrier." In *Cost-Justifying Usability,* ed. Randolph G. Bias and Deborah J. Mayhew, 245–72. Boston: Academic.

Nielsen, Jakob, and Hoa Loranger. 2006. *Prioritizing Web Usability.* Berkeley, CA: New Riders.

NRG Research Group. 2010. *2010 Baccalaureate Survey Report.* MacEwan University.

Ozok, A. Ant, and Gavriel Salvendy. 2001. "How Consistent Is Your Web Design?" *Behaviour & Information Technology* 20, no. 6: 433–47. doi: 10.1080/0144929011009226.

Paterson, Lorraine, and Boon Low. 2011. "Student Attitudes Towards Mobile Library Services for Smartphones." *Library Hi Tech* 29, no. 3: 412–23. doi: 10.1108/07378831111174387.

Pennyfeather, Kevin. 2013. "Library Team Wins Award for Mobile App." *The Griff,* March 27. http://thegriff.ca/2013/03/library-team-wins-award-for-mobile-app/.

Quorus Consulting Group. 2012. *2012 Cell Phone Consumer Attitudes Study.* Canadian Wireless Telecommunications Association. http://cwta.ca/wordpress/wp-content/uploads/ 2011/08/CWTA-2012ConsumerAttitudes1.pdf.

Reidsma, Matthew. 2014. *Responsive Web Design for Libraries: A LITA Guide*. Chicago: ALA TechSource.

Rempel, Hannah Gascho, and Laurie Bridges. 2013. "That Was Then, This Is Now: Replacing the Mobile-Optimized Site with Responsive Design." *Information Technology & Libraries* 32, no. 4: 8–24. American Library Association. doi:10.6017/ital.v32i4.4636.

Seeholzer, Jamie, and Joseph A. Salem. 2010. "Library on the Go: A Focus Group Study of the Mobile Web and the Academic Library." *College & Research Libraries* 72, no. 1: 9–21. doi: 10.5860/crl-65rl.

Shneiderman, Ben, and Catherine Plaisant. 2010. *Designing the User Interface: Strategies for Effective Human-Computer Interaction*. 5th edition. Boston: Addison-Wesley.

CHAPTER THIRTEEN

FIXING FACETS

SEAN HANNAN, STEVEN HESLIP, AND KRISTEN JOHANNES

The Johns Hopkins University (JHU) catalog (Catalyst) is a service provided by the consortium of Johns Hopkins libraries and information groups. Catalyst serves a diversity of users that includes professional and academic staff working in the humanities, engineering, sciences, music, and medicine. This wide range of stakeholders informs both a very wide selection of content types, from online journals and books to musical scores and audiovisual material. Furthermore, Johns Hopkins students, staff, and researchers interact with the same content in different ways. The fact that Catalyst is one of the few services provided to the entire Johns Hopkins community presents unique challenges rooted in how a variety of users interact with different types of information in different ways.

We gained insight into users' strong preferences for interacting with content through a number of use cases in which different user groups and stakeholders failed to find the content they needed by using highly intuitive search strategies. The cases we discuss below are focused on facets within the Catalyst system, a prominent feature of the content organization and user interface. Facets were implemented in Catalyst in order to allow users to delimit their searches on the basis of common properties of the collection such as item format, library location, and language, to name a few. However, preliminary user interviews, in combination with qualitative usage data, revealed that the intended use and engineering of the facet feature was not well aligned to users' search preferences and behavior. These initial observations prompted an in-depth examination of facet structures and user interface and informed a redesign of the facet system in Catalyst.

Background on Johns Hopkins University user populations. There are tens of thousands of Johns Hopkins catalog users, and the population is diverse in many respects. A broad range of academic communities access the collection via the Catalyst interface, including undergraduate, graduate, medical, and preparatory studying in such areas as engineering, humanities, music, nursing, medicine, sciences, and social sciences. Catalyst is used by professional scientists and engineers, clinicians, medical researchers, and hospital staff in the Baltimore, Maryland–Washington, D.C. metropolitan area, and the collection serves academic and professional users at research sites and in community hospitals located across the United States.

Catalog history and change to Blacklight. In 2011 Johns Hopkins moved from Horizon's vended OPAC (Horizon Information Portal—or HIP) to a Blacklight-based discovery layer running atop a HIP back end. Blacklight provided users with more flexibility in discovery as well as much more flexibility in how discovery and access experiences could be improved through customizations. Article search, a related bento box-style search results view, and wayfinding support are three examples of such customizations in Catalyst.

Initial facet configuration. Out of the box, Blacklight offered basic faceting options. However, a customized facet design did not emerge as a priority, owing to complexities associated with rolling out a new discovery layer. The use cases discussed in this chapter motivated a series of studies of and changes to the initial facet design and interface.

The current project: "Fixing the facets." The extensive investigation and later optimization of Catalyst facets that we discuss in this chapter originated from a single but pervasive search problem. Students and other patrons of the Friedheim Music Library were unable, in their Catalyst searches, to locate and access items from Naxos Music Online, an online library of classical music. Users had, intuitively, assumed that an online music library would be "located" at the Friedheim Music Library. However, the documented location according to our facet system was, in fact, the Milton S. Eisenhower Library, which primarily serves the Arts and Science, but not Music, schools. This issue was a simple fix in Catalyst, but the use case was a symptom of a larger class of user concerns with the faceting design.

In this chapter, we outline three complementary approaches to investigating the facet structure of our Catalyst system in the context of the general makeup of the content collection and the preferences and behaviors of those who make use of it. Our first approach made use of quantitative methods to survey both the structure of the collection and the way in which users interacted with it in the Catalyst system, with a focus on facet use. We then considered these quantitative data alongside use cases collected through interviews of different user groups across the Johns Hopkins community. Finally, these quantitative and qualitative results, together, informed a targeted study of user search strategies, in which we collected data on search behaviors that directly addressed the use of facet-based strategies for different types of material in the collection. Our multi-method approach informed a number of changes that were later implemented to improve the structure and interface of faceting in the Catalyst system.

APPROACH 1

QUANTITATIVE SUMMARY OF GENERAL COLLECTION STRUCTURE AND FACET/SEARCH BEHAVIOR

Describing the Content Collection and Facet Structure

The first step to understanding how to improve the catalog facet design was to describe the current Johns Hopkins facet structure, including the number of facet values and how they applied across the collection. Some facets changed how search results were presented differently than others. This was also necessary to account for. Finally, analytics described how facets were used and provided useful insights into user interactions with content using the existing facet structure.

OBSERVATION 1: Facets differ in information density and collection coverage. The current facet categories differ in their collection coverage, number of and clarity of facet values, and their labels and the amount of information gained by choosing a value of the facet for restricting a search. Deciding whether a facet category will be an effective tool for users requires evaluation across multiple characteristics. Table 13.1 lists these characteristics for eight common facet categories currently used in Catalyst.

TABLE 13.1 ——————————————————————————————————————

Eight of the most common Catalyst facets characterized by number of possible values, percentage of collection covered, and average information gain (greater values reflect greater restriction of the search when the facet is applied)

Facet category	Number of facet values	Percentage collection coverage	Information gain in Facet selection (bits)
Format	15	100%	0.649
Location	28	97.2%	0.646
Language	366	99.7%	0.461
Discipline	23	74.1%	1.183
Topic	982	85.9%	2.243
Topic: Era	173	9.7%	2.038
Topic: Region	112	42.2%	1.922
Instrumentation	97	1.5%	1.881

The number of possible values for a facet varies widely across facet categories. Intuitively, we predicted that having a greater number of possible facet values would lead to user confusion and less efficient searching. While having too many facet values may hinder searching, the same is, to some extent, true of having too few facet values. Artificially collapsing values within, for example, the Library Location facet runs counter to users' models of the structure of the collection holdings and leads to confusion.

Facets also vary in their coverage of the collection: facets like Format and Library Location apply to almost every item, while Discipline applies sparsely. As an extreme case, Instrumentation applies systematically to only a subset of the collection.

Finally, facet categories vary in the way that their values are distributed across the collection. In many cases a single facet value, for example English in the Language facet, covers the majority of records, while in other cases values are more evenly distributed. This is captured by a measurement of information gain: higher information gain for a facet means that, on average, a search will be more restricted with the selection of a value of the facet.[1] The Language facet, for example, has low information gain. This is related to the observation that a user searching for material written in English will not, in many cases, dramatically restrict search results by selecting the English value of the Language facet, as the vast majority of the collection (approximately 95 percent) is English material. The information gain of a facet category interacts with other properties, such as coverage of the collection, in critical ways. For example, Musical Instrumentation has low coverage, representing only 1.5 percent of the collection, but has high information gain. This facet category is systematically used by some user populations, and the collection covered by Musical Instrumentation is diverse, so that selecting a particular value (e.g., Bassoon) for the facet restricts the search in relevant ways. Thus, an optimal faceting system for Catalyst should be one that is sensitive to collection coverage and information gain.

OBSERVATION 2: Facet categories vary in their internal organization. Within the Catalyst system, multiple values of a facet can apply to a single item or record. In some cases, this indicates that there are multiple items associated with the record. For example, a record may have multiple values of the Location facet associated with it. In other cases, however, the facet values interact. For example, items are routinely classified with multiple Format values. This can indicate that an item is available in multiple formats (e.g., as both a book and in microform). However, plotting the frequency of co-occurrence of Format facet values, in figure 13.1, reveals that Print and Online values frequently co-occur with all other Format values, essentially cross-cutting the Format facet category. This pattern is consistent with the fact that most items in the collection are either available as (physical) print copies or as part of the online holdings.

FIGURE 13.1 —————————————————————————————————————

The frequency with which different values of the Format facet co-occur in a large sample of the content collection

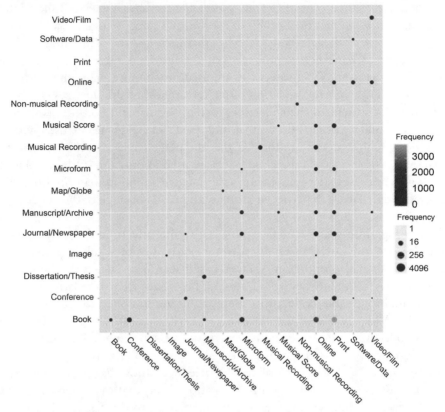

The consequence of interactions between, for example, intuitively access-related facets (Print, Online) and Format facets (Book, Video, Microform, etc.) is ambiguity in item categorization, along with confusion on the part of users. The disconnect between the original Format facet structure and the assumptions that users have about Format as a facet becomes apparent from feedback from research service providers, as we will see in the next section.

EXAMINING USERS' FACET USE AND SEARCH BEHAVIOR

Analytics analysis. Google Analytics records provide data on every search that users performed in the Catalyst system and include information such as the frequency of individual searches, query strings used for searching, and whether or not facets are used as part of a search. Using these data, we compared the frequency and nature of facet-based searches to a popular alternative, which we term query-only searching, marked by detailed query strings and no facet use.

Frequency of facet-based searches in Catalyst. Facet-based searches account for approximately 20 percent of all Catalyst catalog searches. Table 13.2 shows the frequency (raw number of searches) of use for each category of facet, along with the percentage of all facet-based searches that included the facet category. The data in table 13.2 makes two properties of Catalyst users' facet-based searching clear. First, that some facet categories are used much more than others. Moreover, the facet categories used most often in searches are also the ones that have the greatest coverage of the collection, such as Format and Location (see table 13.1). A secondary observation is that multiple facet categories are used within a single search (evident from the fact that the percentages in table 13.2 add to well over 100 percent). Thus, while facets are used in only one-fifth of Catalyst catalog search cases, users employing a facet-based search strategy appear to be using multiple facets, in particular facets with broad coverage of the collection, to narrow the search base.

Looking closely at particular values of frequently-used facet categories like Format and Location reveals a number of additional subtle patterns in facet use. A small proportion of facet-based search cases feature the use of only facets without any keyword queries. These cases are particularly frequent for small, browseable collections such as the video collection: users select the Film/Video value of the Format facet to restrict their searches to the video collection and then browse item records. Examining the interaction of Location facet values with other facet categories also reveals subpopulations of users at the Welch and Friedheim libraries (i.e., those users that select the Welch and Friedheim values for the Location facet) that make very frequent use of facets in their searches, especially in relation to the relative size of the user groups at those locations.

Facet-based vs. query-only search strategies. Facet-based searches accounted for 20 percent of total Catalyst catalog searches; 80 percent of searches used a query-only strategy, where users did not select any facets and entered in a query string, typically 4–5 words or longer. In some cases, keywords within a query-only search were identical to the values of a facet category. For example, users often used values from the Format facet as keywords (figure 13.2). Facet-based searches were often much shorter, and did not include keywords that duplicated values available in facets.

For many item formats, the format was used as a keyword more often than it was chosen as a facet value, as in table 13.2. This pattern suggests that users often intend to restrict searches by, for example, format, but are not making use of facets—the most direct strategy for doing so. In the "Findings and Outcomes" section below we examine the consequences of using keywords in place of facet values for search results and search efficiency.

TABLE 13.2 ——————————————————————————————————————

Raw frequency and percentage of facet-based searches for the eleven top-level facets

Facet	Raw frequency	Percentage of facet-based searches
Format	228, 283	87.9%
Date	179,600	69.1%
Location	37,002	14.2%
Language	18,856	7.3%
Topic	11,898	4.6%
Author	8,357	3.2%
Topic: Region	3,717	1.4%
Discipline	3,510	1.35%
Series	3,309	1.3%
Instrumentation	2,581	1.0%
Topic: Era	2,114	0.8%

FIGURE 13.2 ——————————————————————————————————————

Frequency of facet-based searches vs. query-only searches with facet-like keywords

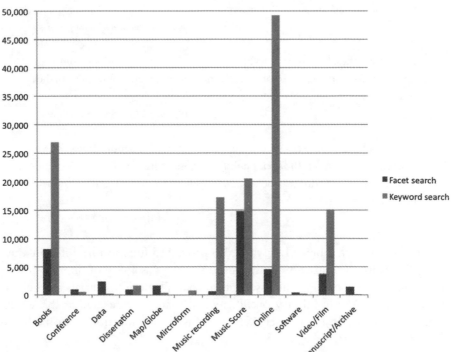

INTEGRATING QUANTITATIVE FINDINGS WITH QUALITATIVE CASE STUDIES

The following vignettes were derived from interviews with library staff at the Welch Medical Library (Medical Campus, Baltimore), Eisenhower Library (Homewood, Baltimore), Friedheim Library (Mt.Vernon, Baltimore), and SAIS Mason Library (Dupont Circle, D.C.). These vignettes demonstrate many of the most common expectations and use scenarios involving Catalyst facets, and yield perspectives that are complementary to findings described in "Approach 1: Quantitative Summary Findings," above.

The following vignettes are also a subset of a larger amount of content provided by staff interview participants. In many cases, concerns overlapped across interviews, further reinforcing the urgency for revision.

Author facet. A group of users across campuses and disciplines took issue with the composition of the Author facet. As implemented, Author contained both traditional named authors as well as corporate authors, conference bodies, and publishers. A related issue was that e-book packages and publisher collections were loaded as a Series, which did not meet the mental model and traditional definition of monograph series of librarian users.

> When looking at the Author facet, I expect to see the names of authors rather than Corporate Authors or Publishers.
>
> —*Welch Medical Library Staff #1*

> For my searches, I often need to limit my searches by publications from large entities (World Bank, International Monetary Fund, etc.) and then further refine with keywords.
>
> —*SAIS Mason Library Student Employee #1*

> When looking at the Series facet, I expect to see unambiguous labels for the series in the result set. Broader, publisher-oriented listings like "LWW Core Collection" and "Springer ebooks" may constitute a series, but it does not help me refine my search.
>
> —*Welch Medical Library Staff #2*

Library location facet. Library Location also proved to function in different ways for different user groups. Some users used the facet as a way of filtering results based on content, making the assumption that all music materials are held at the Friedheim Music Library or all medical materials are held at the Welch Medical Library. Nearly all users were confused by a location option labeled

"Unknown." Implemented as a way to prevent miscataloged items from falling through the cracks, this facet option only served to confuse users.

> When looking for items for patrons, they often want to have a physical copy in their hands. For this purpose, I use the Library Location facet to limit my searches for items at my specific location.
>
> —*Welch Staff #4*

> When looking at the Library Location facet, I expect to see locations that are familiar to me. Broad labeling like "Medical Libraries," "Libraries Service Center," and "Unknown" are not helpful to me.
>
> —*Welch Informationist #2*

> When looking at the Library Location facet, I expect to see the libraries ranked in an order that is relevant to me. Seeing options such as "Libraries Service Center," "Unknown," and "Medical Libraries" does not assist me in getting my hands on the item as quickly as possible.
>
> —*Welch Informationist #5*

> When looking at the location facet specifically for music materials, I expect them to all be located within Friedheim Library since Friedheim is the music library. Seeing large numbers located at MSEL or in a vague place like "Unknown" erodes my trust in the system and makes me question whether I am truly searching what I need to be searching.
>
> —*Friedheim Library Staff*

Format facet. As previously discussed, the Format facet proved to be problematic for some users due to the mixed use of it to represent both physical format and method of access. For users (e.g., film students, musicians) who regularly make use of a wider range of media beyond monograph-centric materials, opportunities to expand this facet were requested. Even among the book-centric patrons, the opportunity to expand Format to include textbooks, specifically, was appreciated.

> My users often need a textbook to read about basic information about a subject. Being able to limit my searches to textbooks would help me fulfill these requests.
>
> When looking at the Format facet, "Format" becomes ambiguous when types or methods of access ("Print," "Online") are listed along with what I understand to be an information format ("Book," "Journal"). The labeling and categorization must be clear and understandable.
>
> —*Welch Informationist #5*

As a music researcher, I expect to be able to see and limit my searches for music recordings by the physical format (either CD, LP, cassette, etc.) in which I will receive it.

—*Friedheim Library Staff*

Facet labels. In a few instances, the actual labeling of the facet did not meet the needs of users. In an attempt to be as broad and inclusive as possible, some facet labels lost meaning for users and became confusing and underused.

When looking at the Topic facet, I see subject terms and keywords. The labeling of "topic" doesn't match my mental model of "subject" search terms and keywords.

—*Welch Medical Library Staff #1*

APPROACH 3

DIRECTLY SOURCING USER REPORTS ON CATALOG/FACET USE

Targeted user studies were developed in two stages. First, we chose a series of library holdings that novice users would later be asked to search for—and conducted pairs of Catalyst catalog searches using first a facet-based strategy followed by a query-only strategy. To illustrate, a single item such as the Russian-language publication of the book *Crime and Punishment* (by Fyodor Dostoyevsky) was searched for in Catalyst first with the facet-based strategy in (1) and then with the query-only strategy in (2). The results of the two strategies are compared, in terms of number of results produced, in table 13.3 for five different items.

(1) Query = Crime and Punishment; Facet Language = Russian (optional Format = Book, Print)

(2) Query = Crime and Punishment Russian; no facets

In all of the five cases examined in table 13.3, facet-based searching yielded a more constrained set of results compared to query-only searching (where the query includes a keyword similar to the relevant facet value). In many cases the dramatic difference between query-only and facet-based search results is due to a calibrated three-term keyword window used by the Catalyst search algorithm. The algorithm is optimized for queries that have three or fewer terms; if a search includes four or more terms (one of which might be a facet term), the search algorithm uses three-term permutation sets to conduct multiple searches, thereby increasing search results.

TABLE 13.3

Number of results for sample item searches produced by facet-based vs. query-only search strategies

Search Item	Facet-based results	Query-only results
Crime and Punishment (novel) in Russian	3–5	*1,264–1,354
Cognitive Psychology (online journal)	18–85	151
Audio recording about stress management	1	415
Human anatomy textbook at MSE Library	9	76
Book about the Crimean War (published pre-1950)	119	267

*Differences in query strategy yielded varying quantities of results for this item.

The second stage of the user study was conducted by asking a sample of novice users (JHU undergraduates in the Milton S. Eisenhower Library) to conduct Catalyst searches for the items listed in table 13.3. For each search, we recorded the query string and facets used along with coarse measures of search success and efficiency, most notably the number of search results and the total time users spent searching for the item. We collected 10–12 search cases for each search item; the coarse breakdown of the frequency of different search strategies is displayed in figure 13.3. Facet–based strategies were used in half or

FIGURE 13.3

Relative frequency (as percentage of total search cases) of facet- based searches, advanced searches, and query-only searches used for selected search items. Unsuccessful searches are not included.

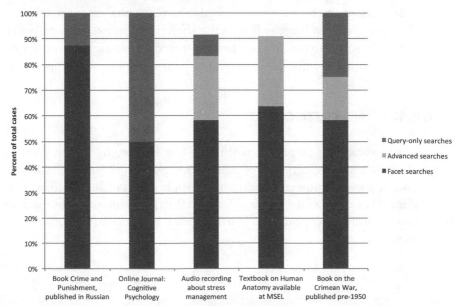

more of all searches for each item, and when users were not using facet-based searching, users employed advanced search strategies (which restrict searches in a way similar to faceting) and query-only strategies. When a facet-based strategy was used, however, the predominant pattern was to restrict searches by Format and/or Location and not through other facet categories, like Language or Date, even though many searches could have been optimally restricted by these secondary facets.

The average number of search results for a search item served as a measure of search success for each of the three strategies (facet-based, advanced searching, and query-only). Search results are a simple and intuitive measure of efficiency: searches for known items that yield a manageable number of results should lead to less browsing and fewer revised searches than those that yield a large, highly varied, or unmanageable number of results. Table 13.4 provides a comparison of results for the three search strategies.

All search cases in which users employed facets resulted in efficient identification of a desired item. The query-only search strategy yielded the only failed search of the study, in addition to two searches that required a facilitator prompt encouraging a second effort for the user to successfully identify a desired item. Users that required a facilitator prompt explained that they would have abandoned their search had they been on their own.

For all of the search cases in which both facet-based and query-only search strategies were used, facet-based strategies led to fewer search results than query-only strategies. This difference is consistent with the case study results in table 13.3, suggesting that, even for novice users who may not have full command of the Catalyst system and facets, the use of facet-based searches is more efficient. In a few of the search cases where users employed both facet-based and advanced search strategies, advanced strategies resulted in fewer results and more efficient search. Looking closely at the search cases that showed this difference, we noticed that, for facet-based searches, the most relevant facet categories—for example, Publication Date—were not being employed by the users in our sample.

FINDINGS AND OUTCOMES

The current set of facet categories within the Catalyst catalog is highly varied in terms of size, coverage, and scale of information gain. Furthermore, individual facets also vary in their internal organization: some facets include information that interacts (online/print vs. format); other facets include separate types of information (author, corporate author) that may be more useful in separate categories.

TABLE 13.4

Average number of users' results using facet-based, advanced, and query-only search strategies

Search Item	Facet-based results	Advanced search results	Query-only results
Crime and Punishment (novel) in Russian	15.9	Not used	49
Cognitive Psychology (online journal)	33	Not used	568
Audio recording about stress management	1	8.3	5
Human anatomy textbook at MSE Library	910	648	Not used
Book about the Crimean War (published pre-1950)	73.3	68.5	229.3

We found that facet-based searches and query-only searches with facet-like keywords produce different sets of results. Facet-based search strategies tend to narrow searches to fewer results than query-only searches, largely owing to the three-term window used by the search algorithm. However, novice users employed both facet-based and query-only (along with advanced) search strategies when searching for known items. Facet use, however, was generally restricted to Format and Location facet categories, even for cases where other facet categories (e.g., Language) would have led to a more optimally restricted set of results.

Our investigations informed two primary design angles to pursue, one being that we improve the effectiveness of the facet strategies that users prefer, and the other being to revise or eliminate unhelpful facets that otherwise distract.

We learned that 87.5 percent of facet searches in Catalyst involved Format facet values even though Format facet information gain was relatively low. By adding DVD, Blu-Ray, VHS, LP, and CD facet values that do not exist in the current facet system we will provide users with additional ways to get maximum utility from the system while engaging in the search behavior that they demonstrably prefer.

Additionally, we learned that more refined facet values would increase user efficiency and minimize confusion. The Author facet was notably valued by users, but was too general to effectively represent the many forms of authorship both covered in and sought from the collection. For this reason, corporate authors and government entities were moved to their own Organization facet.

To address the specific inciting incident of this study, location and online materials were decoupled. All online materials are now location-agnostic. Whether users are using the Location facet to filter by subject area or service proximity, they will have access to all of the online materials.

We learned that confusing facets (Topic, Topic [Era], and Topic [Region]) demonstrated relatively high information gain and represented functionality users ultimately sought, but did not understand because of poor labeling. A simple solution to improve the utility of these facets was to modify the facet labels: Topic became Subject; Topic (Era) became Era; and Topic (Region) became Region.

Finally, there were facets that could not be improved. The Discipline facet proved unreliable and confused users because of a lack of coverage across the collection (specifically, electronic titles), so it was removed. Options with labels such as "Unknown," "Other," or "Unspecified," which were originally included in attempt to provide comprehensive coverage in the collections, were also removed from facets where they appeared because they did not help users to further refine their search.

Note

1. T. M. Cover and J. A. Thomas, *Elements of Information Theory*, 2nd edition (New York: Wiley-Interscience, 2006).

CHAPTER FOURTEEN

ONE SIZE DOESN'T FIT ALL
Tailoring Discovery through User Testing

JOSEPH DEODATO, KHALILAH GAMBRELL, AND ERIC FRIERSON

I mplementing a web-scale discovery service can be a complex and challenging task, but the process doesn't simply end once your service goes live. In order to ensure that your new service is meeting the needs of its users, your implementation plan should include iterative user testing. Different library users have different needs, making it nearly impossible for any discovery product to offer a one-size-fits-all solution. Fortunately, most of these products offer a variety of configuration and customization options to help libraries tailor the experience to the needs of their users.

User testing is an effective and affordable method for libraries to configure their discovery service based on their users' needs and expectations. The following chapter offers practical guidance on how to apply insights from user testing to the customization of web-scale discovery services. However, customization alone only goes so far. To address the full range of challenges uncovered in usability testing also requires close collaboration between libraries and vendors to help develop services and solutions that become a part of future web-scale discovery service offerings. Accordingly, the authors recommend a collaborative three-pronged approach to improving web-scale discovery that includes product enhancement, local customization, and user education.

BACKGROUND

Like other academic libraries, the Rutgers University Libraries (RUL) turned to web-scale discovery services in the hopes of improving access to its collections. For years, users had expressed dissatisfaction with the libraries' search experience, which they found to be confusing, cumbersome, and fragmented. Web-scale discovery promised the ability to deliver a vast amount of high-quality, scholarly content from a single, easy-to-use interface. However, past disappointments with federated search had led some librarians to approach discovery with a bit more caution. RUL undertook a rigorous nine-month evaluation of the leading products that included extensive product and user research, an exhaustive list of product requirements, detailed correspondence with vendors and custom-ers, and an extended period of product trials and testing.[1] At the conclusion of its proceedings, the evaluation team was certain of only one thing: none of the products on the market seemed truly capable of fully satisfying all of the libraries' needs. The linchpin of the team's analysis was a weighted evaluation rubric that was used to score each product in terms of coverage, performance, functionality, and technical architecture. Although one product scored highest overall, the final tally was remarkably close. The team found that each product had its own particular strengths and weaknesses and none had truly stood out from the pack. Library users, who participated in comparative usability testing of the three final candidates, seemed to reach an analogous conclusion. Although users had greater success and more favorable impressions of one product over the others, they struggled with similar problems in all three interfaces. While all agreed that these products made finding library materials easier, they also made it clear that there was ample room for improvement.

Ultimately, the evaluation team recommended that Rutgers acquire EBSCO Discovery Service (EDS). EDS had received the team's highest overall rating and was the favorite in user testing in addition to offering a full range of customiza-tion options. However, the evaluation team's recommendation came with two important caveats. First, the team recommended that additional usability testing be conducted to determine how to customize EDS for the best user experience. Second, the team suggested that Rutgers seek to work directly with EBSCO on testing so that findings could be shared among all stakeholders.

Coincidentally, the EBSCO User Research group had recently shifted from being an internal working group to a team that extends its expertise and ser-vices to customers. User Research has played a critical role in EBSCO's product development life cycle by using various user research methods to understand users' research workflows and in turn ensure that EBSCO products satisfy users' needs and expectations. The group has collaborated with several institutions to understand students' research workflows. Collaborations have been in the form of data analysis, surveys, contextual inquiries, and usability testing. Mostly comprised of librarians with a background in user research, EBSCO User Research was eager to work with Rutgers to observe how students used EDS.

User testing is an important tool for improving library services, but its value is limited when divorced from the ability to control or influence the design of that service. Library-vendor collaboration is critical for improving the user experience of any licensed product or resource. Librarians gain a knowledgeable and committed user experience (UX) partner and vendors get direct feedback from real library users about their product. Furthermore, usability issues cannot be addressed by local customization alone. Some issues can only be solved through product enhancement while others require user education. For this reason, it's important that user testing involve all key stakeholders, including those responsible for developing, customizing, and teaching the library's web-scale discovery service. The following case study is intended to serve as an instructive example of how libraries and vendors might collaborate in user testing to address UX issues holistically using the three-pronged approach of product enhancement, local customization, and user education.

LITERATURE REVIEW

As the adoption of web-scale discovery services continues to rise, a growing body of literature has developed devoted to usability testing of these products. Some studies examine only one product while others offer comparative evaluations of multiple vendor offerings. Regardless of which product is the subject of evaluation, findings have tended to be remarkably consistent. The following is a summary of some common themes found within the usability literature on web-scale discovery services.

One commonly cited problem with web-scale discovery services is that users rarely have a clear understanding of scope and coverage. Studies suggest that students frequently have trouble determining what types of content are searchable within their library's discovery tool. For many users, these tools appear as a black box whose contents and inner workings remain a mystery. As Fagan et al. point out, librarians, themselves, do not always know what titles are covered or what level of indexing is offered by their discovery service provider because this information is not always readily available.[2] Majors, who conducted a comparative analysis of the leading commercial services, concluded that none of these products "offer any transparency about what is being searched and/or indexed, and user behavior reflected a trial and error methodology of figuring out what user tasks were actually supported."[3] In a search log analysis conducted at Montana State University, Meadow and Meadow found that users enter all types of unsupported queries into the library's discovery tool, including the titles of specific databases or journals, the names of frequently used services like course reserves and interlibrary loan, and even the URLs of popular websites like Facebook.[4] As Teague-Rector and Ghaphery point out, a "larger, more visible search box may lead users to falsely assume that the library search functions like an online search engine."[5] Libraries need to make clear the purpose and scope of their discovery tool and ensure that resources and collections which fall outside of that scope are still discoverable. Lown, Sierra, and Boyer recommend that librarians think carefully about how discovery tools are presented on their website and alongside other valuable resources like the catalog and specialized databases.[6] Unlike online search engines, the goal of a library website is not merely to provide useful results but also to promote an understanding of the content, services, and tools that the library offers. Library search interfaces should help users differentiate between the kinds of resources available to them and guide them to those that will best serve their need.

Another frequently mentioned area of concern is search query construction. Although it may not come as a surprise, it turns out that most library users are not expert searchers. Studies suggest that the average user tends to rely on basic keyword searching, rarely modifies default settings or fields, and almost never uses Boolean logic or advanced search operators. This finding is not specific to discovery tools per se and is equally true for other library resources. This behavior is typically attributed to users' habituation to popular search engines where sophisticated ranking algorithms don't require precise queries and tend to be far more forgiving of error. For example, Asher, Duke, and Wilson's comparative study of EDS, Summon, Google Scholar, and conventional library resources found that students "treated almost every search box like a Google search box" using simple keyword searches in 81.5 percent (679/829) of the searches observed.[7] Of the 824 queries studied in Meadow and Meadow's search log analysis, only 27 (3.3 percent) utilized Boolean operators.[8] Foster and MacDonald note that even users who have attended one or two library instruction sessions tend to perform only the simplest of searches.[9]

One could argue that discovery tools are in fact designed to accommodate this sort of behavior. Users are expected to begin with broad keyword searches and progressively refine their results through the use of post-search facets and limiters. However, findings are somewhat mixed on whether or not users take full advantage of these functions. For example, Cassidy et al. assert that the majority of participants in their EDS study did not notice or attempt to use any facets or limiters in their searching.[10] In contrast, Fagan et al. found that their EDS users made frequent use of pre- and post-search refinements to limit searches. In separate studies of Primo, both Nichols and Comeaux noted that the use of facets and limiters increased as testing progressed. These findings suggest that users' awareness and use of search refinements may increase as they learn the system.

The lack of sophisticated user search strategies combined with broad, undefined content coverage produce large, heterogeneous result sets that require careful and attentive evaluation. However, many studies suggest that users often have difficulty interpreting results and distinguishing different types of information. While testing Summon, Gross and Sheridan found that users often had trouble distinguishing between a journal and a newspaper article or between a book and a book review.[11] These observations suggest that the blending of different types of information under one roof may pose serious challenges for novice users who are ill equipped to tell them apart and generally "see all information as being of equal value."[12] Indeed, researchers have shown that many users pursue evaluation superficially by skim-reading titles and abstracts and rarely investigating beyond the first page of results. In the comparative usability study conducted by Asher, Duke, and Wilson, 92 percent (598/649) of the resources used by students were found on the first page of search results.[13] The authors suggest that students attempt to compensate for their lack of evaluation skills by relying on the search engine to determine the quality of resources for them. Even when they know what characteristics to look for, they spend little time actually doing so. Instead, they prefer to put all of their faith in the ranking algorithm and expect the most useful and relevant results to be returned on the first page. As a result, users typically begin a new search rather than refine their current query or navigate to the next page of results.

The usability study conducted at Rutgers follows methods similar to those used in other studies and shares many of the same findings about user behavior. Its uniqueness lies primarily in the collaborative nature of the project, which involved the participation of both library and vendor representatives, as well as the holistic approach to resolving usability problems through a combination of product enhancement, local customization, and user education.

METHODS

Twelve Rutgers students and faculty members were recruited to participate in moderated remote usability testing. Participants were asked to use EDS to complete a series of tasks while sharing their thoughts aloud and having their verbal responses and on-screen activity recorded. Video transcripts of the sessions were analyzed to identify and address usability issues.

Testing was conducted using UserTesting (www.usertesting.com), a commercial online usability testing service. UserTesting offers a full-service user research platform that allows customers to set up usability tests and receive videos of users interacting with their website. Clients can test with their own users or take advantage of UserTesting's on-demand user panel. The researcher dashboard provides useful metrics such as time on task and level of difficulty as well as tools to annotate videos and create highlight reels.

Remote testing was chosen for its ease, convenience, and flexibility. Testing remotely made it easier to reach a wider range of users dispersed across multiple campuses. Users were able to participate at a place and time of their own choosing as long as they had Internet access and a microphone. Remote testing is also arguably less obtrusive since it allows users to be observed in the comfort of their own environment rather than a lab or conference room. Finally, this method made it possible for Rutgers and EBSCO researchers to collaborate virtually without necessitating the time or expense of interstate travel.

Nielsen has famously argued that the majority of usability problems can be uncovered with just five users.[14] However, for the purposes of this study, the investigators wanted to obtain a sample that was large enough to represent the diversity of users that the libraries' discovery service is intended to serve. Sauro has suggested a formula for determining sample size based on the chance of detecting a problem during testing and its probability of occurring.[15]

> **Sample size = log(1-Chance of Detecting) / log(1-Probability of Occurring)**
>
> Using this formula, the investigators decided to recruit 12 participants in order to obtain an 85% chance of identifying any problems that impact 15% or more of users.
>
> **12 = log(1-.85) / log(1-.15)**

Participants were recruited through flyers posted in all campus libraries as well as announcements on the libraries' website, Facebook, and Twitter pages. Users interested in participating in the study were asked to contact the investigators via e-mail and complete a brief online pretest questionnaire. The questionnaire was used to collect demographic information and screen candidates to ensure the selection of a diverse sample representing different campuses, disciplines, and levels of education. The selected candidates were sent a URL with instructions on how to complete the test. Each participant received a $25 Amazon gift card courtesy of EBSCO.

Quota sampling was used to ensure a diverse group of participants. See figure 14.1 for a statistical overview of the sample. Since recruitment ads were posted exclusively within the libraries' physical and virtual spaces, it is highly likely that some amount of selection bias occurred. Generally speaking, the majority of volunteers appeared to be active library users who were well acquainted with library resources and services. Eight out of 12 users (67 percent):

- said they "always" or "often" use library resources in their academic course-work or research;
- had previously attended a library instruction class;
- identified the library catalog or a library database as the resource they use most often when conducting research; and
- rated their ability to find information using library resources to be "good" to "excellent."

Participants were asked to complete five tasks designed to determine how well EDS supports core user needs related to finding, identifying, selecting, obtaining, and using information. Each task was communicated in the form of a hypothetical scenario to provide the participant with an interpretive context for completing the task. In order to test different aspects of the user interface, scenarios typically included two parts. The first part usually required locating a piece of information while the second involved doing something with it. For example, a participant might be asked to find an article on a topic as well as capture its citation for a bibliography. See figure 14.2 for a list of tasks used in testing.

Each session lasted approximately thirty minutes and was moderated by a UserTesting staff member. At the conclusion of the test, participants were asked to complete a brief online questionnaire asking them about their experience and satisfaction with EDS.

FIGURE 14.1

Participant Overview

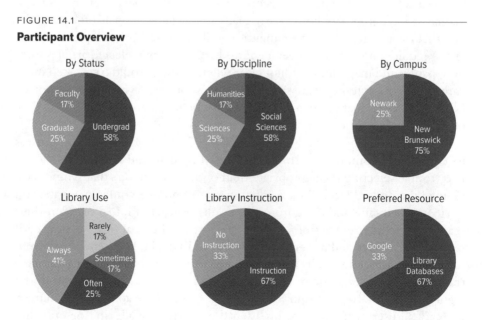

FIGURE 14.2 ———

Tasks

Task	Scenario
1	You are writing a research paper that argues that social networking sites like Facebook are a threat to privacy. Find two scholarly articles that support your argument and e-mail them to yourself.
2	You are working on a group project about wearable technology. Find one article on this topic and decide how to share it with the other members of your group.
3	Find one news article about U.S. foreign debt published in the *New York Times* during the last three years. How would you capture citation information for this article to use in your bibliography?
4	Someone in your department recommended you read an article called "On Magic Realism in Film" by Fredric Jameson. Search for this article and explain how you would obtain a copy of it.
5	You are interested in the latest research on the use of artificial intelligence in perinatal medicine. Find one conference paper on this topic. From the results page, explain how you would broaden your search to find additional results from other sources.

RESULTS

Overall, EDS performed reasonably well, with users achieving an 80–100 percent success rate in three of the five tasks. Most users had little difficulty fulfilling the general requirements of these tasks, but few spent any significant time evaluating the results that were returned. Records were typically selected after a cursory glance and sometimes without a particularly compelling rationale other than the fact that their search terms were mentioned in the title. For example, although task 1 required users to find peer-reviewed articles, some selected articles from newspapers and magazines. It is not clear whether users would have taken more care in evaluation if they were selecting sources for a real assignment or project. Nor is it obvious that participants would have behaved any differently had they been searching a different resource.

Success rates were notably lower for tasks 3 and 5. Task 3 required users to construct a complex search query limited by date and publication. Many had trouble selecting the appropriate field options or limiters that would have yielded the desired result. Task 5 asked users to find one conference paper on perinatal medicine and then, from the results page, attempt to broaden their search to include results from additional sources. The goal here was to see if users would notice and understand how to use EDS's built-in federated search function to integrate results from databases that are not included in the central index. However, none of the users seemed to notice the invitation in the right column to "Expand Your Search" by selecting these additional resources. Instead, all users attempted to broaden their search by altering or omitting a few of their original search terms. In designing the test, the investigators sought to avoid using leading language that might influence user responses, but it's possible that this part of the task might have been too vague. Figure 14.3 shows the average success rate and completion time for each task along with the standard deviation.

In the post–test questionnaire, the majority of participants indicated that they found EDS to be a helpful research tool and said that they would use it again. In their comments, users praised EDS for its simplicity, efficiency, and ease of use. They particularly appreciated the time-saving benefits of searching across multiple library resources. As one participant noted, EDS "made it easier to find articles and cut down my search time." Echoing similar sentiments, another said, "I liked the fact that you were able to get a lot of results all at once." Participants also liked the ability to refine searches using faceted browsing and noted the variety of useful ways to narrow results by subject, language, or date of publication.

However, much of this praise was tempered by reservations. As one participant put it: "It is an effort in the direction of making the university library website the go-to site for research . . . but it has some way to go." In particular, several participants experienced difficulty constructing searches and obtaining relevant

FIGURE 14.3 ————————————————————————————————————

Task success rates

Task	Success		Time		Observations
	Mean	SD	Mean	SD	
1	80%	20%	6:03	3:35	The majority of users completed this task without difficulty, although some had trouble distinguishing between scholarly and non-scholarly sources.
2	100%	0%	2:46	0:42	All users completed this task without difficulty, but several commented that they were not aware or had never used the product's share functions.
3	60%	40%	5:45	2:20	A significant number of users had difficulty formulating an effective search query and/or limiting their results by publication.
4	80%	50%	3:14	1:04	Although most users were eventually successful, many experienced difficulty locating the given article, even when the exact title of the work was entered.
5	50%	10%	4:30	1:45	Most users experienced little difficulty with the first part of this task, but all failed on the second part requiring them to use federated search (which may not have been entirely clear in the instructions).

results. During testing, users often revised their searches multiple times in order to find the requested information. The following comments illustrate some of the frustration users felt when search results did not match their expectations:

> "I did not like the search engine itself and had some trouble finding certain articles when typing in specific authors."

> "It was difficult to figure out what to type in the search engine to help narrow down my search for certain articles."

> "I am most likely not seeing the best results on the first search. You have to modify your search about 2–3 times to find what you're looking for."

Several participants also commented on the design of the user interface. Many found it to be too cluttered, busy, or confusing. This seemed especially applicable to the search results screen. The following comments illustrate users' concerns with and difficulty navigating the interface.

> "The interface was not absolutely clear, but probably I just have to spend more time working with this system."

> "There is a lot going on . . . the tools on the side take away from the main part of the page . . . I didn't need any of it and I'm not even sure what some of the buttons mean."

> "I would have preferred the UI to be more easy and intuitive to use with fewer clicks."

> "The UI still needs to be simplified . . . Make the UI less cluttered visually."

DISCUSSION

This study generated a number of valuable insights about user search behavior that carry implications for those involved in developing, managing, and teaching web-scale discovery services. Based on these observations, the investigators formulated a series of recommendations aimed at improving the user's experience with EDS. Each recommendation was classified into one of three categories based on whether it required product enhancement, local customization, or user education. Figure 14.4 provides a summary of the team's observations and recommendations.

FIGURE 14.4 —————————————————————————————————————

Observations and recommendations

1	Observation	Most users rely on basic keyword or natural language searching more often than Boolean or field searching.
	Recommendation(s)	[User Education] Improve user education on search query construction including keyword selection, field searching, search operators, facets, and limiters. [Customization] Change the default search mode from Boolean/Phrase to Find All My Search Terms, which seems to be more in keeping with how users expect search to function.
2	Observation	Most users find the interface to be too cluttered, particularly the right column of the search results screen.
	Recommendation(s)	[Customization] Remove the right column to simplify the search results screen and find alternative ways of integrating this content into the interface. Replace federated search with a database recommender system and incorporate database and research guide recommendations into a placard that appears at the bottom of the results screen. Replace static chat widget with a dynamic slide-out tab.
3	Observation	Most users have difficulty searching for known items even when the exact title of the article is entered.
	Recommendation(s)	[Product Enhancement] Improve searching and relevance ranking for known items. One possibility may be to boost the ranking of items where the user's search terms are found in proximity. [Update. Since testing, EBSCO Product Management has made significant relevancy ranking improvements to known item searching.]
4	Observation	Most users had difficulty interpreting terms such as "journal" and "peer reviewed."
	Recommendation(s)	[Product Enhancement] Change "Journal Title/Source" in advanced search field dropdown menu to "Publication." [Customization] Change "Journal Name" limiter in basic and advanced search options to "Publication." [Customization] Change "Peer Reviewed" limiter in basic and advanced search options and results list to "Scholarly/Peer Reviewed."
5	Observation	Most users did not navigate beyond the first page of results.
	Recommendation(s)	[Customization] Increase the number of search results per page from 10 to 20. [Product Enhancement] Replace results list pagination with infinite scrolling.
6	Observation	Some users could not accurately distinguish between different content formats.
	Recommendation(s)	[Product Enhancement] Improve icons and display of item formats. Consider including tool-tip format definitions. [User Education] Improve user education about content formats.

Figure 14.4 continued on next page.

FIGURE 14.4 ——

Observations and recommendations (continued from previous page)

7	Observation	Some users did not notice when advanced search limiters from a previous search were being applied to their current search.
	Recommendation(s)	[Product Enhancement] Make applied limiters more prominent. Make advanced search limiters and database facets easier to remove from a search. [Update: Since testing, advanced search limiters are now displayed in and removable from breadbox. Database facet still is not.]
8	Observation	Some users did not notice system error messages notifying them of spelling errors or the need to enter search terms.
	Recommendation(s)	[Product Enhancement] Make system error messages more prominent by, for example, adding a border and/or background color.
9	Observation	Most users had little trouble identifying and using output tools such as e-mail, share, and export although some noted that they do not often use these options.
	Recommendation(s)	[User education] Promote and explain utility and function of output tools such as e-mail, share, and export.

As documented in other studies, users tended to rely on basic keyword or natural language searching more often than Boolean or field searching. They often entered several search terms on a single line without any search operators or fields. These simple queries worked well enough when the bar for precision was low, as in the first two tasks involving broad topical searches. However, users did not fare so well on the next two tasks where they had to find articles from specific publications or by specific authors. For example, when asked to find an article on U.S. foreign debt published in the *New York Times,* the most commonly used query was a keyword search for *u.s. foreign debt new york times.* A similar search strategy was employed when users were asked to find a copy of Fredric Jameson's article "On Magic Realism in Film." Several users' initial query was a variation of *on magic realism in film fredric jameson.* Users were often confused as to why these queries, which seemed both logical and precise to them, did not produce the results they expected. However, the default search mode in EDS is "Boolean/Phrase," which requires search terms to be found in proximity. Therefore, keyword searches combining authors, subjects, and publications in a single undifferentiated query string tend to fail because these terms are not typically found in proximity. Of course, both of the above queries work flawlessly in Google and it seems that users expected EDS to function in much the same way. To make EDS conform more to user expectations, the investigators recommended changing the default search mode to "Find All My Search Terms." This suggestion would remove the proximity requirement and automatically join all search terms in a Boolean AND statement. With this option set as the default, the initial search conducted by users given this task (the title followed by the author's name as keywords, e.g., *on magic realism in film fredric jameson*) returns the desired article as the second result. The investigators also recommended that librarians devote more instruction and tutorials to keyword selection and search query construction as a means to improve overall user efficacy with search systems.

The study also found that users had difficulty searching for known items even when the exact title of an article was entered. Taking the example of the Fredric Jameson article again, many entered the exact title as a keyword search without quotation marks. However, this search strategy tended to be unsuccessful since the article does not appear until result #13 on the second page and most users never navigated beyond the first page of results. Incidentally, the ranking of the sought article actually dropped to #18 even after some users switch from a keyword to a title search. Unfortunately, none of the users utilized quotation marks to increase the precision of their query. A keyword search with quotation marks returned the article as result #4 while a title search with quotations bumped it to #1. Accordingly, the investigators recommended that EDS product management explore ways to improve searching for known items. Since testing, several enhancements have been implemented for known item searching including the following: (1) relevancy increase applied to exact title matches in library catalog, (2) autocomplete has been improved to support common misspellings, popular searches, and current topics, and (3) a publication title placard displays above the results and allows a user to see the exact title match for a book or journal that the library has access.

To counter users' reluctance to probe beyond the first page of results, the investigators recommended customizing EDS to increase the number of results per page and for product management to consider infinite scrolling as a future enhancement.

Many study participants found the EDS results list to be cluttered. Therefore, the investigators recommended minimizing cognitive load by removing the right column of the search results screen and redistributing the content that previously occupied this space. The right column of the EDS search results screen functions as a placeholder for local add-on content. At Rutgers, the right column (see figure 14.5) was used to display EDS's federated search option, a library chat widget,

FIGURE 14.5

Right-hand column display before usability testing

and recommended research guides. However, few participants seemed to use this content and many actually found it distracting. To reduce visual clutter on the interface, content from the right column was transitioned to EDS placards. Placards are call-out boxes that present the user with information related to his or her search and can be placed at the top, bottom, or somewhere in the middle of the results set. In Rutgers's case, the Springshare "Recommended LibGuides" right-column app was replaced with a placard that appears at the bottom of the results list when there are relevant research guides available (see figure 14.6). Rutgers is also considering known-search placards hard-coded to respond to frequent searches that are not intended for the discovery index (e.g., "JSTOR," "parking," "hours") with appropriate information or links.

The investigators found that users were either unaware or unsure of how to use EDS's federated search option. Task 5 asked participants to broaden the results of a preceding search to include results from additional sources. However, none of the users seemed to notice the "Expand Your Search" option that would allow them to incorporate results from external databases. Although the objective of the task may have been too vague for some, it seems fair to conclude that users would not choose this option without explicit instruction to do so. This finding is consistent with several other EDS studies. Williams and Foster, for example, found that users struggled to complete a task requiring them to use federated search without prompting from the test moderator.[16] Cassidy et al. noted that even after the purpose of this tool was explained to users, the majority were still unable to use it successfully.[17] Fagan et al. found that less than 1 percent of all EDS sessions over the course of a semester included any interaction with federated search.[18] With all of this in mind, the investigators recommended retiring federated search and replacing it with a database recommender system that guides users to specialized resources on their topic. It was suggested that these database recommendations be combined with the existing research guide recommendations into a placard that would appear near the bottom of the search results screen. This way, if the user scrolls through the first page of EDS results without finding anything of relevance, they are prompted to consider consulting a specialized database or research guide related to their topic.

FIGURE 14.6 ———

Recommended research guides placard

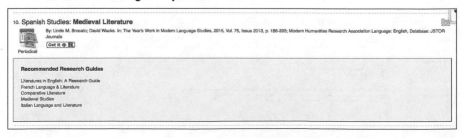

Lastly, the investigators recommended using on-demand controls or modal windows to deliver other content such as the chat reference service so as to minimize use of screen real estate when this content is not needed (see figure 14.7).

Users had difficulty interpreting certain labels, especially when those labels were based on library jargon. For example, when asked to find an article published in the *New York Times,* many users struggled to find the appropriate field or limiter that would allow them to specify this. Although all users eventually made their way to the advanced search screen, most failed or were reluctant to use the limiter labeled "Journal" for this task. As one user rightfully pointed out, the *New York Times* is a newspaper, not a journal, so using this option didn't seem to make sense. If this wasn't problematic enough, the investigators soon noticed that the labels for this characteristic are not consistent throughout the interface. The advanced search limiter uses the term "Journal," but the field menu uses "Journal Title/Source" and the facets use "Publication." Accordingly, the investigators recommended that labels in all three locations be standardized to avoid confusion. "Publication" was recommended as the standard label because it was deemed more user-friendly than "Journal" or "Periodical."

Users also frequently overlooked important system messages during testing. This finding is consistent with Cassidy et al., who noted that users did not always notice EDS's autocorrect suggestions.[19] Similarly, messages indicating spelling errors or the need to input search terms often went unnoticed, even when these errors produced no results. Investigators recommended an EDS product enhancement to make these messages more prominent by, for example, adding borders or background colors.

Finally, as previous studies have suggested, users had notable difficulty interpreting results and distinguishing formats. For example, although task 1 required users to identify two scholarly articles, several participants selected non-scholarly sources. It is unclear whether these users truly did not understand the difference or were merely careless in their evaluation. For example, when one of these users was asked to explain her rationale, she simply noted that the titles of the selected articles contained the word she searched. Interestingly, only one user explicitly used the peer-review limiter to complete this task, which led the

FIGURE 14.7 ——

Right-hand column after usability testing

investigators to recommend changing the label in order to clarify its purpose. Task 5 required users to identify a conference paper and, while all users were successfully able to use the source type limiter to find the requested format, two undergraduate participants admitted that they did not know what a conference paper was.

Recommendations resulting from this study led to further customization of EDS at Rutgers University as well as recent enhancements to the product as a whole. While these changes have yet to undergo another round of user testing, they represent a critical part of iterative testing and improvement by both the library's discovery service administrator as well as the discovery vendor.

CONCLUSION

Web-scale discovery services, while a welcome improvement to the library search environment, are not a panacea. There is still ample room for improvement through product development and local customization. However, the findings from this study and observations at other institutions suggest that library instruction must also play a prominent role in improving users' experiences with discovery services. In particular, users need guidance in developing effective search strategies, distinguishing between different formats, and critically evaluating the quality of sources.

Discovery services often come with out-of-the-box configurations that may not be perfectly suited for every library. However, with the ability to change settings and apply custom code to the user interface, the opportunity for improvement and innovation is high. Librarians should develop a plan of iterative testing and collaborate with vendors in order to address the weaknesses and challenges in discovery systems. While customization options can solve many user experience problems, advancing the state of the art will require vendor commitment to improving their products as well as instructing users on how to get the most out of them.

Notes

1. Joseph Deodato, "Evaluating Web-Scale Discovery Services: A Step-by-Step Guide," *Information Technology and Libraries* 34, no. 2 (2015): 19–75. doi: 10.6017/ital.v34i2.5745.
2. Jody Condit Fagan et al., "Usability Test Results for a Discovery Tool in an Academic Library," *Information Technology and Libraries* 31, no. 1 (2012): 83–112. doi: 10.6017/ital .v31i1.1855.
3. Rice Majors, "Comparative User Experiences of Next-Generation Catalogue Interfaces," *Library Trends* 61, no. 1 (2012): 186–207. doi:10.1353/lib.2012.0029.

4. Kelly Meadow and James Meadow, "Search Query Quality and Web-Scale Discovery: A Qualitative and Quantitative Analysis," *College & Undergraduate Libraries* 19, nos. 2–4 (2012): 163–175. doi: 10.1080/10691316.2012.693434.

5. Susan Teague-Rector and James Ghaphery, "Designing Search: Effective Search Interfaces for Academic Library Websites," *Journal of Web Librarianship* 2, no. 4 (2008): 479–92. doi: 10.1080/19322900802473944.

6. Cory Lown, Tito Sierra, and Josh Boyer, "How Users Search the Library from a Single Search Box," *College & Research Libraries* 74, no. 3: (2013): 227–41. doi: 10.5860/crl-321.

7. Andrew D. Asher, Lynda M. Duke, and Suzanne Wilson, "Paths of Discovery: Comparing the Search Effectiveness of EBSCO Discovery Service, Summon, Google Scholar, and Conventional Library Resources," *College & Research Libraries* 74, no. 5 (2013): 464–88. doi: 10.5860/crl-374.

8. Meadow and Meadow, "Search Query Quality and Web-Scale Discovery."

9. Anita K. Foster and Jean B. MacDonald, "A Tale of Two Discoveries: Comparing the Usability of Summon and EBSCO Discovery Service," *Journal of Web Librarianship* 7, no. 1 (2013): 1–19. doi: 10.1080/19322909.2013.757936.

10. Erin Dorris Cassidy et al., "Student Searching with EBSCO Discovery: A Usability Study," *Journal of Electronic Resources Librarianship* 26, no. 1 (2014): 17–35. doi: 10.1080/1941126X.2014.877331.

11. Julia Gross and Lutie Sheridan, "Web Scale Discovery: The User Experience," *New Library World* 112, no. 5 (2011): 236–47. doi: 10.1108/03074801111136275.

12. Ibid.

13. Asher, Duke, and Wilson, "Paths of Discovery."

14. Jakob Nielsen, "Why You Only Need to Test with 5 Users," *Nielsen Norman Group,* March 19, 2000, www.nngroup.com/articles/why-you-only-need-to-test-with-5-users.

15. Jeff Sauro, "How to Find the Right Sample Size for a Usability Test," *MeasuringU,* December 7, 2011, www.measuringu.com/blog/sample-size-problems.php.

16. Sarah C. Williams and Anita K. Foster, "Promise Fulfilled? An EBSCO Discovery Service Usability Study," *Journal of Web Librarianship* 5, no. 3 (2011): 179–98. doi: 10.1080/19322909.2011.597590.

17. Cassidy et al., "Student Searching with EBSCO Discovery."

18. Fagan et al., "Usability Test Results for a Discovery Tool in an Academic Library."

19. Cassidy et al., "Student Searching with EBSCO Discovery."

PART IV

CONTENT AND METADATA

CHAPTER FIFTEEN

FROM USER STORIES TO WORKING CODE

A Case Study from NYU's Digital Collections Discovery Initiative

DANIEL LOVINS

T he New York University (NYU) Division of Libraries (the "division") embarked on a strategic initiative in 2013 to provide unified intellectual access to locally curated digital collections. The need for such an initiative is, naturally, not unique to NYU. The effort to establish bibliographic control over proliferating repositories, resource types, and metadata standards is a defining challenge of cultural heritage organizations today. NYU is one of the more complex organizations of this type, though, with unique constituencies, collections and mandates, and therefore must tailor its approach to meet local resource discovery challenges.[1]

In this chapter, I begin by describing the context of the initiative at NYU, its roots in the strategic planning process, and the kind of cross-departmental collaboration that was necessary for a successful outcome. I then describe how NYU assessed end-user needs and how these assessments were translated into functional requirements and work packages in order to ensure unified access to curated digital collections. Finally, I discuss lessons learned and recommended next steps, both for NYU and for other institutions engaged in similar efforts.

BACKGROUND

The NYU Division of Libraries, like the university it serves, is a complex and rapidly changing organization. It is a kind of consortium unto itself as well as a service provider to an external consortium. Within NYU, the libraries serve more than 40,000 students and over 3,100 faculty at multiple New York sites including Washington Square, the Health Sciences complex, three major special collections (University Archives, the Tamiment/Wagner Archives, and the Fales Library), the NYU Polytechnic School of Engineering, two additional full-fledged campuses in Abu Dhabi and Shanghai, and multiple smaller-scale research institutes and study sites both in New York and around the world (www .nyu.edu/about.html). Externally, the division facilitates shared borrowing and a union catalog for the Research Library Association of South Manhattan (RLA-SM), which includes Cooper Union, the New School for Social Research, the New York School of Interior Design, the New York Historical Society, and the Brooklyn Historical Society. The NYU Libraries system includes fourteen service locations, while the RLA-SM accounts for eight additional locations (library .nyu.edu/about/locations.html). Core bibliographic processes and applications are managed from the Bobst Library at New York's Washington Square, and its annex facility at 20 Cooper Square.

Within Bobst and 20 Cooper, there are some nonobvious divisions of responsibility worth mentioning here. Knowledge Access Design & Development, or "KADD," the department led by the current author, includes experts in original cataloging, metadata services, and bibliographic systems administration. As the name suggests, the department is responsible for designing new strategies and workflows, and to provide access to new forms of knowledge.[2] This involves going beyond the traditional integrated library system (ILS) and making available websites, blogs, research data, social media archives, full text corpora, or any other objects of interest to our students and researchers.

The concentration of systems and metadata expertise in KADD enabled an unprecedented level of collaboration with other technical units in the libraries, notably Web Services and Digital Library Technology Services (DLTS). Web Services is the department responsible for the division's web presence, including the look and feel of its content management system, integration among diverse software applications, integration with university administrative systems, and custom software development. Among other services (dlib.nyu.edu/dlts/services/), DLTS is responsible for reformatting, preservation, and publication of NYU and affiliated digital collections, as well as grant-funded and custom software development.

Goal Four (out of eight) of the libraries' *Strategic Plan 2013–2017* (library .nyu.edu/about/Strategic_Plan.pdf) is to "establish processes and support structures that ensure we can select, acquire, preserve, and provide access to the full spectrum of research materials." Subsumed under this goal is Initiative Three (out of three), henceforth, "the initiative:" "a plan to provide intellectual access to NYU-curated digital collections via the library's primary discovery-and-access interfaces."

By identifying this work as a strategic priority, the division has been able to leverage the five-year strategic planning cycle to ensure long-term institutional buy-in and regular communication across a wide range of colleagues and stakeholders, including collection curators, metadata specialists, web developers, and usability experts. These communications include internal project meetings (as described below) as well as regular exchanges with the Department Managers Group and with library administrators. Moreover, the strategic plan itself was preceded and informed by environmental scans, department-wide interviews, all-staff forums, and a "Synthesis" report, all of which pointed to collaboration, agile development, and user-centered design as high priorities.

IMPLEMENTING A STRATEGIC INITIATIVE

In July 2013, the initiative charge was drafted and two working groups were established: (1) Collections and Functional Requirements, and (2) Technical Specifications and Prototyping. The first group included representatives from the Fales and Tamiment special collections, along with repository curators and website archivists; namely, individuals who were able to help identify "hidden collections" and submit user stories to inform functional requirements for their discovery. Also in this group was the head of the User Experience (UX) Department, who offered guidance on the efficacy of new features. The current author was a member of both groups, and therefore could facilitate communications between them. Target collections in a first phase included geospatial data sets, numeric data sets, archived websites, Drupal-based digital collections, and files in NYU's DSpace-powered Faculty Digital Archive (FDA).

The second group identified tools and procedures for aggregating, normalizing, enhancing, and disseminating metadata from these digital collections, based, in part, on earlier work on a "Union Catalog for Digital Projects" (2011) and a prototype developed at an NYU Libraries hackfest (2013). This group included developers from Web Services, DLTS, and KADD. It is this second group that settled on the Hydra technology stack and agile project management for implementing user stories submitted by the first group. It is worth noting that, for the initiative, we did not ask students and scholars to submit user stories directly. Rather, we relied on curators and usability specialists to represent their needs and interests.

The shorter-term goal for the initiative was to provide lightweight normalization and remediation for newly received metadata before integrating them with NYU's primary discovery portal, BobCat. This would solve an immediate known problem, namely, that it is often hard to know where to find information on curated digital collections. At the end of this initiative, our patrons would be able to discover many additional NYU digital resources in BobCat, records for which would provide immediate access to resources as well as back-links to the original host repository for richer descriptions and retrieval options. The longer-term goal was to implement a robust internal data model that exposes highly structured, semantically rich metadata to aggregators such as DPLA and WorldCat. Additionally, we see a role for curated library data as part of the "backbone of trust" for the Semantic Web: assertions about authorship and subjects, for example, in knowledge bases like the Google Knowledge Vault.

Like several other projects described in *Exploring Discovery,* ours benefited from having access to the Hydra technology stack and support community. "Ichabod," as we call our discovery solution, is based on Fedora, Solr, Blacklight, and Hydra itself, and is being used at NYU to normalize incoming metadata to a centralized "NyuCore" element set.

In Ichabod we are using the Fedora repository only to store metadata, not the digital objects (for which we have other solutions). Solr is a widely used Lucene-based indexing and searching tool. Blacklight is a discovery layer, maintained by the same community that developed Hydra. The Hydra "gem" (a module of Ruby code) allows web-based management of Fedora objects. NyuCore is a locally defined metadata application profile based on Dublin Core. We are using a "headless" instance of Hydra (hence the name, "Ichabod") as a staging area before exporting metadata to BobCat.[3] We are not (currently) using Blacklight or a Hydra head as a public interface, since we have the Primo discovery tool already embedded in BobCat. We do, however, retain the Blacklight "head" for staff interaction with the Fedora repository.

AGILE DEVELOPMENT AND THE SCRUM FRAMEWORK

"Agile" denotes a way for groups to work together with maximum transparency, accountability, and responsiveness to user needs. It is hard to find a single succinct definition in the literature, but practitioners emphasize the value of face-to-face contact, short-term, iterative development cycles, the relative importance of working code (over complex planning), and treating customers as development partners.[4]

"Scrum" is a particular type of agile development. The official *Scrum Guide* (2013) defines it as "a framework within which people can address complex adaptive problems, while productively and creatively delivering products of the highest possible value" (p. 3). Scrum involves special designations of "roles" and "events." The roles include a "product owner," a "development team," and a "scrum master" (www.scrumguides.org/scrum-guide.html#team). In our case we had two product owners: the current author in his capacity as initiative chair, and the senior manager of NYU's Digital Library Infrastructure. In theory this could pose a problem if the product owners had conflicting agendas. In practice, though, there was no conflict, and the arrangement helped ensure that both digital discovery and digital publishing would inform the Ichabod development process. The two product owners assumed organizational and political responsibilities for prioritizing functional requirements, establishing priorities, and managing relationships with stakeholders. They collected user stories, stored them in a PivotalTracker knowledge base (www.pivotaltracker.com), placed some stories in the "backlog" for short-term assignment, and others in the "icebox" for long-term reference. By having product owners serve as gatekeepers to the backlog and as buffers from outside pressure, developers could be freed up to work on high-value features that had already been vetted.

The development team included two developers from Web Services, three from DLTS, and two from KADD. The Web Services contingent kicked off the project by setting up the initial Hydra instance and sharing their development workflows and infrastructure. DLTS developers had deep knowledge of NYU digitization projects and digital collections and were especially helpful in designing ingest mechanisms into Ichabod. KADD members implemented the NyuCore schema and set up the initial data loaders. They also shared their knowledge of systems underlying BobCat, especially Aleph, which powers our ILS, and Primo, our discovery layer.

"Events" in Scrum include "backlog grooming," "sprint planning," "daily scrums," "sprint reviews," and "sprint retrospectives" (www.scrumguides.org/scrum-guide.html#events). In the case of Ichabod, we did not implement every aspect of Scrum, but only as much as was practicable given our resources and needs. In our case, the product owners met each week with the scrum master in a backlog grooming session to review user stories, document prerequisites and dependencies, and decide which stories to move from the icebox to the backlog before the next sprint planning meeting. At the biweekly sprint planning sessions, the product owners and the development team analyzed user stories, sought clarification on details and acceptance criteria, assigned complexity points, and discussed who might volunteer to undertake a given story for the upcoming sprint period.

From that point on, the developers had two weeks to work on their assigned stories. Two or three times each week the full Scrum team would check in for five-minute Google Hangout meetings ("scrums"), presided over by the scrum master. Members reported on what they accomplished since the last scrum, what they planned to do next, and what, if anything, was blocking them. At

FIGURE 15.1

Evolution of user stories into product features

Roles are in *italics*; Events are in **boldface**

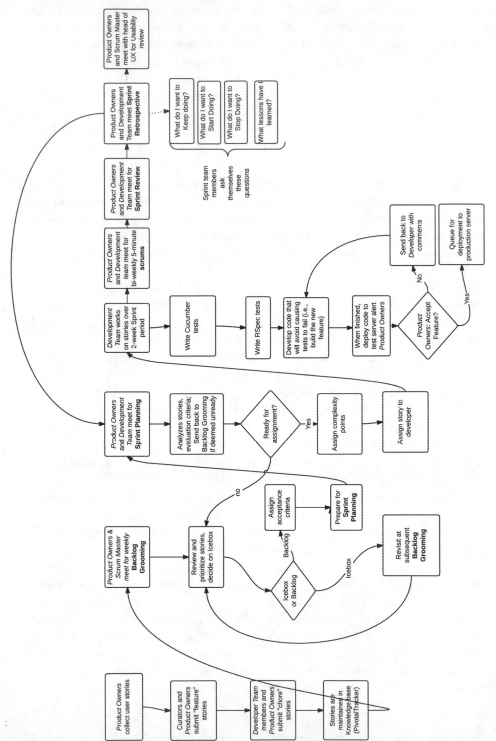

the end of a development cycle the scrum master would sometimes convene a combined sprint review and retrospective, where members would share what they want to keep doing, what they want to stop doing, lessons learned, and any other reflections. Then the cycle would start over with a new sprint planning meeting, continued backlog grooming sessions, and regular scrums. If a developer were unable to finish a story within the two-week sprint, he or she would simply carry it over into the next sprint. Figure 15.1 shows how user stories start as plain English-language requests and evolve into actionable feature specifications and then running code.

FROM USER STORIES TO FEATURES

Here is an example of how a user story was turned into an Ichabod feature: product owners met with managers of the NYU Spatial Data Repository (SDR), who are also members of the Collections and Functional Requirements group. In our discussion on functional requirements, we all understood the need for collocating SDR records within Ichabod, both by original repository (SDR) and by collection (in this case, the name of the GIS software company and platform "ESRI").[5] Toward that end, we documented this user story:

"As an NYU patron, I want to be able to filter my search results by the collection 'Spatial Data Repository' and the collection 'ESRI,' so that I can home in on the GIS datasets that I am interested in."

FIGURE 15.2 ——

SDR story in PivotalTracker

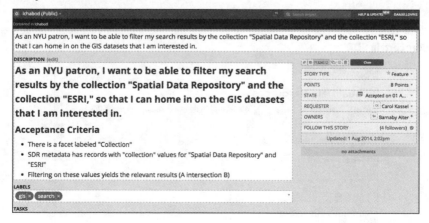

At a backlog grooming session, we developed the following acceptance criteria:

- There is a facet labeled "Collection"
- SDR metadata has records with "collection" values for (A) "Spatial Data Repository" and (B) "ESRI"
- Filtering on these values yields the relevant results (A intersection B)

At a subsequent sprint planning session, developers asked questions and sought consensus on the complexity level of this story. Developers would discretely write down a complexity score (a kind of educated guess, represented by a Fibonacci number between zero and twenty-one), and then share them with the group all at once. This would then lead to discussion on why some developers assigned a higher score than others, and they would negotiate until consensus was reached, thus affording a more nuanced understanding of the nature of the challenge. We used the Fibonacci sequence (en.wikipedia.org/wiki/Fibonacci_number) to remind ourselves that the more highly scored stories were often *significantly* more complex than the less highly scored ones. Finally, a member of the group volunteered to take on the story (which, incidentally, had received a complexity score of 8). In this case, it involved modifying a Ruby-based data loader, aligning incoming records with NyuCore, assigning the collection name as a new element, and testing the feature with RSpec (www.rspec .info/) and Cucumber (www.cukes.info/). This testing step is critical in the evolution of plain English user stories into working code. As one project member put it, "With Cucumber, you may describe a feature in plain English, then define the steps in Ruby (with RSpec), and finally let it fail. This will have the added benefit of documenting what your code is doing and what you are testing for."[6] See figures 15.3–15.6 for screenshots of an SDR record as it appears and moves through three different systems.

FIGURE 15.3

SDR record in SDR

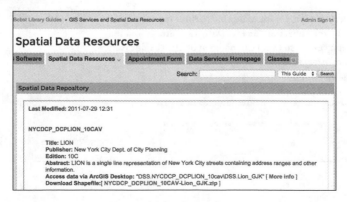

FIGURE 15.4

SDR record in Ichabod

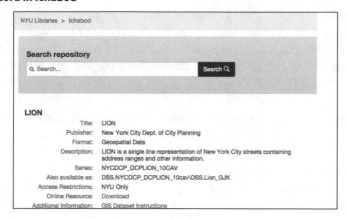

NYU Libraries > Ichabod

Search repository

Search... [Search Q]

LION

Title:	LION
Publisher:	New York City Dept. of City Planning
Format:	Geospatial Data
Description:	LION is a single line representation of New York City streets containing address ranges and other information.
Series:	NYCDCP_DCPLION_10CAV
Also available as:	DSS.NYCDCP_DCPLION_10cav\DSS.Lion_GJK
Access Restrictions:	NYU Only
Online Resource:	Download
Additional Information:	GIS Dataset Instructions

FIGURE 15.5

SDR record edit in Ichabod

Edit Item   My Workspace

Identifier
DSS.NYCDCP_DCPLION_10cav\DSS.Lion_GJK
Restrictions
NYU Only
Resource set
spatial_data_repository
Available
http://mapetlan.home.nyu.edu/datasets/zips/NYCDCP_DCPLION_10CAV-Lion_GJK.zip

[ ]

[+]

Citation

[ ]

[+]

Title
LION

[ ]

FIGURE 15.6

SDR record in BobCat

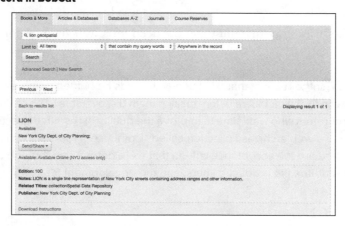

Books & More | Articles & Databases | Databases A-Z | Journals | Course Reserves

lion geospatial

Limit to: All items ⇕ that contain my query words ⇕ Anywhere in the record ⇕

[Search]

Advanced Search | New Search

Previous | Next

Back to results list   Displaying result 1 of 1

LION
Available
New York City Dept. of City Planning;
[Send/Share ▾]

Available: Available Online (NYU access only)

Edition: 10C
Notes: LION is a single line representation of New York City streets containing address ranges and other information.
Related Titles: collectionSpatial Data Repository
Publisher: New York City Dept. of City Planning

Download Instructions

This was a fairly straightforward example, since we had complete control over collection names and could assign them as a kind of rubber stamp at ingest time. More challenging user stories go beyond the insertion of text strings like collection names, though, and require careful thinking about levels of organization. For example, here are two other user stories related to the first:

(1)   "As a curator, I want to be able to describe existing resources at the collection level, so that I can add information to them."

Here are the acceptance criteria:
▸ All existing collections in Ichabod are changed to use Collection object rather than Resource Set to store collection information.
▸ Collection Abstract field exists, is editable.
▸ UI (user interface) is unchanged as a result of this modification.

(2)   "As a collection curator, I want to see my resources organized in Ichabod by collection, because that's the way I think."

And here is the acceptance criterion:
▸ There is a Collection object in Rails with these fields: Collection Name, Abstract, Rights, Discoverability Flag, Provider, Department.

Curators have told us they need to be able to modify aspects of the Collection class and have them inherited by members of that class. In this example, the access rights for the entire collection might change, so rather than having to revise access restrictions item-by-item, we want the Collection class to contain the information and cascade down to all of its instances. Having a Collection object with properties like "rights," along with editing forms and instance inheritance, makes this possible.

Here is another user story that illustrates the need for a well-defined collection object.

"As a curator, I want to request that a set of new records be hidden from view in Ichabod, so that I can fix the metadata before making them discoverable." This feature was requested by curators who want time to improve the quality of resource descriptions before exposing a web archives collection called "Composer Web Sites" in Ichabod and BobCat. Here are the acceptance criteria that were determined through consultation with the curator, the product owners, and the development team:

- On load, the Composer Web Sites records are marked as non-discoverable.
- A search for "louiskarchin.com" (i.e., the URL for one of the curated composer sites) shows 0 results when not logged in.
- A search for "louiskarchin.com" shows a result when logged in as (curator).
- The ability exists to mark the records as discoverable from Jenkins (our continuous integration server).[7]

These user stories require specific implementation decisions in Fedora and Rails, but even before that happens, they require a consensus on our data definitions, namely, how we define the "collection" object and enumerate its attributes. We do not want to make these decisions just for Ichabod and BobCat, however, since a longer term goal is to enable interoperability with higher-level aggregations. Thus, we note that the Digital Public Library of America's (DPLA's) *Metadata Application Profile (MAP)* uses the label "Collection" for a "collection or aggregation of which described resource is a part,"[8] while the *Europeana Data Model (EDM)* uses "Is Part Of" for "a related resource in which the described resource is physically or logically included," and both are reusing the DCMI Metadata property: "dcterms:isPartOf" (dublincore.org/documents/dcmi-terms/).

We have similar user stories around the concept of language. At the application level, we want to avoid literal character strings like "English" or codes like "eng." We prefer an RDF-type object with a unique persistent identifier, a preferred label, alternate labels, position within its language family, and so on. The Library of Congress maintains a list of ISO language terms, where the URL that identifies the English language (id.loc.gov/vocabulary/iso639-1/en.html) represents a complex object (see figure 15.7). We want Ichabod to point to this kind of URL and benefit from its persistence, its cross-references, and its RDF serializations.

Ichabod is an aggregation of discrete digital library collections curated at NYU. We do not know exactly what new collections will be added or what will happen as Ichabod collections get combined with BobCat (another aggregation), or WorldCat or DPLA. By building linked data concepts into Ichabod and aligning our data model with those of the wider web and cultural heritage communities, we can fulfill the need for data consistency and collocation as reflected in our user stories, while also benefiting other constituencies through improved interoperability, shared identifier schemes, and a lower maintenance burden on any one institution. Additionally, the Ichabod team is contributing its own work back to the wider Hydra community and helping refine a common data model.

FIGURE 15.7 ──

English-language object as linked data

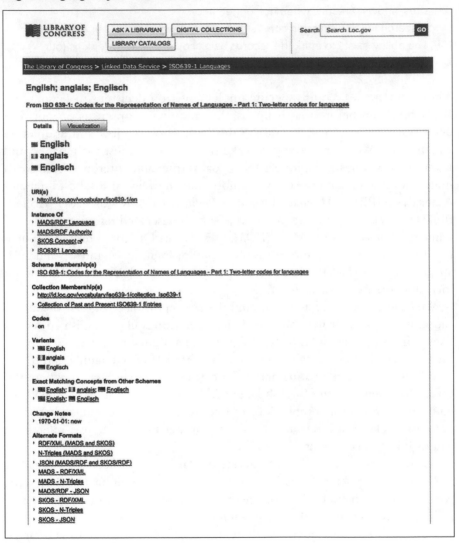

LESSONS LEARNED AND NEXT STEPS

The strategic planning process cannot prevent conflicting priorities and competition over scarce resources, but it can help ensure that only the highest-priority initiatives become part of that competition. And in the case of new discovery services, projects can be mutually reinforcing. For example, overlapping with the

Ichabod project at NYU has been an effort to rebuild our archives discovery portal to improve indexing, display, system logging, responsive design elements, and other features. This, too, involved Scrum methodology, Ruby on Rails, and Blacklight development, and many of the same developers and specialists. Since much of the infrastructure was the same, the project members continue to build up common NYU infrastructure and skills and can be even more effective when returning to Ichabod. Moreover, the archives portal was able to ramp up quickly because of the precedent set by Ichabod.

We need to continuously revisit what it means for something to be a "curated collection," as specified in the initiative. For example, the NYU Faculty Digital Repository is largely self-service. Some of the contributions may appear out of scope or inappropriate for wide dissemination. Some metadata may be irregular or absent, and fail to map to our data model and therefore fail to generate useful access points and collocation in the discovery interface. The former challenge (i.e., what counts as "curated") will remain a grey area and require case-by-case evaluation before being included in Ichabod. The latter (i.e., inadequate metadata) can be mitigated through quality assurance routines, metadata remediation, and vocabulary reconciliation.

While we have in place a basic data model for NYU resources, we envision future iterations that are more fully articulated. Moving forward, we intend to align ourselves with larger-scale aggregators and discovery systems, including DPLA.

As the number of collections grows, and the Ichabod mapping becomes more complex, we want to incorporate usability review more tightly in the development process. This will become even more important if we decide to make Ichabod a discovery platform in its own right, that is, in addition to its role as an aggregator, remediation platform, and staging area. We also should consider expanding the range of assessment inputs to include application transaction logs, web analytics, and interviews directly with students and researchers.

CONCLUSION

NYU has undertaken a strategic initiative to make its distributed digital collections discoverable through the libraries' central portal, BobCat, and has completed its short-term goal of being able to represent high-priority curated digital collections in BobCat via Ichabod. The "user story," a component of agile development, has proven an effective means of understanding patrons' needs on their own terms, and allowing them to remain at the center of conversation among developers, product owners, and stakeholders. In the case of Ichabod, we see how plain English feature requests are captured in PivotalTracker, assigned priority level and acceptance criteria by product owners, then assigned complexity points by the developer team. The developers instantiate the acceptance criteria in the form of natural-language Cucumber and Ruby RSpec tests and proceed to write the code. Once the features have been realized within the application, curators and usability specialists help us determine how well they satisfy the original stories. Product owners decide whether to "accept" the story as complete, and, if so, whether the implemented feature warrants future changes or enhancements (in which case they will need new user stories).

Our longer-term goal involves enhancing the NyuCore application profile to exploit its value in a linked open data environment. At the same time, we are following data modeling efforts at Hydra, DCMI, DPLA, Europeana, Schema .org, W3C, and other communities to ensure that NYU collections data can be aggregated effectively for discovery at any level. This work will need to continue being rooted in the needs of our real users, so user stories will remain essential. Here is a made-up (but plausible) example of a long-term goal user story: "As a researcher, in order to build up a collection of images as quickly and comprehensively as possible, I want to be able to search DPLA for images of Indian Ocean postcards, and find NYU's contributions interfiled with those of other institutions."

The path from user story to product feature is supported by the commitment to a common development environment and work culture: the Hydra framework for its community and shared code libraries, Cucumber and RSpec for test-driven development, NyuCore for a local metadata hub, and Scrum for communication and project management. By embracing a shared vision and infrastructure, we are able to take plain English user stories and find a path to implementing them as tangible product features.

Notes

1. For example, the division oversees rapidly growing physical and electronic resource collections, extensive special collections, a strong digitization program, NYU TV channel operations, and the university press. All of these include important intellectual assets that need to be made available to the NYU community and beyond.

2. Carlen Ruschoff, "Reality Check: A New Framework for Technical Services: Interview with New York University's Carol A. Mandel and Martin Kurth," *Technicalities* 33, no. 5 (September/October 2013): 1ff. In 2010 the division created a new directorate called Knowledge Access and Resource Management Services (KARMS). KARMS comprises three new departments: Resource Management (RM), Metadata Production & Management (MPM), and KADD. RM manages, among other things, workflows around budgets, vendors, and e-resource knowledge bases. MPM "is responsible for providing intellectual access to a continuing flow of physical materials acquired from all over the

world, along with maintaining the bibliographic database and doing the necessary work to keep information accurate, current, and fresh."

3. The reference is to Ichabod Crane, the schoolteacher who engages the Headless Horseman in Washington Irving's *Legend of Sleepy Hollow.*

4. "Manifesto for Agile Software Development": http://agilemanifesto.org/; Agile Alliance, "What Is Agile?" www.agilealliance.org/the-alliance/what-is-agile/; Martin Fowler, "The New Methodology": http://martinfowler.com/articles/newMethodology.html.

5. That is, the "Environmental Systems Research Institute" (ESRI), which, in 1982, released "the first commercial GIS," the ARC/INFO system. See www.esri.com/about-esri/history/history-more.

6. Based on a previous user story, there was already a workflow in place to ingest data from source, map them to NyuCore elements, persist (i.e., store) metadata values to Fedora, index them in Solr, and convert Ichabod's HTTP JSON output to Primo Normalized XML (PNX), with could then generate resource descriptions and delivery options in BobCat's current discovery layer, Primo.

7. "About Jenkins CI": https://jenkins-ci.org/content/about-jenkins-ci.

8. "DPLA Metadata Application Profile, version 4.0": http://dp.la/info/wp-content/uploads/2015/03/MAPv4.pdf.

References

Agile Alliance. "What Is Agile Software Development?" www.agilealliance.org/the-alliance/what-is-agile/.

Definition of the Europeana Data Model v5.2.6. http://pro.europeana.eu/files/Europeana_Professional/Share_your_data/Technical_requirements/EDM_Documentation//EDM%20Definition%20v5.2.6_01032015.pdf.

DPLA Metadata Application Profile. Version 4. https://docs.google.com/a/nyu.edu/document/d/1Jh8ULpw0jb8kyxV-Ygw9U0n-XqXkM6_V3jxfmnkebqo/edit.

Fowler, Martin. "The New Methodology." http://martinfowler.com/articles/newMethodology.html.

"Manifesto for Agile Software Development." 2001. http://agilemanifesto.org.

NYU Libraries. "Report on Strategic Initiative to Provide Enhanced Intellectual Access to NYU Curated Digital Collections." https://archive.nyu.edu/handle/2451/33869.

————. *Strategic Plan 2013–2017.* http://library.nyu.edu/about/Strategic_Plan.pdf.

Pivotal Labs. "PivotalTracker." https://www.pivotaltracker.com.

Ruschoff, Carlen. 2013. "Reality Check: A New Framework for Technical Services: Interview with New York University's Carol A. Mandel and Martin Kurth." *Technicalities* 33, no. 5 (September/October): 1–5.

Schema.org Data Model. http://schema.org/docs/datamodel.html.

Schwaber, Ken, and Jeff Sutherland. 2013. "The Scrum Guide." www.scrumguides.org/docs/scrumguide/v1/Scrum-Guide-US.pdf.

CHAPTER SIXTEEN

REGIONAL AGGREGATION AND DISCOVERY OF DIGITAL COLLECTIONS

The Mountain West Digital Library

ANNA NEATROUR, REBEKAH CUMMINGS, AND SANDRA MCINTYRE

The Mountain West Digital Library (MWDL) is a digital collaborative of over 180 partners from six states in the U.S. West, sharing free access to over 800 digital collections with over 950,000 resources. Partners of the MWDL work together on providing regional discovery via an online portal at mwdl.org and facilitating, on behalf of the region, the on-ramp to national discovery via the Digital Public Library of America (DPLA) portal at dp.la.

MWDL was organized around these common goals:

- ‣ Establish a distributed digitization and hosting infrastructure to support memory institutions in sharing their digital collections
- ‣ Increase public access to digital collections materials through aggregation and discovery via open search portals
- ‣ Promote interoperability of metadata via common standards and enhancements
- ‣ Share expertise and training

This chapter describes how these goals have been met for MWDL partners through a coordinated network of distributed repositories supporting collections and a central harvesting system for searching. Key to the success of regional discovery has been the establishment of common standards and practices, along with the development of useful data enhancement practices, also described below. How MWDL has adapted over its years of growth and adoption of changing technologies, and particularly how it has served the emergence of the new national digital library, are also discussed. Finally, future directions for collaborative discovery are suggested, with notes about the challenges ahead.

BUILDING A REGIONAL COLLABORATIVE FOR DIGITAL DISCOVERY

The Mountain West Digital Library was created in 2001 as a collaborative program among the member libraries of the Utah Academic Library Consortium (UALC). Several of the libraries had started digital collections and wanted to learn from each other's efforts. Leaning on the consortium's lengthy history of successful collaboration among higher education libraries in Utah and Nevada, leaders of the nascent digitization centers in UALC libraries looked to each other for support in establishing servers running CONTENTdm software for digital asset management and in sharing the costs of training and purchasing of equipment and software. Initial partners in the network included the University of Utah's J. Willard Marriott Library, Brigham Young University's Harold B. Lee Library, Southern Utah University's Gerald R. Sherratt Library, and Utah State University's Merrill-Cazier Library. Other libraries in UALC were also represented on the UALC Digitization Committee, which met regularly to set standards and policies for the new network (Arlitsch and Jonsson 2005).

Working with DiMeMa, the creators of CONTENTdm, the digital assets management system, the UALC partners implemented the CONTENTdm Multi-Site Server to harvest and share the indexed metadata from all the repositories in a central search interface, which they named the Mountain West Digital Library. Partners were encouraged to share digital resources openly, with clearly assigned usage rights and other metadata assigned according to agreed-upon standards. In 2007 harvesting moved to the Public Knowledge Project's Open Archives Harvester, to allow for aggregation of non-CONTENTdm repositories as well, using the harvesting protocols of the Open Archives Initiative Protocol for Metadata Harvesting (OAI-PMH). As the size of the central index grew, PKP Harvester proved inadequate for harvesting, and in 2011 harvesting moved again to a more robust discovery system, Primo by Ex Libris Group.

FIGURE 16.1 ───

Hub and spoke service model of the Mountain West Digital Library, showing aggregation of hosting hubs into a central MWDL portal. Smallest circles represent collection partners.

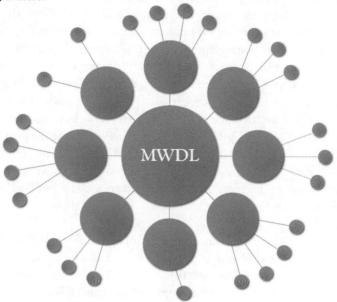

The early work of these UALC pioneers led to a strong, distributed network of regional hosting hubs, each providing digitization services and hosting not only for the digital collections of the host library but also for the collections of additional libraries, museums, and archives. This hub and spoke model is illustrated in figure 16.1.

The supported partners are typically located nearby or, in the case of several hubs, within the hub's administrative structure, regardless of physical location. Over time the MWDL network added CONTENTdm repositories from more Utah and Nevada academic libraries, the Utah State Archives, and the Utah State Library, and then expanded in the late 2000s to harvest both more CONTENTdm repositories and more repositories based on other systems. Recently, collaboration has expanded again to include repositories using additional software systems, and the network has expanded to include partners in additional states. The network now includes collections from partners in six states—Utah, Nevada, Idaho, Arizona, Montana, and Hawaii (through BYU–Hawaii). Hosting hubs and supported partners include academic libraries, public libraries, archives, historical societies, museums, state agencies, and county and municipal governments (mwdl.org/aboutPartners.php).

From the start of collaboration in 2001, the UALC Digitization Committee has provided a forum for collaboration among the MWDL partners. Meeting twice a year, the group established common standards for metadata, ensuring the interoperability of the data created by many partners around the region. Members of the committee share information and advice about the decisions and tasks involved in running a digital curation center, including equipment purchases, digital assets management systems selection, digitization workflow, and digital imaging best practices. In addition, partners collaborate on training about content selection and metadata assignment. In 2008, to facilitate support of a growing number of partners, representatives of the hosting hubs created a common set of competitive prices for digitization and hosting services offered at all hubs; the MWDL Digital Services Price List was revised in 2015 and continues to help partners estimate the costs of working on digital projects. No outside vendor prices are included in the list, nor does MWDL negotiate with outside vendors. Partners are encouraged to use the network of hosting hubs for digital services, but are also free to establish their own relationships with outside vendors.

In 2009 the Digitization Committee established the first of its task forces, and soon much of the practical work of the committee was being accomplished via smaller working groups. These task forces and interest groups help the whole network to move forward on various topics of interest, typically at the forefront of new technology and practice, from geospatial metadata best practices and digital preservation policies to institutional repository management, linked data, and research data curation.

As a collaborative enterprise, MWDL is funded and governed largely by the hosting hubs that maintain the repositories and digitization centers. Core funding is provided by the UALC Council from Utah legislative funds, and technology infrastructure and overhead have been provided by MWDL's host institution, the University of Utah's J. Willard Marriott Library. Grant funding has played an important role at several points. In the early years, Library Services and Technology Act (LSTA) grants from the Institute of Museum and Library Services via the Utah State Library helped to fund the new collaborative. Sub-awards to MWDL from four federal and private foundation grants accorded to the Digital Public Library of America provided the foundation for growth of the MWDL network from 2013 to 2015. Through a recent six-month advisory committee process, the MWDL funding model was revised to include membership dues from harvested repositories. Supporting one full-time and two part-time staff positions, the new model was implemented in the summer of 2015 and will maintain regional aggregation and data enhancement services, as well as provide a sustainable base for future growth.

BENEFITS OF REGIONAL DISCOVERY

Fifteen years after the formation of the Mountain West Digital Library, the benefits of regional collaboration for discovery are readily apparent. The diversity of curators who contribute collections to MWDL ensures a variety of viewpoints and representation, while the hub and spoke model has enabled growth to a large scale. The MWDL portal at mwdl.org now provides close to one million records of unique and historical content available for discovery.

The MWDL collaboration is largely imperceptible to end users, yet provides them great benefits in terms of online access and usability. Prior to the widespread digitization of historical content, searching for archival materials was the province of dedicated researchers and historians. These privileged few would correspond directly with institutions likely to have materials of interest and would travel, sometimes great distances, to view special collections in person. To the general public, these collections were largely invisible. While the physical items in special collections are still of great interest to scholars, digitized special collections are now available to anyone with an Internet connection.

In the Mountain West Digital Library, the metadata records for large and small special collections sit side-by-side in a navigable user interface driven by interoperable metadata. The aggregation of these metadata records greatly enhances serendipitous discovery for users who may have previously searched the digital collections of only one or two institutions. For example, Mormon pioneer history is an important area of interest for researchers investigating the settling of the American West. Materials of interest to these researchers include pioneer diaries, hand-drawn maps, personal correspondence, and drawings, and these materials are held by hundreds of collecting institutions around the West. Using the single MWDL search portal, a user can search the collections of larger institutions such as Brigham Young University, Utah State University, and the Utah State Historical Society, alongside those of smaller institutions such as the Darby Community Public Library, Emery County Archives, and the Sharlot Hall Museum. In fact, a search for "pioneer history" in MWDL provides metadata records from forty different partners (figure 16.2). With access to so many records from multiple institutions, the Mountain West Digital Library has become an obvious starting point for regional research.

The benefits of a regional library collaborative are just as significant to MWDL partners as MWDL users. While the discoverability of their content is the primary reason most partners join MWDL, the benefits of partnership within a robust digital library community provide equal value. Many new partners approach MWDL when they are considering how to digitize their first collection and offer it online. After conducting a new partner interview, MWDL staff present

FIGURE 16.2 ────────────────────────────────────

A partial list of MWDL institutions that have materials related to "pioneer history"

Refine Search		
Include	Exclude	Collection Partner
☐	☐	University of Utah - J. Willard Marriott Library (1,021)
☐	☐	Brigham Young University - Harold B. Lee Library (720)
☐	☐	Utah State Library (168)
☐	☐	Utah State University - Merrill-Cazier Library (157)
☐	☐	Utah State Historical Society (146)
☐	☐	Brigham Young University-Idaho (77)
☐	☐	Arizona State Library, Archives and Public Records (43)
☐	☐	Weber State University - Stewart Library (28)
☐	☐	Idaho Commission for Libraries (25)
☐	☐	Uintah County (UT) Library (17)
☐	☐	Utah State Archives (16)
☐	☐	Show Low (AZ) Historical Society Museum (15)
☐	☐	Billings (MT) Public Library (15)
☐	☐	Utah Valley University Library (12)
☐	☐	Darby (MT) Community Public Library (11)
☐	☐	ImagineIF Libraries, Flathead County (MT) (11)
☐	☐	Southern Utah University - Sherratt Library (9)
☐	☐	University of Montana - Maureen and Mike Mansfield Library (9)
☐	☐	University of Utah - American West Center (8)

options for creating a digital collection. Although some partners choose to create their own digital repository, MWDL staff members often pair the new partner with an established partner for training, digitization, and hosting assistance. Over time, as new partners gain expertise, many of them go on to assist other institutions with their new collections. This ripple effect, along with the distributed, tiered nature of provided services, has allowed MWDL to continue to expand with minimal central staff.

MWDL creates an invaluable platform for leveraging expertise and equipment across the regional network. Many partners have invested significant resources into developing new digital library skills, tools, and workflows. Rather than working in isolation, MWDL partners have a venue to share their recent discoveries and accelerate progress for other partners by leveraging both in-person and virtual training. In 2014 MWDL hosted twenty webinars on digital library topics, featuring guest speakers from both inside and outside of the network. The MWDL Webinar Series was a great opportunity for our partners to stay on the cutting edge of digital library topics and share their expertise with a broader audience. Some partners have also invested in specialized equipment such as high-speed robotic scanning, that others in the network can use for a reasonable fee.

The most recent benefit to the partners in the network is the opportunity to have their records included in the national digital library, the Digital Public Library of America. The Mountain West Digital Library was one of the inaugural six service hubs for the DPLA and the largest contributor of records to DPLA at its April 2013 launch. As a result of this new partnership, the metadata records of MWDL partners are now available at local, regional, and national levels, greatly increasing the discovery of their collections. The process of serving records to DPLA and the impact of this partnership are explored in more detail below.

ENHANCING DISCOVERY THROUGH METADATA AGGREGATION

The Mountain West Digital Library has a history of collaboration in developing best practices for discovery through metadata aggregation. The regional network provides a forum for librarians and library staff engaged with digitization and metadata creation to explore best practices and metadata improvements in a supportive environment. The collaborative adopted the Western States Dublin Core Best Practices, a document developed in 2003 by organizations in eight western states, including early MWDL partners, led by the Colorado Digitization Project, later called the Collaborative Digitization Project. These best practices were complemented by a locally developed document, "Metadata Guidelines for the Mountain West Digital Library," which provided examples of metadata records for various types of digital objects in conformance with the Western States standards.

The need to expand metadata standards to include Dublin Core Metadata Terms refinements led to the founding of the Metadata Task Force of the UALC Digitization Committee (sites.google.com/site/mwdlmetagroup), which developed the *Mountain West Digital Library Dublin Core Application Profile,* first released in 2010 and revised in 2011 (mwdl.org/docs/MWDL_DC _Profile_Version_2.0.pdf). The MWDL standard calls for eight required fields: date, description, format, identifier, rights, subject, title, and type, along with two mandatory-if-applicable fields: conversion specifications (for local use only) and creator. These fields are searchable, along with several others that are not required but commonly included, such as language and geospatial location. The greater specificity of Dublin Core Metadata Terms allows for a finer granularity for discoverability. For example, while in Dublin Core Metadata Terms the properties temporal and spatial refine the core element coverage with distinct meanings, the metadata provision in Dublin Core Elements conflates the two, making an accurate harvest of geospatial information impractical.

The extensive instructions in the *MWDL Dublin Core Application Profile* assist MWDL partners in creating robust and consistent metadata records at the local level, where librarians and archivists are most familiar with the materials. Training and support to local memory institutions are enhanced by the specific directions in the profile, along with additional, less formal information in the *General Guidelines for Digital Collections Metadata* provided on the MWDL website (mwdl.org/getinvolved/guidelines.php). The combination of standards documents continues to be widely used.

There is high awareness of the *MWDL Dublin Core Application Profile* in the Mountain West region, and it is often used as a base for customization by other digital libraries. For example, the Montana Memory Project Guidelines (msl.mt.gov/Statewide_Projects/Montana_Memory_Project/Documents/15 .MMPMetadataGuidelines.pdf) were informed by MWDL's standards, with additional required local fields added to reflect Montana-specific information. The Consortium of Church Libraries and Archives for the Church of Jesus Christ of Latter-day Saints (ccla.byu.edu) has also adopted the MWDL document with the addition of fields specific to the church's worldwide hierarchy for administration and worship. An MWDL task force is currently exploring controlled vocabulary and best practices for geospatial metadata (sites.google .com/site/mwdlgeospatial), and the conclusion of that process is likely to lead to a new revision of the *MWDL Dublin Core Application Profile*.

Records are normalized by MWDL at the time of aggregation to provide additional discoverability. Minor normalization routines are run to standardize item type, separate subjects for faceting, display date ranges in an expected fashion, and to enable other search and display functionality within Ex Libris Primo.

More significantly, MWDL adds values that indicate the context of individual resources. Since the default architecture of the Primo discovery system did not support the exploration of collections from a single partner or source repository, MWDL hard-codes fields for hosting center, repository, collection, and partner identifiers, allowing resources to be retrieved according to the context under which they were provided. For example, the hard-coded value "usu-16-363-2166" attached to all items in one collection coordinates retrieval of values from four customized Primo mapping tables, with "usu" identifying the hosting center at Utah State University's Merrill-Cazier Library, "16" identifying that library's CONTENTdm repository, "363" identifying the North Logan Public Library as the partner, and "2166" identifying the North Logan History Collection (mwdl. org/collections/2166.php). Users can retrieve all items in this collection if they wish, or all items from this partner, or repository, or hosting center. Likewise, they can limit their advanced searches to a specific collection, partner, and so on, or facet their search results after a search to narrow to a specific context. MWDL users can use these search strategies to retrieve only resources from selected—presumably the most trusted—partners. Each partner and each collection is represented with a landing page on the MWDL website, providing valuable information to search engine crawlers as well as end users of the portal. This assignment of values also allows users to browse and discover materials across platforms for a given partner. For example, they need not consider that a hosting center may provide metadata from one or more repositories, or that a partner may work with more than one hosting center because of available equipment or bandwidth for digitization. Similarly, if a collection moves from one repository to another, because of changing preferences or technology, the user can continue to find the materials by searching on the collection name.

The tiered nature of the MWDL network creates opportunities for users to encounter digitized objects in a variety of contexts. For example, while a public library may host a collection web page with local branding, collection materials may also be hosted within the technical infrastructure of a larger statewide collaboration like the Montana Memory Project (mtmemory.org). Likewise, a hosting hub like the Utah Valley University Library will also host collections for local memory institutions like the Utah Territorial Statehouse State Park Museum (mwdl.org/partners/351.php). Users may encounter digital objects through a Google search, direct links on a partner's web page or library catalog, via search on the hosting repository, via search at mwdl.org, or through a DPLA search. Rodger C. Schonfeld explored the variety of places where discovery for library users happens in a 2014 Ithaka report (Schonfeld and Ithaka S+R 2014). Recognizing that driving traffic to a single portal like mwdl.org will not capture all the users of digital collections in the area, MWDL encourages metadata improvements and best practices at the local level, as opposed to taking on more complicated metadata normalization and transformation at the repository level. Since users of MWDL are directed to the local repository to view the digital object, the metadata is best improved at the location of the source object, and then updated through frequent harvesting and reindexing.

To ensure consistency of application of metadata standards across hundreds of collections, MWDL staff members audit metadata at different stages of ingestion. A detailed audit report is prepared for a small number of pilot collections for each new repository before harvest, including suggestions for changes in field mapping and find-and-replace routines for field values. For already harvested repositories, new collections offered for harvest are reviewed for conformity as well.

Serving as a regional aggregator of metadata for a variety of partners and service hubs across multiple states creates challenges when approaching the goal of providing a consistent index for discovery. MWDL currently harvests from twenty-three repositories. While more than half of the aggregated repositories use CONTENTdm, MWDL also harvests from other systems, including other vendor products and open source systems, often adapted with locally coded OAI-PMH provision. To date MWDL has harvested from ArchivalWare, APPX AXAEM, IxiaSoft, and bepress, and efforts are under way to adapt Equella, SalesForce, and SimpleDL repositories for harvest. MWDL staff members are often called upon to consult on OAI-PMH support and development issues, especially for new repositories that have not been harvested before.

NATIONAL DISCOVERY: SERVING METADATA TO THE DIGITAL PUBLIC LIBRARY OF AMERICA

The idea of a national digital library had been discussed for almost a decade and after a three-year planning process, the Digital Public Library of America launched in April 2013. Rather than create a centralized digital library akin to the Library of Congress, the DPLA founders elected to build a lightweight portal aggregating metadata records from digital records sources around the country. DPLA's metadata records are harvested from content hubs and service hubs (dp.la/info/hubs/). Content hubs are large institutions, such as the Smithsonian Institution, that contribute over 200,000 records directly to DPLA. Service hubs, like MWDL, are records sources that have content from a variety of institutions and provide an on-ramp to DPLA for many institutions' materials. Service hubs are critical to the scalability of DPLA, as they remove the need for DPLA to maintain a one-to-one relationship with every memory institution in the country. Like MWDL, DPLA's hub and spoke structure has allowed DPLA to increase the amount of shared content rapidly and to focus on discoverability. In its first two years, DPLA harvested over ten million records and became a force for innovation on library technology, standards, and discoverability (Matienzo and Rudersdorf 2014).

MWDL was selected as one of the DPLA's six inaugural service hubs as part of the DPLA Hubs Pilot Project in 2012 and is still the only hub that represents a multistate regional collaborative. The other five initial hubs—Minnesota Digital Library, Digital Commonwealth (Massachusetts), Digital Library of Georgia, Kentucky Digital Library, and South Carolina Digital Library—were established as state-based collaboratives with more centralized models for digitization and hosting services. These other service hubs are often supported primarily by a single institution and have dedicated state-based or institution-based funding for staffing. In contrast, MWDL is affiliated with all institutions of higher learning in Utah, represents partners throughout the Mountain West, and has a more distributed funding model.

Involvement with the new national network of DPLA hubs has offered greater opportunities to connect with and share best practices with other librarians and information professionals engaged with issues of providing resources for discovery. Similar issues arise for all service hubs with regard to standardization, normalization, and OAI-PMH, and exploring these topics as a community of practice has been beneficial. Hubs have also developed and shared new tools for metadata management, for example the Metadata Aggregation Tools (github .com/ncdhc/dpla-aggregation-tools) developed by the North Carolina Digital Heritage Center (Gregory and Williams 2014). These tools allow service hubs engaged in OAI-PMH metadata harvesting to check for required fields and locate areas for improvement by providing a visual way to browse the contents of OAI streams of collections prior to harvest.

Having our records included in DPLA makes the digital collections of our partners visible to a national audience and increases the chances of serendipitous discovery by providing an additional high-profile access point. In its first year, the DPLA website and open application-programming interface (API) received over ten million hits, and, among all DPLA hubs, the Mountain West Digital Library received the second highest usage. Of the top twenty-five partners in DPLA, five of them were from the Mountain West Digital Library (mwdlnews .blogspot.com/2014/06/mwdl-statistics-from-dpla.html). This additional visibility predictably boosts the use of digital collections in MWDL and provides new opportunities for promotion and press. At the one-year anniversary of the DPLA launch, an MWDL image was featured in both the *Chronicle of Higher Education* and the *New York Times* "ArtsBeat" blog. The image, shared by a museum in Murray, Utah (population 48,612), became the most-viewed item in DPLA in April 2014. The inclusion of MWDL partners' images in DPLA's well-curated national exhibits (dp.la/exhibitions) has also raised their visibility and demonstrated the complementarity of content from around the country. Some of the recent exhibits, such as "Staking Claims: The Gold Rush in Nineteenth-Century America" (dp.la/exhibitions/exhibits/show/gold-rush), rely heavily on contributions from MWDL partners and highlight the depth of our collections in the Mountain West.

DPLA's experimentation with new user-friendly interfaces has also been a boon to MWDL partners, staff, and users. Unlike a traditional digital library interface that tends to require some searching expertise, DPLA has integrated user-friendly search features such as map and time-line interfaces. Users can search for materials by zooming in on a map interface to locate items in a particular part of the country or scroll through the time line to find primary source material from a particular year. Traditional facets can still be exposed if the user would like to narrow a search, but the default search mechanisms are more visual and intuitive than traditional library tools.

DPLA actively supports experimentation and use of the harvested and enhanced metadata available through its API (dp.la/info/developers/codex/).

To the extent that DPLA partners may hold any rights to the metadata, they agree to dedicate those rights to the public domain; a Creative Commons public domain dedication is applied upon harvest. At the time MWDL initially explored providing records to DPLA, partners were given the opportunity to opt out of dedicating metadata to the public domain. Not a single partner opted out. Since DPLA metadata is dedicated to the public domain, this has the effect of encouraging innovation and creativity with the use of that metadata. Hackathons have frequently been hosted to encourage the development of new uses of the API via apps, which point to new possibilities in discovery. DPLA apps range from twitter bots centered on specific topics such as Historical Cats, (dp.la/apps/20) to the virtual scrapbook Culture Collage (dp.la/apps/7), discovery through a user's geolocation with DPLA Map (dp.la/apps/5), a Wikipedia Editing browser extension (dp.la/apps/22), and a variety of metadata visualization apps (deanfarr .com/viz/index.php). Recent creative usage of DPLA's API has resulted in discovery interfaces such as Color Browse (colorbrowse.club), to explore selected photos by color, and DisasterView, which browses the Library of Congress and DPLA for images of catastrophes (disasterview.laurawrubel.org/).

Involvement with DPLA has provided MWDL staff an additional forum for exploring best practices for discovery at a national level. The new community formed by the service hubs and content hubs of DPLA often consists of the only individuals for a particular state or region concerned with harvesting metadata and working with a variety of local partners. MWDL has relied on DPLA expertise when developing our emerging recommendations for geospatial metadata, and representatives from other DPLA service and content hubs have contributed to MWDL task forces. The DPLA Metadata Application Profile (dp.la/info/developers/map/) provides guidelines for service and content hubs, and MWDL staff ensure that the MWDL Dublin Core Application Profile conforms with DPLA's expected practices.

ASSESSING THE IMPACT OF REGIONAL DISCOVERY

MWDL staff members have explored several means to gauge the impact of providing aggregation for regional discovery, as well as the sharing of records on the national platform of DPLA. With each round of assessment, staff members have also implemented changes that enhance discovery. This process is an ongoing, iterative one.

Google Analytics (GA) usage tracking was put into place in 2013, and the GA configuration has been tailored by the search engine optimization team at MWDL hosting institution, the J. Willard Marriott Library at the University of Utah, to collect cross-domain statistics, that is, to gather information about the usage of metadata records pages in Primo and static "About" pages on a conventional web server. The staff produces usage reports with GA statistics, along with "Page Insights" statistics from the MWDL Facebook page. Similarly, DPLA provides GA statistics to all its hubs monthly.

Search engine optimization is an ongoing process as well for the MWDL portal. Basic site maps have been implemented, and MWDL staff members are working with Ex Libris staff to create a more crawler-friendly environment in Primo. Early actions for linked data readiness and exposure are also being investigated, such as inclusion of microdata elements and recommendations for linked data URIs in certain fields.

Because participation in the collaborative is motivated by increased exposure and usage for digital collection materials, MWDL will be expanding its assessment strategies in the coming year.

SUCCESS TO DATE AND EVOLVING ISSUES

MWDL has succeeded in meeting its initial goals, serving as a locus for the digital community, sharing valuable resources with the world, and tailoring retrieval for maximum discovery using current tools, systems, and standards. That strong foundation of collaboration will continue to be highly useful as we plan improvements to our regional discovery services. As we look forward to new frontiers, we will continue to leverage our successful collaborative model and a history of collaborative goodwill and experience.

Future areas of growth include more integration with K-12 educational curriculum development and encouraging discovery for the classroom. This may involve integrating data delivery for learning management systems and developing metadata that reflects educational standards-specific learning objectives, learner level, and other fields. Also, MWDL will examine how to provide more focused collection development for building out important regional themes, as well as providing direct topic access to retrieve thematic materials.

Linked data for digital collections is another emerging issue MWDL is keenly aware of. DPLA's infrastructure is moving from linked-data-ready towards direct implementation of linked data, and Ex Libris is creating mechanisms for MWDL and other customers to expose data as JavaScript Object Notation (JSON), so a "perfect storm" of opportunity is likely to emerge shortly. MWDL is also interested in exploring the opportunities that a shared regional controlled vocabulary might provide for describing cultural heritage objects.

The role as a regional portal will doubtless adapt to complement the work of the DPLA on national discovery. Serving as a service hub to DPLA offers us the opportunity to experiment with frontiers for both levels of discovery. DPLA is developing better discovery options for digital items with its "Getting It Right on Rights" initiative (dp.la/info/about/projects/getting-it-right-on-rights/), and, along with other service hubs, MWDL will help to roll out recommendations for rights statements that will better help users locate items they can use or adapt. In addition, DPLA's Hydra-in-a-Box (imls.gov/assets/1/Asset Manager/LG-70–15–0006–15_Proposal.pdf) development project, funded under a National Leadership Grant from the Institute of Museum and Library Services, has the potential to modernize digital repository software, as well as make the harvesting process more standardized and streamlined both for national portals like DPLA and regional ones like MWDL.

As the national context for sharing access to digital collections matures, whether the size of MWDL's regional scale continues to feel "just right" remains to be seen. Personal relationships and reciprocal services have been at the heart of MWDL's success, and it is difficult to predict how further expansion will affect the important trust, goodwill, and social aspects of the collaboration. As a discovery portal that started out with the focus on a single state, and then expanded to serve multiple states, retaining the right mix of staffing and services to collaborate on discovery at a regional scale is an ever-changing puzzle.

References

Arlitsch, Kenning, and Jeff Jonsson. 2005. "Aggregating Distributed Digital Collections in the Mountain West Digital Library with the CONTENTdm Multi-Site Server." *Library Hi Tech* 23, no. 2: 220–32. doi: 10.1108/07378830510605179.

Gregory, Lisa, and Stephanie Williams. 2014. "On Being a Hub: Some Details behind Providing Metadata for the Digital Public Library of America." *D-Lib Magazine* 20, nos. 7/8. doi: 10.1045/july2014-gregory.

Matienzo, Mark A., and Amy Rudersdorf. 2014. "The Digital Public Library of America Ingestion Ecosystem: Lessons Learned After One Year of Large-Scale Collaborative Metadata Aggregation." In *Proceedings of DC-2014: The International Conference on Dublin Core and Metadata Applications,* 12–23. Austin, TX. http://dcevents.dublincore.org/public/dc-docs/2014-Master.pdf.

Schonfeld, Roger C., and Ithaka S+R. 2014. "Does Discovery Still Happen in the Library? Roles and Strategies for a Shifting Reality." Ithaka S+R. www.sr.ithaka.org/sites/default/files/files/SR_Briefing_Discovery_20140924_0.pdf.

CHAPTER SEVENTEEN

OPEN ACCESS AND DISCOVERY TOOLS

How Do Primo Libraries Manage Green Open Access Collections?

FRANÇOIS RENAVILLE

The open access (OA) movement gains more and more momentum, with an increasing number of institutions and funders adopting OA mandates for publicly funded research. Consequently, an increasing amount of research output becomes freely available, either from institutional, multi-institutional, or thematic repositories or from traditional or newly established journals.

As of the beginning of December 2015, there were about 2,980 OA repositories (Green OA) of all kinds listed on OpenDOAR (www.opendoar.org). Scholarly OA repositories contain lots of treasures, including rare or otherwise unpublished materials and articles that scholars self-archive, often as part of their institution's mandate (Harnad et al. 2004). But it can be hard to discover this material unless users know exactly where to look.

Since the very beginning, libraries have played a major role in supporting the OA movement. Next to all services they can provide to support the deposit of research output in the repositories, they can make OA materials widely discoverable by their patrons through general search engines (Google, Bing, etc.), specialized search engines (like Google Scholar), and library discovery tools, thus expanding their collection to include materials that they would not necessarily pay for.

In this chapter, we focus on two aspects regarding Green OA and the Primo discovery tool.

In early 2013 Ex Libris Group started to add institutional repositories into Primo Central Index (PCI), their mega-aggregation of hundreds of millions of scholarly e-resources (journal articles, e-books, reviews, dissertations, legal documents, reports, etc.) (www.exlibrisgroup.com/category/PrimoCentral). PCI is an additional service available to Primo discovery tool customers. It may now be interesting to take stock of the situation of PCI regarding OA institutional repositories.

On the basis of a survey carried out among members of the Primo community, we will see how libraries using the Primo discovery tool integrate Green OA contents in their front end. Two major ways are possible for them. First, they can directly harvest, index, and manage any repository in their Primo instance and display those free materials next to the more traditional library collections. Second, if they are PCI subscribers, they can quickly and easily activate any, if not all, of the institutional OA repositories contained in PCI, thus making the contents of those directly discoverable to their end users. This chapter shows what way is preferred by libraries, if they harvest or not their own repository (even if it is included in PCI), and suggests efforts that Ex Libris could take to improve the visibility and discoverability of OA materials included in the "Institutional Repositories" section of PCI.

SURVEY RESULTS

The survey contained multiple-choice and open questions related to OA local sources and the usage and perception of the "Institutional Repositories" section of PCI. It was posted to the electronic discussion list PRIMO-DIS-CUSS-L in March 2015 and was open from March 16 until April 10, 2015. PRIMO-DISCUSS-L has about 1,500 subscribers, who are typically local Primo administrators or managers. As it was an institutional survey, only one response per institution was expected.

The survey received 34 responses from 15 countries: Australia (2), Austria (1), Belgium (1), Brazil (1), Canada (2), Denmark (1), France (5), Iceland (1), Netherlands (2), New Zealand (1), Norway (1), Sweden (1), Switzerland (3), United Kingdom (5), and United States (7).

HARVESTING OF LOCAL OA COLLECTIONS

Of the 34 respondents, 20 (59 percent) said they harvest a local institutional repository (IR) in their Primo instance, 7 did not, and 7 did not at the moment of the survey, but planned to do so.

Respondents were also asked if all the records they harvest (or plan to) have at least one OA file. Of the 27 concerned respondents, 6 said it is the case and 6 admitted they didn't know. For most of the respondents, not all local records they harvested have an OA file, to varying degrees. However, harvesting few OA contents does not necessarily mean harvesting few records: some large repositories, especially if they also act as an institutional bibliography, may have more OA content than smaller repositories with a higher percentage of OA content.

An institutional bibliography aims to offer a web-based instrument to capture, process, use, and disseminate bibliographic information on the output and ongoing research of a university or research institution. One of its goals is to increase the external and internal visibility of the research done. Of the 27 respondents that harvest or plan to harvest an institutional repository (IR), 15 have admitted that their repository also acts as an institutional bibliography, at least partially for some departments.

Of the 34 respondents, 17 said they also harvest or plan to harvest an additional OA repository in their Primo for their end users. Examples given are various: they may be other selected traditional OA repositories (2 respondents), or OA repositories with contents of research or regional interest, but not necessarily with scholarly research output (e.g., "University's repository of learning objects"; "archival photos, videos of researchers talking about their work, old university publications . . . including Creative Commons licenses for all material"; "digitized manuscripts and rare books, pictures, videos, sound recordings . . . which belong to our institution or to partner institutions within the country and are freely available to all").

Survey participants were also asked if they have defined or intend to define any specific configuration in the Primo Back Office administration for their local OA scholarly materials in order to prominently display their OA institutional research output within the results of the discovery tool. Five methods for achieving this goal were suggested to the respondents:

1. *Boosting.* The Primo discovery tool allows the library to negatively boost records that are not from the institution. In other words, PCI records or records from a partner institution (e.g., in the case of a consortium) may be placed below records of the institution in the Brief Results page. However, this option does not make any distinction between bibliographic records coming from the ILS and records coming from any harvested repository, both sources being local data.

2. *Indexes.* Particular indexes for OA local contents can be created in the Simple or Advanced Search interface.

3. *Display.* Any display configuration like label, logo, or specific information in the Details tab.[1]

4. *Links.* Primo allows the library to display additional links in the full bibliographic record description. In the case of OA content, such links could, for example, lead to the original record, to the full text, to copyright information, and so on.

5. *Facets.* Facets are links in the Brief Results page that allow users to filter their search results by a specific category, such as creator, language, topic or, in this particular case, for institutional OA materials.

Respondents could also enter text into an "other" option.

Figure 17.1 shows the frequency of these 5 responses from the 27 respondents who harvest or plan to harvest a scholarly OA repository. Seven answered that they use boosting options so that local data may be displayed before PCI records. Two will use specific indexes. Five use particular display rules, for example by displaying a Creative Commons license where applicable on the Details tab or by adding a line like "Open Research Online—a research publication from the University" to the Brief Results page. Six use links to promote their OA contents ("The associated OA files appear in the links section of detailed view pages"; "Direct link to the reference via View It + additional link to the reference in the Details tab").[2] Finally, eleven respondents answered that they use facets; two mentioned that they promote their local OA research output with a top-level

FIGURE 17.1 ————————————————————————————————————

Specific configuration to prominently display local OA contents in Primo

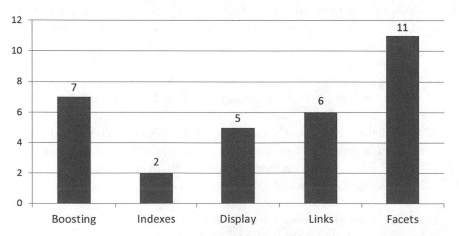

institutional facet.[3] Moreover, one respondent has explained they have created a specific search scope containing part of the contents of their OA repository (theses and dissertations), and one more intends to create an additional scope for their harvested OA research output.

Finally, one respondent intends to combine four of these promoting options (links, facets, display, indexes), two use three of them (boosting, facets and links), and six use or will use a combination of two means.

PRIMO CENTRAL INDEX

Primo Central Index (PCI) is the name for Ex Libris's mega-index of "hundreds of millions of scholarly e-resources of global and regional importance. These include journal articles, e-books, reviews, legal documents and more that are harvested from primary and secondary publishers and aggregators, and from open-access repositories."[4] Those records are mainly provided by publishers (for example, Wiley, Springer, Elsevier, and Thomson/Reuters), which provide the metadata from their publication platforms (Wiley Online Library, Springer-Link, ScienceDirect, Scopus, Web of Science) to PCI, and by aggregators (e.g., ProQuest) and their databases. PCI allows direct access to the metadata but not full texts, which are only available to the customers and their end users if the institution subscribes to that service. Therefore, PCI works in close relationship with link resolvers (like SFX) and makes it possible to display to end users only records for which an access to the full text is available. In addition to publishers' and aggregators' content, Ex Libris has also included in PCI large collections and archives of free scholarly materials, for example ArXiv.org, HAL (Hyper Article en Ligne), OAPEN: Open Access Publishing in European Networks, SwePub, and Norwegian Open Research Archives.

In January 2013 Ex Libris "released a new service for institutional—and open access—repositories [in order to] simplify the process of allowing their content to be indexed in Primo Central" (Ex Libris Group 2013a). This registration service was open to all institutions, not only to Primo customers. The goal was to enable users at Primo institutions to discover more easily such OA materials. The IR registration service was part of a wider Ex Libris initiative to support OA. In addition to adding more OA material to their indexes, Ex Libris also worked on improving access to OA articles in subscription (hybrid) journals (Ex Libris Group 2013a).

Activating collections in PCI is a very easy task. A widget displays all the available collections, sorted by publisher, with brief descriptive information related to the update frequency and the day the resource was included in PCI. Some collections are restricted for search and delivery: they may only be activated by the customer if the institution has a valid subscription at the original provider (e.g., *Scopus* [Elsevier], *Web of Science* [Thomson/Reuters], *MLA Institutional Bibliography* [MLA], ProQuest databases [ProQuest], *L'Année Philologique* [Société Internationale de Bibliographie Classique], *GeoRef* [American Geosciences Institute]).

INSTITUTIONAL REPOSITORIES IN PCI

Following the release of the registration service, the first IRs were integrated and available to PCI subscribers in March 2013. More than two years later, at the beginning of December 2015, seventy-five IRs were integrated in PCI.

As figure 17.2 shows, the number of IRs has mainly increased from spring to autumn in 2013 and 2014 while it stagnated at the end and the beginning of the year. Only five repositories were added in 2015. Two years after the new registration service was launched, the service link is surprisingly not available anymore and has disappeared from the Ex Libris website.[5]

The 75 IRs come from 20 countries: United Kingdom (17), United States (14), Spain (7), Germany (6), Australia (4), Canada (4), Belgium (3), Netherlands (3), Norway (3), Czech Republic (2), Peru (2), Switzerland (2), Austria (1), Brazil (1), Chili (1), Ireland (1), Italy (1), New Zealand (1), Sweden (1), and Taiwan (1).

FIGURE 17.2 ──

Growth of institutional repositories in PCI (from March 2013 to November 2015)

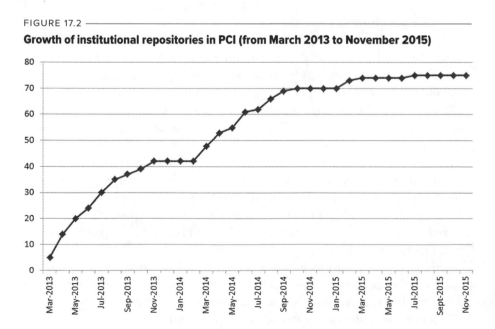

RESOURCE TYPE AND NUMBER OF RECORDS

PCI aggregates various sources with various contents.[6] Therefore, all original resource types from the IR are mapped by Ex Libris with one of the twenty-three PCI resource types:

- Article
- Audio
- Book
- Book Chapter
- Conference Proceeding (includes proceedings volumes as well as individual papers)
- Database
- Dissertation (PhD and master thesis)
- Government Document (publications issued by government agencies, including patents, excludes court opinions, case briefs, etc.)
- Image
- Journal (includes journal issues)
- Legal Document (court opinions, case briefs, etc.)
- Map
- Newspaper Article
- Reference Entry (individual entries in dictionaries, encyclopedias)
- Research Dataset (raw data produced as the output of research)
- Review (book, product, film reviews)
- Score
- Statistical Data Set (tables, graphs containing statistics)
- Technical Report
- Text Resource (unclassifiable textual sources)
- Video
- Website
- Other (unclassifiable non-textual sources)

For library administrators in charge of Primo, successfully managing those resource types in relation with their local data is not always an easy task (Koster 2012).

Among those resource types, "Text Resource" is a particular one. Ex Libris relies on the metadata given to them by the provider. Some providers supply appropriate resource types like "article" or "book chapter" while some providers simply state that the resources are "text." Therefore, depending on the quality of the provided metadata, many books, articles, reports, reviews, and so on may be hidden behind a generic and unclear "Text Resource" which represents 29 percent of all materials coming from IRs (n = 400,316). As of March 31, 2015, dissertations represent 27.6 percent (n = 381,222) of the whole content coming from IRs in PCI, articles 25.2 percent (n = 348,102), images 7.4 percent (n = 102,358), and conference proceedings 3.6 percent (n = 49,487).

After text resources, dissertations and articles are the most two frequent materials provided by IRs. In some cases, those contents represent the entire harvested content of repositories (tables 17.1 and 17.2).

As of March 31, 2015, PCI contained more than 1,600,000 records coming from IRs. According to Ex Libris policy, all those included records should provide access to an OA full text. The rule is that "only content which is 100% Open Access should be included in the Institutional Repositories collections" (Ex Libris Group 2014). In the case a repository is not fully OA (e.g., in case of an institutional bibliography) it is possible to ingest only the records which contain specific values in an OA tag so that "only records which include links to unrestricted Full Text or to a publisher's landing page where unrestricted Full Text is available" (Ex Libris Group 2014) are indexed in PCI.

However, experience and remarks from survey participants (see below) have revealed this was far from the case. It should also be emphasized that at the very beginning candidate repositories were not required to be entirely OA, or that metadata must include clear, consistent OA indicators. The very

TABLE 17.1 ──

Top 10 institutional repositories in PCI—dissertations (March 31, 2015)

Institutional Repositories	Dissertations	% of the Harvested IR Content
DiVA—Academic Archive Online (Uppsala University Library)	138,761	76.1%
ETDs Repository (VŠKP—University of Economics, Prague)	37,757	99.6%
BRAGE (BIBSYS)	33,836	45.1%
National Chung Hsing University Institutional Repository (National Chung Hsing University, Taiwan)	28,168	41.9%
ThinkTech (Texas Tech University)	17,622	90.7%
Dokumentenserver der FU Berlin (Freie Universität Berlin)	10,587	100.0%
Digital Dissertations (Universitätsbibliothek der LMU München)	10,497	100.0%
Digital Library of the University of Pardubice	8,399	80.7%
Diposit Digital de Documents de la UAB (Universitat Autonoma de Barcelona)	6,771	11.5%
RiuNet (Universitat Politècnica de València)	6,500	24.0%

TABLE 17.2

Top 10 institutional repositories in PCI—articles (March 31, 2015)

Institutional Repositories	Articles	% of the Harvested IR Content
Repository Utrecht University	38,717	57.9%
Infoscience (École Polytechnique Fédérale de Lausanne [EPFL])	30,762	100.0%
Diposit Digital de Documents de la UAB (Universitat Autonoma de Barcelona)	21,189	36.1%
ORBi (Open Repository and Bibliography) (University of Liège)	19,665	49.2%
ZORA (University of Zurich)	19,152	70.6%
National Chung Hsing University Institutional Repository (National Chung Hsing University, Taiwan)	17,499	26.0%
VU-DARE (VU University Amsterdam)	16,271	66.8%
DiVA—Academic Archive Online (Uppsala University Library)	15,431	8.5%
Digital Access to Scholarship at Harvard (DASH) (Harvard University, Office for Scholarly Communication)	15,076	80.9%
Lirias (KU Leuven Association)	12,736	49.0%

first prerequisites for submitting an IR for inclusion in PCI (Ex Libris Group 2013b) were indeed:

- "Content should be of scholarly interest
- Content should contain sufficient metadata using standard formats such as Dublin Core or MODS
- Initially we will be focusing on OAI-PMH as the harvesting method"

These soft and very basic requirements from the beginning may partially explain why some content provided by repositories may be without any OA file.

USAGE AND PERCEPTION OF PCI

Institutions that have an institutional repository whose content is harvested in PCI *and* also subscribe to the PCI service may choose to directly harvest and index in their Primo instance or to activate their own repository in the Primo administrative interface.[7] When activating one's own repository via PCI, the institution benefits from automatic weekly updates. New OA content coming from the repository is added in PCI and made available via the institution's Primo. On the other side, directly harvesting its own repository allows more flexibility, but requires more investment from the library staff. For example, specific configuration in order to prominently display local OA contents in Primo is possible (see above). The institution also has the possibility to include repository items with restricted access (campus only) and to make them searchable via Primo for end users, and more frequent updates can be scheduled. On the other hand, that flexibility requires local Primo administrators to carry on and monitor the whole harvesting and indexing process.

All survey participants (34) belong to an institution that subscribes to PCI. Of these, 18 include their own institutional OA materials in PCI; for 14 of them, the local IR is directly harvested by PCI. In the 4 other cases, even if the IRs are not directly harvested in PCI, they are actually *indirectly* harvested since their OA materials are harvested by another resource such as a national scholarly repository, which is then harvested by PCI. For 10 respondents, the OA repository is not yet included in PCI; 2 of them already requested Ex Libris to add it. The last 6 respondents have no institutional repository that is harvested by PCI at the time of the survey.

The survey aimed to determine whether libraries whose IR is harvested by PCI prefer to activate it in their PCI administrative interface and by doing so effortlessly get their own OA materials available in Primo or if they prefer instead to harvest their IR. This second option requires some additional work for Primo administrators, but it allows more flexibility and more frequent harvesting and indexing of new and updated records archived in the repository and the possibility of putting forward local OA materials (boosting, specific indexes, particular facets, scopes).

Table 17.3 shows that of the 14 respondents whose IR is harvested by PCI, 7 have not activated it in PCI, while 7 have. Surprisingly, of the 7 that have activated their IR in PCI, 5 also directly harvest their local IR in their own Primo. Of the 7 that have not activated their own IR PCI, 6 directly harvest it and one does not.

TABLE 17.3 ————————————————————————————————————

Repository in PCI: activated or not? Directly harvested or not?

	Activated in PCI	Not Activated in PCI
Directly harvested	5	6
Not harvested	2	1
Total	7	7

One respondent also explained they activated their IR in PCI, but only for a brief testing period. They considered that information presented in Primo via PCI was not good enough and regretted that "all resources were considered available" while their "default configuration of Primo is set to display available resources only."[8] Another respondent (a PCI subscriber whose IR is not included in PCI) noticed a similar defect, arguing that "PCI cannot differentiate between no [OA] full text and [OA] full text records." According to Ex Libris's basic requirements (see above), this should not occur.

Of the 34 PCI subscribers, 19 (56 percent) admitted that they decided not to activate some IRs included in PCI or to deactivate others. The reasons they gave are closely related to the potentially negative effect that those unwanted collections could have on their users. Seven respondents (21 percent) explained that for some collections there is not always an OA full text available and that full text—if there is any—is only available after logging in on the original platform (restricted access):

▸ "They were causing errors in Primo search results, such as showing up as available, until you tried to access them and then you get a 'no full text available' message or it turns out to be just a record with no full text."
▸ "When it appears that a record is only accessible when logged in, we deactivate the collection. This happens quite regularly."

The second most frequent reason, given by 5 respondents (15 percent), is that some IRs might be deactivated if their content is considered to be not relevant or out of scope for the end users:

▸ "To prevent from noise, lack of interest for some contents."
▸ "Some repositories which do not content real scholarly production—like images related to the history of a particular institution—or whose content is for a very local usage, and of very few interest for our users."

Two respondents mentioned both reasons.

Survey participants were also asked if they applied a specific selection policy before activating new resources added to the PCI "Institutional Repositories" section (table 17.4). Four main policies (direct activation, analysis based on the content, on the availability of open access content, and on the metadata quality) and their combinations were proposed.

While 21 percent of respondents complained that there is not systematic OA content in records from IRs—and this in contradiction with Ex Libris's policy—that same percentage is reflected in the selection workflow that libraries have set up. Surprisingly, more than one in five respondents concede that they rarely

TABLE 17.4

Specific selection policy before activating new IRs in PCI

Selection Policy	Number	Percentage
(a) We usually directly activate any new repository in the Production environment (or in both Staging and Production environments) (no checking).	10	29%
(b) We first activate new repositories in the Staging environment, and activate in the Production environment after we have controlled that its content is appropriate for us (discipline-oriented).	1	3%
(c) We first activate new repositories in the Staging environment, and activate in the Production environment after we have controlled that its content is (mainly) in Open Access.	0	0%
(d) We first activate new repositories in the Staging environment, and activate in the Production environment after we have controlled that metadata are good enough.	0	0%
Combination: (b) + (c)	3	9%
Combination: (b) + (d)	1	3%
Combination: (c) + (d)	2	6%
Combination: (b) + (c) + (d)	2	6%
(e) We rarely or never activate resources from the "Institutional Repositories" section.	7	21%
(f) Other workflow	8	24%
Total	**34**	**100%**

or never activate resources from the "Institutional Repositories" section. Two respondents explain that they had not considered such OA collections carefully yet and that it is a project that is under way, in conjunction with an analysis and revision of their entire collection of subscriptions (periodicals and databases). Another argues that library policy prevents activating those collections, while a second explains that they "have an ongoing debate on displaying OA resources in [their] discovery system." Finally, one last respondent explains it is a content and access issue ("Content often not relevant to our specialist institution. Percentage of OA material would also need testing—don't want something coming up as full text access and then users clicking through and finding it's not full text after all").

Among those who have another workflow, one respondent explains they have set up an internal decision-making process, in association with other librarians, since in their opinion the Primo administrator should not be alone in activation decision. For another, they directly activate in their production environment any new repository that has appropriate content, without checking on the staging server before. Finally, one respondent specifies that since they are part of a consortium, their PCI is centrally managed by the consortium office.

Among the respondents who regularly activate OA resources in PCI's "Institutional Repositories" section, five do not see any repository that should be removed from PCI. On the other hand, five respondents are not against that possibility. The reason that is put forward by four of them is related to those IRs whose harvested results do not always contain an OA file:

> "Some resources have too many false-positives (online access without any full text). It is frustrating to the users and gives us a lot of error reports to handle manually."

> "That IR section should only contain repositories that provide 100% OA content to Ex Libris. Unfortunately, it is not always the case and it is terribly frustrating for the end-users."

> "If there is no link to full test from the 'view it' tab, it frustrates our users, or if there is no full text available at all. We might consider de-activating if we get recurrent complaints."

> "All of those which require an institutional log-in."

Survey participants were also asked to give their opinion about the necessary efforts that Ex Libris should make to improve the "Institutional Repositories" section of PCI. Seventeen respondents made different suggestions which can be spread into six categories. Many enhancement requests concern repository records where OA availability is incorrectly indicated (false positives) and that should normally not be made available through PCI:

1. Providing *only OA contents* in the "Institutional Repositories" section or at least making more checks for the availability of full text (systematic monitoring), so that libraries can be sure they will activate only the repositories which have at least one OA file attached (pointed out eight times).

2. Providing *more detailed information* about each OA repository for local PCI administrators (number of records, percentage of eventual non-OA entries [*sic*], types of documents, disciplines . . .) (pointed out three times).

3. Adding *more OA contents* (by improving the awareness within the international academic community about the existence of harvesting activity repositories by Ex Libris, by adding more available free resources such as national library collections, and special governmental collections) (pointed out three times).

4. Requiring OA content providers to provide *good metadata quality* and to adhere to OA indicator standards (for example as defined by a standards body like NISO) (pointed out twice) (NISO 2014).

5. Establishing a *better collaboration* between Ex Libris and the host of the metadata to ensure that the content can quickly and correctly be integrated into PCI (for example, the final result could be approved by the metadata provider before the new OA repository is available in PCI for other customers) (pointed out twice).

6. Allowing richer and more extended *record formats* for harvesting purposes (DIDL, MODS . . .) (pointed out twice).

When asked about the general efforts that could be deployed to bring together OA content so that it is not so laborious to add and make it easily and quickly visible for end users, five respondents suggested improving the way OA collections are displayed in the front end. Respondents suggested the use of consistent facets for OA content or specific OA flags (for example, in the Brief Results) like the <free_to_read> XML element "to indicate that content can be read or viewed at its current location by any user without payment or authentication" (NISO 2015). Improvement can also be made in the back-end interface by getting more information about the various collections which are regularly added in PCI (e.g., number of records, types of documents included, thematic coverage, etc.) so it becomes easier for local Primo administrators to determine which collections should be activated or not. Those expectations are confirmed by a recent survey (Bulock, Hosburgh, and Sanjeet 2015):

> Another common theme . . . involved frustration with inaccurate information in OA management systems affecting patron discovery and staff workflows.
>
> Hosburgh noted that databases and discovery services often include facets designed to limit result sets to OA items. Librarians praised knowledge bases for helping them provide more OA resources, and appreciated link resolvers that clearly labeled OA items as "FREE" on the result screen.

One respondent suggested the possibility of choosing a rank of boosting (of results) for each resource, and not only for local contents vs. PCI records. One respondent also pointed out that smart grouping of records is "very important, and even more for green OA where different versions of the same document can be offered from various sources (publisher platform, one or more institutional repository/ies or subject repository . . .) with varying metadata quality."[9] Finally, two respondents also recommended that Ex Libris harvest first and foremost national or global repositories instead of smaller repositories with less content.

CONCLUSIONS

The survey shows that most of the respondents (59 percent) harvest a local institutional OA repository in their Primo instance. Several have defined specific configurations in their Primo in order to put forward their institutional OA research output within the results of the discovery tool; facets and boosting local data being the two most popular ways. All survey participants belong to an institution that subscribes to PCI, and for fourteen of them their local IR is directly harvested by PCI. Some respondents have admitted that in addition to directly harvesting their repository they have also activated their own IR in PCI.

All survey participants are also PCI subscribers. Fifty-six percent of them admitted that there are in PCI some IRs they decided not to activate, or to deactivate. The two main reasons are related to potential negative effects that those collections could have on their end users: materials of some IRs are considered to be not relevant for the end users and, for some IRs collections, there is not always an OA full text available, contrary to what Ex Libris requires from repository content providers. One in five respondents confessed they always check the availability of announced OA contents before activating them in the production environment.

In terms of number of records, the "Institutional Repositories" section of PCI *theoretically* allows subscribers to display more than 1,600,000 OA records, of which about half are clearly identified as scholarly articles or dissertations. Even if 21 percent of the respondents concede they rarely or never activate resources from the "Institutional Repositories" section in PCI, many participants stress that improvement is necessary for those materials, notably by providing *only* OA contents in the "Institutional Repositories" section, by providing more detailed information about each OA repository, and by adding more OA repositories. Improving the way OA collections are displayed in the front end is also encouraged. By improving *quality* and *quantity* of the "Institutional Repositories" section in PCI, Ex Libris can certainly hope to gain gratitude from its customers.

Notes

1. In Primo, the Details tab displays the item's full record and additional links.
2. In Primo, the View Online Tab (or View It) displays items that are available online inside the tab.
3. In Primo, top-level facets are static facets that display in the "Show only" section (first section above) of the Brief Results page. Unlike other kinds of facets, top-level facets always display even if there is only one matched record in the category.
4. Ex Libris Group, Primo Central Index, www.exlibrisgroup.com/category/PrimoCentral.
5. However, the service page can be found with the help of the Internet Archive's Wayback Machine (http://web.archive.org/web/20130509051917/http://dc02vg0047nr.hosted .exlibrisgroup.com:8080/IRWizard/wizard.html).
6. See details in Appendix.
7. Theoretically, they can also do both: activating their IR in PCI for OA contents and directly harvesting records with no OA full text, but this is additional work and may display duplicates in the front end.
8. However, this is configurable in the Primo administrative interface with a slight adaptation of the Real-Time Availability (RTA) rules. By default, the RTA feature allows Primo sites to get real-time availability statuses for physical items directly from the source system, but local Primo administrators can also use them to display a particular availability text for repository records with no OA full text.
9. In PCI, grouping is based on an existing FRBR workflow that is used to prevent duplicate records in the results list. In the Primo front end, the system displays the preferred record in the brief results list. Preference is always given to the original publisher's record over an aggregator record, a pre-print or a record coming from an institutional repository. Users can easily access to additional versions by clicking the "View all versions" link.

References

Bulock, C., N. Hosburgh, and M. Sanjeet. 2015. "OA in the Library Collection: The Challenges of Identifying and Maintaining Open Access Resources." *The Serials Librarian: From the Printed Page to the Digital Age* 68, nos. 1–4: 79–86. doi: 10.1080/0361526X.2015.1023690.

Ex Libris Group. 2013a. January 31. "Institutional Repositories in Primo Central: Registration Is Now Open." (Blog post). http://initiatives.exlibrisgroup.com/2013/01/institutional -repositories-in-primo.html.

———. 2013b. "Institutional Repositories Registration." http://web.archive.org/ web/20130509051917/http://dc02vg0047nr.hosted.exlibrisgroup.com:8080/IRWizard/ wizard.html [Capture from May 9th, 2013, by Wayback Machine].

———. 2014. "Institutional Repository Submission Requirements."

Harnad, S., T. Brody, F. Vallières, L. Carr, S. Hitchcock, Y. Gingras, C. Oppenheim, H. Stamerjohanns, and E. Hilf. 2004. "The Access/Impact Problem and the Green and Gold Roads to Open Access." *Serials Review* 30, no. 4: 310–14. doi: 10.1016/j.serrev.2004.09.013.

Koster, L. 2012. "Wizards and Tables or How the Primo Back Office Could Work Better."
    Paper presented at IGeLu 2012 Zurich. http://igelu.org/wp-content/uploads/2012/09/
    Wizards-and-Tables_Koster.ppsx.
NISO. 2014. "Open Discovery Initiative: Promoting Transparency in Discovery." www.niso
    .org/apps/group_public/download.php/14821/rp-19–2014_ODI.pdf.
———. 2015. "Access License and Indicators. A Recommended Practice of the National
    Information Standards Organization." www.niso.org/apps/group_public/download
    .php/14226/rp-22–2015_ALI.pdf.

APPENDIX

The number of records per resource type was retrieved from a Primo instance where all IRs had been activated at least two weeks earlier in Primo Central Index. It was not possible to get any results for "Digital Repository @ Iowa State University (Iowa State University)" and "eScholarship (University of California, California Digital Library)." Therefore, the following table contains results for seventy-two repositories. Only the results for the nine most common resource types (article, book, conference proceeding, dissertation, image, map, review, text resource, and video) are presented; all other resource types (database, journal, legal document, newspaper article, reference entry, research dataset score, technical report, statistical data set, website, and other) have been grouped into one general category (all others).

Searches were made in two steps on March 31, 2015. First, for each repository, meaningful keywords were used to retrieve a maximum number of potential records:

- "Utrecht" to search for "Repository Utrecht University"
- "Leeds University" to search for "Leeds Met Open Search (Leeds Metropolitan University)"
- "London School of Economics" to search for "LSE Research Online (London School of Economics and Political Science)" and "LSE Theses Online (London School of Economics and Political Science)."

Secondly, collection facets were used to retain only records coming from the IRs. It was not possible to use facet filtering for four repositories:

- Manchester eScholar (Manchester University)
- Opus: Online Publications Store (University of Bath)
- ETDs Repository (VŠKP—University of Economics, Prague)
- Dokumentenserver der FU Berlin (Freie Universitat Berlin)

However, with the used search terms ("Manchester eScholar," "Online Publications Store" AND "University of Bath," "VŠKP," and "Dokumentenserver der FU Berlin") and their results, there was no room for uncertainty.

In some cases, the total number of records is lower than the sum of all resource types. The reason is that when multiple records from different sources (IRs or not), with a different resource type, are FRBRized, facets take the different values into account (for instance, if an item that is an article is grouped with an item which is a review, both of them will have both facet values).

Institutional Repositories	Total number of records	Number of records per resource type									
		article	book	conference proceeding	disser-tation	image	map	review	text resource	video	all others
ARAN (National University of Ireland Galway)	3,331	1,262	155	506	720	1	0	36	481	0	894
Bergen Open Research Archive (University of Bergen)	7,578	1,892	52	101	5,303	1	0	11	401	4	0
BRAGE (BIBSYS)	75,026	6,842	1,075	492	33,836	14	2	7	22,788	63	4
CERES (Cranfield Collection of E-Research) (Cranfield University)	445	400	0	28	0	0	0	10	7	0	1,210
Constellation (Université du Québec à Chicoutimi)	2,436	137	106	21	2,015	0	0	67	88	0	848
Die digitale Landesbibliothek Oberösterreich (Upper Austrian Federal State Library)	3,515	3,515	0	0	0	0	0	0	0	0	0
Digital Access to Scholarship at Harvard (DASH) (Harvard University, Office for Scholarly Communication)	18,629	15,076	525	780	1,715	0	0	186	2,440	0	255
Digital Commons @ SPU (Seattle Pacific University)	3,017	0	0		0	124	0	0	2,222	671	2,155

Institutional Repositories	Total number of records	Number of records per resource type									
		article	book	conference proceeding	dissertation	image	map	review	text resource	video	all others
Digital Dissertations (Universitätsbibliothek der LMU Muenchen)	10,497	0	0	0	10,497	0	0	0	0	0	74
Digital Library of the University of Pardubice	10,412	1,451	21	522	8,399	0	0	0	23	0	5
DigitalCommons@McMaster (McMaster University Library)	13,310	12,231									44
Digitale Sammlungen (Universitätsbibliothek Paderborn)	3,191	639	1,632	0	867	0	0	0	24	0	0
Diposit Digital de Documents de la UAB (Universitat Autonoma de Barcelona)	58,675	21,189	571	397	6,771	0	0	0	16,756	0	0
Diposit Digital de la Universitat de Barcelona	16,462	7,219	272	40	5,444	189	0	16	2,955	48	0
DiscoverArchive (Vanderbilt University)	6,241	815	137	0	323	138	5	6	1,063	2,287	0
DiVA—Academic Archive Online (Uppsala University Library)	182,337	15,431	5,624	6,984	138,761	0	0	1,508	12,864	0	892
Dokumentenserver der FU Berlin (Freie Universität Berlin)	10,587	0	0	0	10,587	0	0	0	0	0	345
DSpace@ Cambridge (University of Cambridge)	188,334	229	7	2	17	5,223	2	0	6,823	0	9,932
DUGiDocs (Universitat de Girona)	8,402	4,429	101	0	1,839	0	0	0	2,033	0	3,474

| Institutional Repositories | Total number of records | Number of records per resource type ||||||||||
		article	book	conference proceeding	disser-tation	image	map	review	text resource	video	all others
DUGiFonsEspe-cials (Universitat de Girona)	720	720	0	0	0	0	0	0	0	0	65
DUGiMedia (Universitat de Girona)	2,789	0	0	0	0	0	0	0	0	2,789	7
Edinburgh Research Archive (University of Edinburgh)	5,524	212	257	46	4,930	1	0	0	68	0	0
ELEA (Universita Degli Studi di Salerno)	1,043	133	0	1	472	0	0	0	513	0	967
espace @ Curtin (Curtin University of Technology)	16,610	6,131	1,089	4	1,952	0	0	0	3,960	0	0
ETDs Repository (VŠKP—University of Economics, Prague)	37,923	166	0	1	37,757	0	0	0	0	0	11
Fraunhofer ePrints (Fraunhofer Gesellschaft)	12,884	1,742	578	4,734	744	0	0	0	4,743	1	0
Ghent University Academic Bibliography (Ghent University)	22,623	10,409	950	7,638	2,034	0	0	81	2,048	0	25
Infoscience (École Polytechnique Fédérale de Lausanne (EPFL))	30,762	30,762	0	0	0	0	0	0	0	0	4,164
Iowa Research Online (University of Iowa Libraries)	16,303	1,590	188	65	2,393	34	0	57	12,037	256	24
Kent Academic Repository (University of Kent)	4,270	2,045	387	0	75	6	0	38	1,695	0	0
Leeds Met Open Search (Leeds Metropolitan University)	3,546	1,694	611	122	12	15	0	13	1,113	0	342

Institutional Repositories	Total number of records	Number of records per resource type									
		article	book	conference proceeding	disser- tation	image	map	review	text resource	video	all others
Leiden University Repository	14,675	8,638	1,677	76	2,574	0	0	157	661	0	8
Lirias (KU Leuven Association)	26,011	12,736	1,753	5,467	1,309	7	0	410	4,323	1	866
Loughborough University Institutional Repository	8,008	4,866	157	824	592	3	0	23	786	25	0
LSE Learning Resources Online (London School of Economics and Political Science)	152	152	0	0	0	0	0	0	0	0	170
LSE Research Online (London School of Economics and Political Science)	12,044	2,615	4,880	374	8	0	0	0	4	0	7
LSE Theses Online (London School of Economics and Political Science)	969	0	0	0	969	0	0	0	0	0	1,467
LSHTM Research Online (London School of Hygiene and Tropical Medicine)	6,208	5,636	8	44	368	0	0	69	323	11	0
MADOC Publikationsserver (Mannheim University Library)	4,037	137	32	86	551	0	0	115	3,118	0	29
Manchester eScholar (Manchester University)	5,891	3,764	114	948	735	0	0	0	318	1	0
National Chung Hsing University Institutional Repository (National Chung Hsing University, Taiwan)	67,245	17,499	117	729	28,168	0	0	0	20,733	0	0

Institutional Repositories	Total number of records	Number of records per resource type									
		article	book	conference proceeding	disser-tation	image	map	review	text resource	video	all others
Open Access LMU (Universi-tätsbibliothek der LMU München)	18,547	9,152	2,258	1,073	295	0	0	0	5,769	0	169
Opus: Online Publications Store (University of Bath)	4,834	2,711	304	430	945	0	0	0	419	0	1,408
ORBi (Open Repository and Bibliography) (University of Liège)	39,981	19,665	2,470	10,449	1,084	0	47	592	4,474	0	0
OUR@oakland (Oakland University)	3,185	0	28	0	36	4	0	0	162	48	0
Portal de Revistas PUCP (Pontificia Universidad Catolica del Peru)	10,179	10,179	0	0	0	0	0	0	0	0	103
PUCRS Institutional Repository (Pon-tifical Catholic University of Rio Grande do Sul)	5,759	1	0	0	1	0	0	0	5,757	0	4
Repositori Digital de la UPF (Universitat Pompeu Fabra)	4,208	373	18	79	280	0	0	4	2,081	0	176,032
Repositorio Digital de Tesis PUCP (Pontificia Universidad Catolica del Peru)	2,847	0	0	0	2,847	0	0	0	0	0·	0
Repository Utrecht Uni-versity	66,879	38,717	8,165	972	5,299	0	725	6,469	5,638	0	0
Research Re-pository (RMIT University)	3,124	634	46	438	1,996	0	0	0	10	0	0
RiuNet (Univer-sitat Politècnica de València)	27,036	5,215	211	534	6,500	0	5	29	14,623	0	2

Institutional Repositories	Total number of records	Number of records per resource type									
		article	book	conference proceeding	disser-tation	image	map	review	text resource	video	all others
ROAR (University of East London Repository)	2,383	910	200	464	681	0	0	4	141	5	0
Scholar Commons (University of South Florida)	17,264	0	0	0	0	0	0	0	17,264	0	0
ScholarWorks @ UVM (University of Vermont)	863	0	0	0	0	0	0	0	863	0	0
SDEIR (Université du Québec à Chicoutimi)	600	0	0	0	0	0	12	0	212	0	81
SHAREOK Repository (University of Oklahoma/ Oklahoma State University)	13,776	45	17	0	6,493	0	0	0	7,221	0	0
Swinburne ImageBank (Swinburne University of Technology)	3,322	0	0	0	0	3,281	0	0	29	12	0
Sydney eScholarship Repository (University of Sydney)	5,118	0	40	0	3,371	4	0	0	1,607	22	0
TEORA (Telemark University College)	1,093	282	9	0	237	2	0	0	559	0	0
The Portal to Texas History (University of North Texas)	281,388	0	0	0	0	85,342	15,276	0	180,678	92	74
ThinkTech (Texas Tech University)	19,430	570	2	1	17,622	164	8	0	880	15	0
UBIRA ePapers (University of Birmingham)	1,138	35	300	0	0	463	0	0	258	1	0
UBIRA eTheses (University of Birmingham)	4,397	0	0	0	4,397	0	0	0	0	0	0
UCL Discovery (University College London)	19,899	12,484	495	1,444	3,913	0	0	1	1,524	0	2,907

Institutional Repositories	Total number of records	Number of records per resource type									
		article	book	conference proceeding	disser-tation	image	map	review	text resource	video	all others
Unitec Research Bank (Unitec Institute of Technology)	1,344	330	0	178	607	0	0	1	128	0	0
University of Guelph Theses and Dissertations	1,928	0	0	0	1,928	0	0	0	0	0	0
UNT Digital Library (University of North Texas)	57,511	556	1,115	2	5,455	7,342	26,451	18	14,883	286	0
VCU Scholars Compass (Virginia Commonwealth University)	758	623	15	23	0	0	0	1	96	0	0
VU-DARE (VU University Amsterdam)	24,373	16,271	786	1	3,006	0	0	227	3,827	0	376
White Rose Research Online (White Rose University Consortium)	8,091	5,793	1,568	661	0	0	0	0	12	0	0
ZORA (University of Zurich)	27,146	19,152	247	1,706	1,492	0	0	4	3,790	0	0
TOTAL	**1,601,063**	**348,102**	**41,370**	**49,487**	**381,222**	**102,358**	**42,533**	**10,160**	**400,316**	**6,638**	**209,440**

CHAPTER EIGHTEEN

DISCOVERY PLATFORMS AND THE DATABASE OF RECORD

ALAN MANIFOLD

The limitations of traditional online public access catalogs (OPACs) brought such frustration to library automation mavens that they finally gave up on improving them and came up with a way to replace them (Tennant 2006, 30). This is the origin story of discovery platforms, whose design principle "involves the separation of resource management from resource discovery" (Breeding 2010, 31–32). This separation makes possible the inclusion of data from multiple systems including "bibliographic records, digital collection materials, and items within institutional repositories, and provides a common interface for discovery of these materials," breaking down what used to be rigid barriers between records for different types of materials (Vaughan 2011, 39).

These innovations contribute to a new challenge for libraries and their staff: "the waning fortunes of the ILS" and the consequent crumbling of the primacy of the database at the heart of the integrated library system (ILS), which has served as a de facto database of record for the library (Caplan 2012, 114). The concept of a database of record is that, whenever there are multiple places where data is stored, one of those places is the final and indisputable reference for the current and correct value of a given piece of information. If these locations are out of sync, it is the one to be believed. The notion of a database of record must be considered as we move forward with discovery systems.

EARLY LIBRARY APPS

The first library systems "involved widespread experimentation which helped to train the first generation of practitioners" (Groenewegen 2004, 39). Access to computers was new, but pioneering libraries began to take some of the most routine tasks and create programs that would streamline those tasks. De Gennaro (1968) mentions the automation of "various housekeeping functions such as circulation, ordering and accounting, catalog input, and card production" (76). These experiments encouraged libraries to continue dabbling and even chancing larger and more complex systems.

Due to limitations in computer capacity, the data included could be extremely abbreviated. For one early serials list, "each journal issue was contained on a single card that included a 5-digit identification number, a code indicating whether the title was indexed in *Index Medicus,* an abbreviated title, subscription price, a source code, current volume number, current issue number, publication frequency, number of issues in a volume, and subject code" (Peay and Schoening 2008, 264). Auld (1968) recounts a story about Oakland University's book order application, which had to undergo a basic design change after just three months due to lack of disk space (94).

Because storage space was so limited and data sharing was difficult, these small stand-alone systems typically managed their own data. Circulation, order tracking, and serials management programs might each store a different version of an item's title separately. Changing the title in one system would have no effect on it in another. The card catalog continued to serve as the database of record for most bibliographic information.

EMERGENCE OF THE ILS

As reliance on computer systems grew, frustration began to arise from this situation. Data was entered into one system to order a book, but when it was received, its information had to be entered on catalog cards and in three or four other systems. Receiving the latest issue of a serial might have been relatively simple, but subscribing to a new serial could involve mountains of work. It was virtually impossible to keep the data consistent everywhere.

Early systems required off-line (i.e., batch) data entry and updating. At Purdue University, our Library Systems Department employed three keypunch operators who created the cards necessary to input new serials issues received for our "Library—Other—SERials" program or "LOSER." Updates were run each night on a schedule. Later, the availability of CRT terminals simplified data input, but updating was still done by overnight batch processing. The year 1981 saw the implementation of "holdup," our program to update MARC holdings in real time. The process was not only vastly more efficient, it also meant that data changes were available immediately.

As the capability of computers expanded, it was possible for multiple programs to share data more easily. The consolidation of automated systems culminated in the creation of integrated library systems, which "enabled libraries to create bibliographic records at the time of ordering materials and to augment them with data needed for acquisitions, accounting, and cataloging" (Borgman 1997, 222). The record that Acquisitions staff entered to order an item was finalized by Cataloging, then used to track circulation. Most information was only entered and stored once, which made out-of-sync data impossible.

Having reusable data made possible the creation of OPACs. Borgman (1997) wrote, "by combining circulation, acquisitions, and cataloging data, integrated systems changed the nature of the catalog from a record of materials owned to a database indicating what is owned, available, and on order" (223). The data was there just waiting to be reused, so an additional module could be developed that would pick out the data the library wanted to display to the public, reformat it so it was readable by nonlibrarians, and open it up to public use. An update in cataloguing or circulation status would immediately be reflected to the patron.

ESTABLISHMENT OF A SINGLE DATABASE OF RECORD

Having all of the data for the library system in a single database gave the ILS database an important stamp of authority. Retrospective conversion immediately became a very high priority because "there was concern that catalogue users would overlook one or other catalogue and not find the material they were looking for" (Bowman 2007, 332). Having an OPAC for the public and a single, reliable data store for staff was enough to allow libraries to close their card catalogs.

It is essential for all data that there is a "single version of truth":

> Companies often tend to end up with a hodgepodge of databases, many of them containing the same or similar data, such as names and addresses. The value of a data object may not necessarily be the same in the different databases. For instance, a customer may have moved; and the new address may have been put in one database but not in another. . . . In this case, there is only one "version of the truth"; and this database is known as the database of record. Having a database of record is . . . necessary for correct operations and good customer relations. (Highleyman, Holenstein, and Holenstein 2008)

Early automated systems abounded in duplicated data, often with no connections between the various instances of a piece of data. In this context, the ILS was an answer to prayer, as "many things became possible, including library systems that aggregated a number of different functions, now called modules, around a single, shared MARC database" (Caplan 2012, 113). Potter (1989) mentions "the unifying function of the catalog, the ability to locate any item from a single source" (107). There was a new standard, "centered on an integrated library system, including an online catalog for search and patron services related to lending such as viewing checkouts and renewals, placing holds, or paying fines" (Breeding 2011, 28). Libraries had agreed on their database of record.

DISCOVERY PLATFORMS

The first step in the evolution from the OPAC to present-day discovery platforms was what are often called next-generation catalogs or OPAC 2.0 interfaces. These were not so much new products as additions to the OPAC functions of an ILS. Vendors developed "next-generation catalogs with many features and cues understood and expected by today's researchers, such as faceted navigation, tag clouds, and Web 2.0 social features" (Vaughan 2011c, 6). The first big step forward was the inclusion of relevancy ranking, although the ranking algorithms were not highly refined.

These variations on the OPAC did not change their fundamental nature. They searched the data that was present in the ILS. The format of the data in the ILS is MARC, which was developed for the purpose of interchange of data between disparate systems. The format was remarkably well designed for this purpose, and continues to provide a solid foundation for data exchange (Williams 2009, 8). It stores, in a mix of coded and text fields, all of the information used by catalogers to describe a bibliographic entity.

The MARC format was not designed as a basis for searching or browsing, nor was it intended for use on every resource that might be of interest to library patrons. The structure of a MARC record is obscure and difficult to parse (Tennant 2002, 26). Additionally, author fields are formatted for catalog cards, titles and series can begin with articles, field tags are arbitrary three-digit numbers, most fields are optional and repeatable, and fields are split up into subfields, sometimes with a great deal of disruption. The punctuation is defined very precisely, but really, punctuation? Most integrated systems treat code validation as optional, so there is no guarantee of data quality. The definition of some "fixed" fields varies according to record format. And there are multiple flavors of MARC for particular contexts or countries.

Also, the MARC format was created for the description of bibliographic materials, such as books and serials. It has been extended for use with visual and audio media, music scores, computer files, and other types of materials, but there are limits to how far it can be extended without fundamental changes to the structure:

> The rapid evolution of digital information media and communications networks has posed significant challenges for the continued development and viability of the MARC format. Adapting the format to the demands of this new environment entails more than simple incremental enhancement to format specifications; it requires extensive re-examination of the underlying logical structure of the format and its application. (Delsey 2002, 4)

Among other things, library collections now routinely include images, e-books, electronic documents, websites, finding aids, tablet computers, video games, and full-text objects, which are handled more or less well within MARC. Libraries have always had serials and other multilevel objects whose relationships cannot be easily represented through MARC.

The answer to this dilemma was to "harvest" the data out of the ILS and put it into a different format in a different application where it could be tuned for efficient and effective searching (Vaughan 2011b, 23). Unfortunately, this answer has its own undesirable implications. Data which was formerly stored only in the database of the ILS is now also stored in the discovery system's database. This leads to the possibility of the two databases getting out of sync. Smith-Yoshimura (2014) says, "Maintaining the same metadata across multiple databases takes significant effort. Out-of-synch databases can result in frustrating users who cannot find items even though they are held or licensed by the library. Inconsistency and inaccuracy across databases can confuse users."

Fortunately, the concept of harvesting data comes with the concept of refreshing the data. If there is any concern that the data between the two systems has gotten out of sync, one can simply harvest the data again and replace the copy in the discovery system with fresh data. While this can be difficult, as it basically means reloading the entire discovery system database and reindexing all of the data in it, it is a sure way to bring the two databases back into harmony.

Although this appears to make it safe to follow a data harvesting model, that is only true if there is no additional data in the discovery system that is not in the ILS. But, of course, one of the primary purposes of creating an advanced user interface is to "give end users tools for organizing, saving, and exporting results ... tagging, user ratings and reviews, integration with personal accounts, and sharing with external sites, such as Facebook" (Hoeppner 2012, 39). These highly desirable additions mean that the discovery system contains data that is not present in the ILS. The single database of record definition has been broken.

EXPANSION OF THE LIBRARY CATALOG

The ILS never really was a single database of record. The ILS traditionally includes only primary library materials such as books and serial titles. Every library used other search methods "that are separate from the catalog such as printed indexes, CD-ROM databases, or commercial online services" to find articles, pamphlets, government documents, book reviews, poems, and a vast array of other materials (Potter 1989, 107). As time went on, not only were a plethora of print sources missing from the ILS, but there was a growing array of digital content outside of the ILS. For example, the University of Virginia has "a significant collection of TEI XML documents, EAD finding aids, and digitized images" that were little used because they were not searchable in the OPAC (Sadler 2009, 64).

Discovery platforms made the scope of library collections more obvious than ever before: "In essence, these tools create a unified space for integrating access to a diverse group of digital and print resources" (Luther and Kelly 2011, 4). Discovery systems can also be extended to "previously hidden collections . . . thus providing a more comprehensive view of all of the materials available . . . regardless of whether it has been formally collected by the library" (Sadler 2009, 64). So-called mega-aggregate indexes or web-scale discovery tools such as Primo Central and Summon allow a user to retrieve "catalogue records and journal records in a single search, thus alleviating the searching 'silo effect' of previous resource discovery solutions" (Gross and Sheridan 2011, 238). Finally, the inclusion of application program interfaces (APIs) in discovery means that both libraries and outside developers "have been able to use the API to create completely new applications that exist independently of the OPAC" (Sierra, Ryan, and Wust 2007, 6).

The problem is clear. Discovery systems, which both duplicate data from the ILS and augment it, which combine into a single database and search interface records from multiple sources, which integrate collections from the library with collections from external sources, which aggregate metadata and full text for journal and newspaper articles harvested from the widest possible array of publishers and indexes, and which permit the development of a multitude of differently oriented interfaces through the exploitation of APIs, have thoroughly changed libraries' understanding of their data. It is no longer possible for librarians to delude themselves into thinking that the ILS can serve as the "single source of truth" about library data.

DIRECTIONS FOR SOLUTIONS

At the State Library of Victoria, we perform ongoing data syncing to maintain our ILS as the single database of record. All materials are cataloged in the ILS, then records are exported to other systems, such as our digital object management system (DOMS). Fields which get added in the DOMS are published out and integrated back into the ILS source record. For a number of reasons, we have recently acknowledged that it is no longer possible nor desirable to do this in all cases.

Another possible solution would be to insist that all data is added or updated directly into the ILS. This would require turning off any of the update features in the discovery platform, such as tagging and reviews. It would also limit the ability for users to maintain "a personal profile (academic degree and one or more disciplines) to activate personalized relevance ranking," one of the features of Primo Central (Breeding 2014, 39). Strictly speaking, a library would also need to turn off the ability for patrons to save searches, to create and manage portfolios of results, or to set up "current awareness" searches that e-mail new results to the user each day. Since these features are one of the primary reasons for implementing a discovery system, this strategy is clearly a nonstarter.

The final possibility is to accept the existence of multiple databases of record and work out ways to ensure that the primary source of all data is clear. Katherine Hammer (1996) describes the issue:

> Another key type of metadata is *data primacy*. It addresses which database should be considered the *database of record* for a replicated data value. This is an example of metadata that is rarely recorded electronically; users of the system often consider data primacy to be a matter of common sense. For example, a customer's address may be stored in multiple databases, but in case of a conflict in the record content, the user is likely to consider the address in the billings database to be the most accurate. In other cases, it may be difficult to determine the database of record.

To the issue that Hammer specifically address, data primacy for replicated data, should be added the issue of keeping track of all the places where non-replicated data is stored, for example, bibliographic records are stored in the ILS, metadata for digital objects is stored in a digital asset management system, tags and reviews are in a discovery system, and so forth.

As long as systems are stable, the data goes where it is supposed to and appears when and where it is supposed to and there is no need to think about the primary or unique location of stored data. When change comes, however, it is good to be prepared. Change includes system failure, upgrade, or replacement, or simply an evolution in the library's needs. In all of these cases, it is essential to know what data is where and even better to have a plan in place to capture it all.

System vendors will usually have utilities to migrate what they consider the core data of a system. So, if the library is moving from an ILS to a replacement system, the vendor will almost certainly provide a pathway to migrate bibliographic data to the new system. Vendors are less likely to have the capability of migrating user-entered data such as tags and reviews from one discovery platform to another. By keeping track of where this data resides and in what format, the library can increase the chances of being able to extract the data in a usable form and to preserve it, even if it is impossible to integrate it immediately into a new system.

It is also helpful to have a "map" that shows the relationships between various pieces of data. For example, if patron data resides primarily in the ILS, but there is also patron-related data in the discovery system, any recoupling of these two data sources will require knowledge of the identifying numbers or other data points they have in common. For academic institutions, the ILS may not be the actual database of record for some of the patron information, because the library may get data feeds from the university's student and HR systems. Consequently, if the university switches from one unique identifier to another, it may be necessary for the library to negotiate with its vendors to replace the old number with the new one in the ILS and discovery system. Having the relationships between the data in these systems well documented may be the difference between success and failure in this project. While it is tempting to trust the automation vendors to document and manage the data that is entrusted to their systems, ultimately the library is responsible for maintaining its own data.

I am not aware of any library that has undertaken the task of identifying and recording the database of record for all the data in the library's various systems. I am aware, however, of a number of cases where data was lost in the course of a migration or upgrade. In some of these cases, the loss of data was anticipated, but in others, it wasn't even discovered until after it was too late to do anything about it.

CONCLUSION

The emergence of discovery systems as a new element in library automation brings with it what at first appears to be the destruction of the concept of a single database of record in the library through the ILS. Further reflection, however, reveals that this was never more than an illusion, because there have always been a myriad repositories of data in every library, of which the ILS was only one. Adding a discovery system to the mix does, however, bring the issue to the fore.

Libraries have choices in how to deal with this newly identified problem. They can try to extend their ILS with the additional data to keep it as the primary database as much as possible, or they can turn off the very features in their discovery systems that justified their purchase. A better strategy is to carefully identify and document, for each unique bit of data, "what fields constitute a record definition, the characteristics of each field, where and how the data defined by the record definition is stored and other characteristics" (Hammer 1996), as well as the primary source, or database of record for each of them. Proceeding very far down the broad road of the expanding library catalog without addressing this problem is irresponsible at best and dangerous at worst.

References

Auld, Lawrence. 1968. "Automated Book Order and Circulation Control Procedures at the Oakland University Library." *Journal of Library Automation* 1, no. 2 (June): 93–109.

Borgman, Christine L. 1997. "From Acting Locally to Thinking Globally: A Brief History of Library Automation." *Library Quarterly* 67, no. 3 (July): 215–49.

Bowman, J. H. 2007. "Retrospective Conversion: The Early Years." *Library History* 23, no. 4 (December): 331–40.

Breeding, Marshall. 2010. "The State of the Art in Library Discovery 2010." *Computers in Libraries* 30, no. 1 (January/February): 31–34.

———. 2011. "Transformations in Academic Libraries Demand Transformed Automation Support." *Computers in Libraries* 31, no. 4: 27–29.

———. 2014. "Major Discovery Product Profiles." *Library Technology Reports* 50, no. 1 (January): 33–52.

Caplan, Priscilla. 2012. "On Discovery Tools, OPACs and the Motion of Library Language." *Library Hi Tech* 30, no. 1: 108–15.

De Gennaro, Richard. 1968. "The Development and Administration of Automated Systems in Academic Libraries." *Journal of Library Automation* 1, no. 1 (March): 75–91.

Delsey, Tom. 2002. "Functional Analysis of the MARC 21 Bibliographic and Holdings Formats." www.loc.gov/marc/marc-functional-analysis/source/analysis.pdf.

Groenewegen, Hans W. 2004. "Four Decades of Library Automation: Recollections and Reflections." *The Australian Library Journal* 53, no. 1 (February): 39–53.

Gross, Julia, and Lutie Sheridan. 2011. "Web Scale Discovery: The User Experience." *New Library World* 112, nos. 5/6: 236–47.

Hammer, Katherine. 1996. "Metadata Tracks a Moving Target." www.uniforum.org/publications/ufm/may96/infotech.html.

Highleyman, Bill, Bruce Holenstein, and Paul J. Holenstein. 2008. "Achieving Century Uptimes Part 9: Where Is My Database of Record?" www.gravic.com/shadowbase/pdf/Achieving%20Century%20Uptimes%20Part%209%20%28Database%20of%20Record%29.pdf.

Hoeppner, Athena. 2012. "The Ins and Outs of Evaluating Web-Scale Discovery Services." *Computers in Libraries* 32, no. 3 (April): 6–10, 38–40.

Luther, Judy, and Maureen C. Kelly. 2011. "The Next Generation of Discovery: The Stage Is Set for a Simpler Search for Users, but Choosing a Product Is Much More Complex." *Library Journal* 136, no. 5 (March): 66–71.

Peay, Wayne, and Paul Schoening. 2008. "Estelle Brodman and the First Generation of Library Automation." *Journal of the Medical Library Association* 96, no. 3 (July): 262–67.

Potter, William. 1989. "Expanding the Online Catalog." *Information Technology and Libraries* 8, no. 2 (June): 99–104.

Sadler, Elizabeth. 2009. "Project Blacklight: A Next Generation Library Catalog at a First Generation University." *Library Hi Tech* 27, no. 1: 57–67.

Sierra, Tito, Joseph Ryan, and Markus Wust. 2007. "Beyond OPAC 2.0: Library Catalog as Versatile Discovery Platform." *Code4Lib Journal*, no. 1 (December): 10–16.

Smith-Yoshimura, Karen. 2014. "Synchronizing Metadata among Different Databases." http://hangingtogether.org/?p=4524.

Tennant, Roy. 2002. "MARC Must Die." *Library Journal* 127, no. 17 (October): 26–28.

———. 2006. "Fixing Library Discovery." *Library Journal* 131, no. 11 (June): 30.

Vaughan, Jason. 2011a. "Ex Libris Primo Central." *Library Technology Reports* 47, no. 1 (January): 39–47.

———. 2011b. "Serials Solutions Summon." *Library Technology Reports* 47, no. 1 (January): 22–29.

———. 2011c. "Web Scale Discovery: What and Why?" *Library Technology Reports* 47, no. 1 (January): 5–11, 21.

Williams, Jo. 2009. "MARC Data, the OPAC, and Library Professionals." *Program: Electronic Library and Information Systems* 43, no. 1: 7–17.

CHAPTER NINETEEN

KNOW THY METADATA
Metadata Challenges in Discovery Services

MYUNG-JA K. HAN AND WILLIAM FLETCHER WEATHERS

T he new discovery services offered by library technology vendors, locally created or available as open source, have generated excitement in the library community because they promise Google-like search and discovery functions for library users. In addition, these systems offer other functionalities specific to libraries, including faceted refinement, record de-duplication, and grouping records of Functional Requirements for Bibliographic Records (FRBR) group 1 entities (Tillett 2004; IFLA 1998) that are solely based on metadata. However, this new excitement brings with it challenges as well. In order to provide optimal discovery services and Google-like search and discovery functions, the systems need to ingest, index, and search against heterogeneous metadata that comes from many different sources, is encoded in a variety of formats, and describes resources at different levels of granularity. The metadata that these systems are built upon can be divided into two categories: metadata that discovery system vendors provide with the system by default, and metadata that each institution adds to the system. Understanding and knowing how to evaluate, manipulate, and maintain metadata from a library's collections in a discovery system's heterogeneous metadata environment is critical when implementing discovery services.

The importance of having quality metadata to provide better user services has been discussed for both traditional and digital library environments over the years. As many libraries try to implement discovery interfaces within their main gateway, the literature has already stressed that metadata is an integral part of the discovery service design and implementation process, since all searches are performed against the metadata that has been indexed in the system. Although some systems allow keyword searches to be conducted across an index that contains abstracts and full text, the metadata still plays an important role in relevance ranking and categories for advanced search design. For this reason, Sadeh (2008) said that it was important to understand how to work with metadata of collections from different sources, using different metadata standards and controlled vocabularies when implementing a discovery service system. Yang and Hofmann (2011) also posited that different levels of access to materials is one of the features that users want the most, and this requires the system to work with metadata that describes different levels of granularity. The literature also discussed the challenges posed by metadata in a discovery service system as well, especially in regard to metadata quality. Denton and Coysh (2011) found that inconsistencies, inaccuracies, and incompleteness of metadata caused less than ideal results of faceted navigation display. Emanuel (2011) also found that inconsistencies in cataloging records, such as using uncontrolled vocabularies, impeded effective use of the faceted navigation display feature. In consequence, if the metadata does not have specific information or if controlled vocabularies are not consistently used, some of the resources may be excluded from the search results page when the discovery service provides a faceted navigation view (Han 2012).

While the literature discusses metadata challenges and the importance of metadata quality in discovery service systems, less attention has been given so far to how libraries might work to solve these challenges. This chapter will discuss common metadata challenges that libraries may encounter when implementing discovery services, and suggest ways to work with these challenges.

DISCOVERY SYSTEMS

Libraries currently have many options to pursue when implementing a discovery service. Of these options, Breeding tracks some of the more prominent and widely used discovery products on his Library Technology Guides website (http://librarytechnology.org/discovery/). Among the options are open source, vendor-based, and "web-scale" discovery products. As of April 29, 2015, Breeding mentions that these products "tend to be independent from the specific applications that libraries implement to manage resources, such as integrated library systems, library services platforms, repository platforms, or electronic resource management systems."This tendency towards independence from these management systems speaks to their overall design in that metadata from these systems is ingested into a separate single (or central) index, results from which are returned through the discovery system interface.The selection of resources and the ingestion of the corresponding metadata into a discovery product is up to an individual library. In the case of web-scale discovery systems, however, libraries can typically build an index of metadata from the aforementioned management systems and provide access to the metadata from the vendor's massive central index of largely article-level metadata from publishers, abstracting and indexing services, open access databases, and more.

The University of Illinois at Urbana-Champaign (UIUC) Library implemented a vendor-based web-scale discovery product, Ex Libris's Primo, for a trial period of two years from 2012 to 2014.The library has been using a locally developed search engine called Easy Search (www.library.illinois.edu/it/helpdesk/service/es.html) that facilitates federated search. For the investigation, the library ingested into the discovery system not only all catalog records available in its integrated library system (ILS), but also metadata from digital collections stored in its digital asset management system, CONTENTdm, items from the Institutional Repository, and LibGuides created by departmental libraries and subject librarians.When ingesting the metadata, the implementation team developed different workflows based on the original metadata standards of each source system. For the library catalog records, consisting of about six million records in MAchine-Readable Catalog (MARC) format, a metadata librarian for web-scale discovery adjusted the vendor's default crosswalk between MARC fields to the discovery system's metadata schema. CONTENTdm uses Dublin Core as its default metadata schema but allows for the creation of additional custom elements in order to provide more precise description of resources. In order to preserve the contextual information of each collection in CONTENTdm, the metadata librarian for web-scale discovery reviewed the use of customized elements and created a crosswalk that best represented local elements in an aggregated central index environment. LibGuides is not a typical collection included as a target resource for discovery systems. However, since many library-specific instructions and resources are included in LibGuides, the library decided to add them as one of the target resources. Since no preexisting ingestion path existed for LibGuides, a new Extensible Stylesheet Language Transformations (XSLT) stylesheet was created to map the appropriate information from LibGuides metadata to Dublin Core. Initially, the instance of the UIUC Library's discovery service system started with fifteen elements in its central index, but added several additional customized elements to better work with metadata for locally created unique resources. Lessons learned from the process are shared in both the "Challenges" and "Suggested Best Practices" sections below.

CHALLENGES

There is tension between what discovery systems allow a library to do in order to improve discovery services and what metadata will allow a library to do. Discovery systems provide many ways for libraries to improve the discoverability of resources by leveraging metadata available in the system. However, although using these functions can improve the discovery experience for the end user, they must be implemented with careful deliberation in order to ensure the maximum effect and to minimize any potential deleterious side effects. For example, as previously noted with the faceted refinement functionality, if attention is not paid to the metadata used in the implementation of a discovery service, the result is decreased discoverability of otherwise available resources.

As with any library system, be it an ILS or digital repository, one of the most important challenges to overcome in implementing a discovery service is in ensuring quality metadata. Discovery service systems, being index-based systems, rely on metadata to provide the functionality that users need to complete the common FRBR User Tasks of finding, identifying, selecting, and obtaining (IFLA 1998). With discovery services, however, the importance of metadata quality is compounded by the added functionality that is reliant on metadata from various sources.

In the context of discovery services and the heterogeneous metadata upon which they are built, quality metadata must also be shareable metadata. Shreeves, Riley, and Milewicz (2006) noted that 6C's—content, consistency, coherence, context, communication, and conformance to standards (such as metadata standards, vocabulary and encoding standards, descriptive content standards, technical standards)—make metadata sharable in a digital environment. These qualities are even more important in the discovery service environment, especially when a new service is being built. The only difference is that in the discovery service environment the library has to make all harvested metadata shareable metadata before the ingestion process so the central index can have quality metadata that improves the discovery of resources available from a variety of sources. Common challenges arise because of the aggregated nature of the discovery systems' metadata, which libraries have to provide as shareable quality metadata.

METADATA FROM VARIOUS SOURCES

Unlike a traditional library's online public access catalog, a discovery service uses metadata from various sources, from both inside and outside of an institution. This means that metadata standards, content standards, controlled vocabularies, and the way each metadata field is used in each metadata source may be different.

Collections can lose their overall identity when intermingled and indexed with a vast amount of other collections and resources. In addition, meanings associated with each metadata element within collections in a local context may be lost in a similar fashion.

METADATA QUALITY

The quality of metadata varies by collection or even by item within the same collection. However, since there is no systematic way to measure metadata quality, the only thing that matters for a discovery service is whether the metadata includes the specific information that is going to be used for certain discovery functions, for example, options for a faceted browsing service or FRBR groupings. Simply checking whether the elements are present and information is added from a controlled vocabulary will work as a minimum measurement for metadata quality.

MAPPING TO DISCOVERY SERVICE SYSTEM METADATA

A discovery service system typically uses the metadata stored in its central index, which has its own set of metadata elements. Because all harvested metadata will be mapped to the metadata elements used by the central index, mapping has a direct impact on the performance of discovery services. While a library may have control over the way how harvested metadata are mapped to the discovery system's metadata schema, it has no control over how the metadata from the service's central index gets mapped. Thus, if a library pursues a mapping it feels is correct, but does not necessarily match the mapping of the central index, search results and faceted refinement will be affected negatively.

GRANULARITY OF METADATA AND RESOURCES

As Yang and Hofmann (2011) found in their research, users liked when discovery services provided different types of resources, such as articles, images, journals, and books, together in the results page. However, this means that the system needs to work with metadata that has different levels of granularity. For example, a journal vendor usually provides metadata at the article level, digital collections housed in each institution's digital asset management system have metadata at the individual-item level (usually an image), archives maintain metadata at the collection level (finding aids), and metadata from an ILS is usually at the title level for monographs or serials. Since the granularity of metadata information is used for type-faceted browsing options, identifying the granularity of metadata description and enhancing the needed information into the metadata is challenging but highly desired.

SUGGESTED BEST PRACTICES

The following best practices serve to prevent or solve the common metadata challenges outlined above.

Metadata from Various Sources

Once the sources of content are identified, their metadata should be reviewed, including metadata standards and controlled vocabulary used, as well as the resources described by the metadata. It should be verified that information is added correctly in the resources' metadata by using controlled vocabularies within standardized metadata fields. For example, if the metadata comes from a digital asset management system and the collection contains audio resources, the type of item should be present in each metadata with the same term, such as "Audio," and this information should be present in the same metadata element, such as <dc:type> or <mods:typeOfResource>. Some institutions and collections have detailed documents (metadata application profiles) that explain how they use the metadata fields and controlled vocabularies. These documents help to plan mapping and metadata remediation work.

Mapping to Discovery Service System Metadata

Reviewing the metadata process greatly improves the mapping. Mapping metadata elements from the source schema to the discovery system schema can be done in four different ways: one-to-one, many-to-one, one-to-many, and many-to-many. There is no need to be constrained to a one-to-one mapping (St. Pierre et al., 1999). Based on the metadata analysis and the way in which the discovery service will use the metadata, many-to-one and one-to-many mappings can be considered. There may also be an additional mapping relationship: no mapping at all. Not all information included in the metadata needs to be mapped to the central index metadata schema, because not all information available in the metadata is relevant in a discovery service. If the metadata includes information about administration or preservation of a resource, this does not need to be mapped to the central index (Han et al. 2009). In order to avoid a possible change of mapping, documenting each collection's mapping before implementation is also ideal. This can show overall mapping practices, for example, how similar elements and values are mapped to the central index metadata element. This will make the changing of mappings easier and painless.

Granularity of Metadata and Resources

Information about granularity should be included in the metadata using a controlled vocabulary. The controlled vocabulary for the granularity of resources can be developed locally based on the discovery service design—how to provide faceted browsing options and what types of resources are included in the central index. In case the metadata does not have that information, there should be a plan for enhancing the metadata with that information on granularity, either in the original metadata if the metadata comes from the local system, in the central index, or both (Foulonneau et al. 2006).

Metadata Quality

When it is apparent that the metadata quality is not ideal for use in a discovery service, metadata remediation work can be considered. However, metadata remediation requires careful planning and follow-up work as well as the resources to carry out the work. A plan can be devised by type of remediation, automatic or manual, and scope of the remediation, adding specific information to a certain metadata element, for example, type of resource, or changing the controlled vocabulary used for a certain resource or element. Metadata remediation can also be planned in conjunction with mapping and metadata granularity work.

OTHER CONSIDERATIONS

In addition to suggested best practices that would solve these metadata challenges, there are other considerations that would improve the performance of discovery services.

Metadata as a Living Thing

Metadata can be updated at any given time as well as the contents they describe (Ellero 2013). Some collections are static, so their metadata does not need not to be updated. However, it is safe to assume that metadata can be changed or deleted. In order to provide an accurate description of resources within a discovery service environment, a regular metadata harvesting schedule should be coordinated. The frequency can be determined depending on the resources that each institution has for discovery service system maintenance work.

Understanding Your System

While there may be some shared characteristics between all discovery service systems at a very high level, each system will have some degree of variance in how the base functionality is carried out. Vendor-based web-scale discovery systems, for example, are built upon a combined index of harvested metadata and a massive aggregation of metadata that each vendor has licensed from abstracting and indexing services, publishers, journal article aggregating services, and other metadata sources. Understanding how the system works with metadata and understanding the flexibility that the system allows in adding customized metadata elements can greatly improve overall metadata work flows.

Documentation

All decisions about metadata work flows and processes should be documented and shared within the group responsible for the implementation and maintenance of the discovery system. This is important because any changes made affecting metadata can have a direct impact on the search functionality and the user experience. Documentation provides not only a history of the work done, but also the underlying reasons for why decisions were made, so that over time this information can be preserved and used as institutional memory. Depending on the composition of the working group and the institution's policy, the documentation could be shared via a wiki or a closed server.

Collection Development Policy

Libraries have been building their collections based on collection development policies that are specific to each institution. While it is expected that a library should have a well-defined collection development policy for its traditional collections, it is safe to say that the same policy is not usually applied when implementing a new discovery service. One possible reason may be because it is easy to add new collections or resources that are not owned or curated by the institution to the discovery system. However, the ease of working with any available collection should not make libraries overlook the collection development policy. Because the collection development policy is required to best serve the users and their needs, the discovery service implementation process should have its own collection development policy or should use the library's overall policy as its guiding principle.

CONCLUSION

Metadata plays a critical role in the function of any discovery service. Search, relevancy ranking, faceted refinement, and record grouping all function and respond to the metadata present. The quality of outcomes for end users of discovery systems is directly linked to the quality of metadata indexed by each system and can best be achieved by having a comprehensive metadata strategy at the outset of any discovery service implementation. Such a strategy ought to be informed not only by the common metadata challenges presented by discovery services, but also by the characteristics unique to a library's collections. However, this understanding is only one component of an overall strategy that a library needs to undertake when implementing a discovery system.

Before working with metadata a library should form a group of representatives from the public services and technical services divisions to identify how their specific users find, search, identify, and obtain the resources they need (from public services), and where this information is stored in the metadata (from technical services). After an assessment of user experience and information-seeking user behaviors, decisions can be made as to what functionalities will be needed by a library's user group(s). Once a library has a clear picture of its unique user needs and a thorough understanding of how a discovery system leverages metadata, then it can begin to form and execute the metadata strategy component of implementing and maintaining an optimal discovery service.

References

Breeding, Marshall. "Major Discovery Products." *Library Technology Guides: Product Directory.* http://librarytechnology.org/discovery/.

Denton, William, and Sarah J. Coysh. 2011. "Usability Testing of VuFind at an Academic Library. *Library Hi Tech* 29, no. 2: 301–19.

Ellero, Nadine P. 2013. "Integration or Disintegration: Where Is Discovery Headed?" *Journal of Library Metadata* 13, no. 4: 311–29.

Emanuel, Jennifer. 2011. "Usability of the VuFind Next-Generation Online Catalog." *Information Technology & Libraries* 30, no. 1: 44–52.

Foulonneau, Muriel, Timothy W. Cole, Charles Blair, Peter C. Gorman, Kat Hagedorn, and Jenn Riley. 2006. "The CIC Metadata Portal: A Collaborative Effort in the Area of Digital Libraries." *Science & Technology Libraries* 26, nos. 3/4: 111–35.

Han, Myung-Ja. 2012. "New Discovery Services and Library Bibliographic Control." *Library Trends* 61, no. 1: 162–72.

Han, Myung-Ja, Christine Cho, Timothy W. Cole, and Amy S. Jackson. 2009. "Metadata for Special Collections in CONTENTdm: How to Improve Interoperability of Unique Fields Through OAI-PMH." *Journal of Library Metadata* 9, nos. 3/4: 213–38.

IFLA (International Federation of Library Associations and Institutions). 1998. "Functional Requirements for Bibliographic Records: Final Report." www.ifla.org/files/assets/cataloguing/frbr/frbr.pdf.

Sadeh, Tamar. 2008. "User Experience in the Library: A Case Study." *New Library World* 109, nos. 1/2: 7–24.

Shreeves, Sarah L., Jenn Riley, and Liz Milewicz. 2006. "Moving towards Shareable Metadata." *First Monday* 11, no. 8. http://journals.uic.edu/ojs/index.php/fm/article/view/1386/1304.

St. Pierre, Margaret, Sandra K. Paul, Albert Simmons, and Bill LaPlante. 1999. "We Used to Call It Publishing—Issues in Crosswalking Content Metadata Standards." *Against the Grain* 11, no. 4: 74.

Tillett, Barbara. 2004. "What Is FRBR?" www.loc.gov/cds/downloads/FRBR.PDF.

Yang, Sharon Q., and Melissa A. Hofmann. 2011. "Next Generation or Current Generation? A Study of the OPACs of 260 Academic Libraries in the USA and Canada." *Library Hi Tech* 29, no. 2: 266–300.

ABOUT THE CONTRIBUTORS

JULIA BAUDER is the social studies and data services librarian and associate librarian of the college at the Grinnell College Libraries, where she has worked since 2008. She received her MLIS degree from Wayne State University in 2007. Prior to becoming a librarian, she worked as a freelance writer and editor of reference books.

SONYA BETZ is digital initiatives projects librarian at the University of Alberta, in Edmonton, Canada, where she is responsible for the project management and coordination of a broad spectrum of digital initiatives, including digital repository services, digitization, research data management, web archiving, and digital preservation. Betz also spent several years as the web and user experience librarian at MacEwan University in Edmonton, Alberta, where she conducted regular user testing with students and faculty, and led the implementation of a number of digital initiatives, including the Virtual Services Integration Project, described in this chapter. Betz has presented frequently on emerging technology initiatives at national and international conferences, including Computers in Libraries, Internet Librarian, Access, and IFLA.

STEPHEN BOLLINGER has been working in information technology for twenty years, including library technology for over ten years, in both public and academic libraries. After library school, he worked for five years as an information architect and consultant with clients including General Motors, Steelcase, and Borders Group. When he started working in libraries, he worked on catalog redesigns, deploying content management systems, and web services. His interests include user-centered design broadly applied to library services and providing powerful library technological solutions that are both accessible and usable. He is currently the head of Library Systems at the North Carolina Agricultural and Technical State University. He is a graduate of the School of Information at the University of Michigan, Ann Arbor.

JENNIFER COLT is a user experience designer in the department of Digital Scholarship & Preservation Services at Cornell University Library. She has provided front-end development on a number of recent projects including the library website, search page, and catalog; the Law Library website; and the Library's Hydra pilot project. Colt has a master's degree in mass communications from the University of South Carolina–Columbia, and a BA in anthropology from Hamilton College.

MATTHEW CONNOLLY is an application developer in the Web Development Group of Cornell University Library's Information Technology Department. He writes code for a variety of internal- and external-facing library projects, including the library catalog, search interface, and discovery systems. Connolly is a longtime member of the library's Usability Working Group and lends technical support to experimental technology projects. He is also a coauthor of *Using iPhones, iPads, and iPods: A Practical Guide for Librarians.* Connolly holds a BS and a M.Eng. degree in electrical engineering from Cornell University.

REBEKAH CUMMINGS is the research data management librarian for the social sciences and humanities for the J. Willard Marriott Library at the University of Utah, and previously held the position of assistant director/outreach librarian for the Mountain West Digital Library. She received her BA in philosophy from California State University, Long Beach, and her MLIS from the University of California, Los Angeles. Prior to her work with MWDL, Cummings was a graduate student researcher on the UCLA Knowledge Infrastructures research team studying the social and technical structures surrounding data and data practices.

JOSEPH DEODATO is the digital user services librarian at Rutgers University, where he applies insights from user research to the design, implementation, and evaluation of system-wide digital library services. Toward this end, he works closely with librarians, IT staff, and vendors to improve the functionality and effectiveness of digital services used to deliver library content and provide a seamless, consistent, and engaging online user experience. Deodato has published and presented on a variety of emerging trends in library technology including Web 2.0, mobile devices, and web-scale discovery.

ERIC FRIERSON is a senior discovery services engineer with EBSCO. Prior to joining EBSCO, he was head of library systems at St. Edward's University, reference and instruction librarian at the University of Texas at Arlington, and instructional technology librarian at the University of Michigan. He received his MS degree in information from the University of Michigan and an under-graduate degree in computer science from the University of Texas at Austin and was a high school teacher at Richardson High School in Texas. He is coeditor of *Planning Our Future Libraries: Blueprints for 2025*, is the primary developer for EBSCO's Curriculum Builder, an LTI-based tool for learning management systems, and works directly with front-line librarians to optimize the discovery experience at their institution.

KHALILAH GAMBRELL is a user research consultant at EBSCO Information Ser-vices and is focused on understanding and enhancing users' research experience with web-scale discovery. Prior to this role, she worked for over seven years in software product management at EBSCO, leading the user requirements effort on several products including EBSCO Discovery Service. Gambrell received an MA degree in history from Boston College and a master's degree in library and information science from Simmons College. She is an active member of the Special Libraries Association and has held several leadership positions in the organization, including SLA New England president and the 2015 Annual Conference Planning Council.

MYUNG-JA HAN is a metadata librarian at the University of Illinois at Urba-na-Champaign. Her main responsibilities consist of developing application profiles for digital collections and evaluating and enhancing cataloging and metadata work flows. Her research interests include interoperability of metadata, relationships between collection description and item-level metadata, issues on bibliographic control in the digital library environment, and the Semantic Web and linked data.

SEAN HANNAN is user interface developer at Johns Hopkins University, Sher-idan Libraries and Museums. He has backgrounds in information technology and library science. His work is focused on front-end web development on information retrieval systems. He has a master's degree in library and informa-tion science.

DARREN HARDY is a geospatial software engineer at Stanford University, where he develops open-source geospatial digital library software and services. His interdisciplinary research focuses on crowd sourcing geographic information, geospatial data discovery and management, and spatial effects on information behaviors. He earned PhD and master's degrees in environmental science and management from the University of California, Santa Barbara, and BS and MS degrees in computer science from the University of Colorado at Boulder.

MARGARET HELLER is digital services librarian at Loyola University in Chicago. She is a regular writer for the ACRL *TechConnect* blog, and speaks regularly on issues of scholarly communication, digital projects, and user experience. She is also active in the Library and Information Technology Association.

STEVEN HESLIP is user experience and service design officer at the William H. Welch Medical Library at the Johns Hopkins Medical Institutions. He has academic backgrounds in anthropology and human–computer interaction. His current work is focused on describing how researchers and staff interact with clinical data and designing services to support researchers and clinicians. He has a master of science degree.

WILLIAM HICKS is the head of the User Interfaces Unit at the University of North Texas Libraries. He oversees the presentation, information architecture, content strategy, and other aspects of user experience of the library's public-facing websites and services.

NATHAN HOSBURGH has worked in academic libraries for over ten years. He has a broad range of experience, including circulation, interlibrary loan/document delivery, reference, instruction, collection development, electronic resource management, library technology, and systems. Hosburgh has held previous librarian positions at the Florida Institute of Technology and Montana State University. Currently, he serves as the discovery and systems librarian at Rollins College, a small liberal arts institution in Winter Park, Florida.

COLE HUDSON is a digital publishing librarian and adjunct instructor for Wayne State University (WSU). A member of the Digital Publishing team, he helps build and maintain digital library infrastructure as well as WSU's institutional repository, DC@WSU.

GRAHAM HUKILL is a digital publishing librarian at Wayne State University. His primary focuses are the library's digital collections platform, library website, and helping manage the institutional repository.

KRISTEN JOHANNES, MA, PhD, is a research associate in science, technology, engineering, and math (STEM) education at WestEd Inc. and applies experimental and statistical methods to improve education outcomes. Johannes received her doctorate in cognitive science from Johns Hopkins University.

T. LOUISE M. KIDDER is the discovery services librarian at the University of Texas Medical Branch in Galveston, Texas. She previously served as acquisitions and electronic resources manager at Rosenberg Library, the oldest continually operating public library in Texas, and she is an alumnus of the University of North Texas and Angelo State University.

JOANNE LEARY is an assessment analyst in the Department of Assessment and Communication at Cornell University Library, specializing in creating custom queries and reports using the Voyager Access database. Leary has worked extensively with Access Services and is responsible for configuring system settings for circulation-related operations in Voyager's SysAdmin client. Leary has an academic background in mathematics and has worked with Cornell University Library for thirty-eight years.

DANIEL LOVINS is head of knowledge access design and development at New York University's (NYU's) Division of Libraries. Before coming to NYU he served as Yale University's Hebraica Cataloging Team leader, and then as Yale's metadata and emerging technologies librarian, at which time he co-led an implementation of the VuFind discovery system. His research interests include multilingual resource discovery, open-source software development, and linked open data for libraries.

HONG MA is head of library systems at Loyola University in Chicago. She is a regular writer and speaker on implementing large-scale digital projects and systems. She is also active in the Library Information Technology Association (LITA).

ALAN MANIFOLD has more than thirty years' experience in library automation, from manager of library enterprise applications at Purdue University to Primo and Voyager support manager at Ex Libris to digital and library applications manager at the State Library of Victoria. Through developing Purdue's first integrated library system, then working extensively with NOTIS, Voyager, and Aleph, he is an expert on the subject of the integrated library system. Over the past five years, he has begun to develop a high level of expertise on discovery tools as well. He has consulted with and presented training workshops to libraries around the world. He has served on NOTIS, Endeavor, and Ex Libris User groups.

SANDRA MCINTYRE is the director of the Mountain West Digital Library (MWDL). She earned an M.Ed. in science education from Georgia State University and is pursuing an MS(LIS) from Drexel University. She has worked in digital libraries since 2002 and has been with the MWDL since 2007. Prior to her work with MWDL, she was the program manager for the Health Education Assets Library at the UCLA School of Medicine.

ANNA NEATROUR is a metadata librarian for the J. Willard Marriott Library at the University of Utah. She previously served as the digital metadata librarian for the Mountain West Digital Library. She received her BA from Kalamazoo College and a master's degree in library and information science from the University of Illinois, Urbana-Champaign. Prior to joining the Mountain West Digital Library she was project manager for the Western Soundscape Archive and also worked with the Western Waters Digital Library.

MARK PHILLIPS is the associate dean for digital libraries at the University of North Texas. He oversees the division responsible for resource discovery, digitization, digital preservation, and digital library system development. His research areas include web archiving, digital preservation infrastructure, and metadata quality and analysis.

SAM POPOWICH graduated with an MLIS degree from Dalhousie University in 2007, and was the emerging technologies librarian at the University of Ottawa from 2008 to 2011. Since then, he has worked at the University of Alberta as the discovery systems librarian. He has presented on discovery and open-source development at the Access and Netspeed conferences, and is active in the Edmonton chapter of Code4Lib.

JACK REED is a geospatial web engineer at Stanford University. He works on increasing access to geospatial data at Stanford University Libraries. A contributor to open-source software, Reed is active in the geospatial, library, and open data communities. He also serves on the executive committee of the International Association for Geoscience Diversity.

FRANÇOIS RENAVILLE has worked at the University of Liege Library (Belgium) since 2001 and as a systems librarian in the same university since 2007. He is notably responsible for Ex Libris solutions (Alma, Primo) and has been involved in institutional open-access projects. He acted as chairman of the French-speaking group of Ex Libris users from 2010 to 2014. He is also the editor of "Discovery Tools, a Bibliography" (http://discoverytoolsbibliography .wordpress.com).

IAN ROBERTON is a librarian at MacEwan University in Edmonton, Alberta. He is currently responsible for usability testing and management of the library's website. His research interests include user-experience design, urban informatics, and library marketing.

BESS SADLER is the manager for application development in the Digital Library Systems and Services Department at Stanford University Library. She has been building open-source library software for over a decade and is a cofounder of the widely used Project Blacklight (http://projectblacklight) and Project Hydra (http://projecthydra.org).

KATE SILTON has worked in academic libraries for nearly a decade, serving varied institutions in multiple capacities. While she has specialized in electronic resources for the past seven years, her initial interests in libraries were outreach and instruction, which motivates her passion for effective access and discovery of online content. A graduate of the School of Information and Library Science at the University of North Carolina at Chapel Hill, Silton is currently the electronic resources librarian at North Carolina Agricultural and Technical State University.

JASON THOMALE has been the resource discovery systems librarian at the University of North Texas (UNT) since 2011. His work has focused on helping support and incrementally improve the systems and interfaces that serve library resources to users, including the library's III catalog, Summon instance, and bento box search interface.

JENNIE THOMAS has worked in libraries and archives since 1998. She holds an MA in the humanities from Central Michigan University, an MLS from the University of Maryland, and a BA in music from St. Mary's College in Maryland. After nearly a decade as the Marilyn Crandell Schleg Archivist and special collections librarian at Albion College, she came to the Rock and Roll Hall of Fame and Museum to implement and manage the archival program for the new Library and Archives. At the Library and Archives, Thomas continues to collaborate with her colleagues on new and innovative ways to present library, archival, and digital materials to the public through a single catalog interface.

MELISSA WALLACE is a user experience designer in the department of Digital Scholarship and Preservation Services at Cornell University Library. Wallace's responsibilities include visual design, information architecture, and front-end development and usability testing for a variety of library websites. Her recent projects include the Cornell University Library website, search page, and catalog; the Management Library website; eCommons, the library's institutional repository; and web interfaces for various digital collections. Wallace has an MS in library and information science from Pratt Institute and a BA in art history from the State University of New York at Albany.

ADAM WEAD has been active in the fields of library science and technology for over fifteen years. After working at Indiana University where he supported the music technology efforts at the Cook Music Library, he went on to the Rock and Roll Hall of Fame's new Library and Archives, where he built the systems and software for the most comprehensive repository of materials relating to the history of rock and roll. Today, Wead continues his work with repository software development at Penn State University, where he supports institutional repository solutions using the Hydra open-source software platform.

WILLIAM FLETCHER WEATHERS is a web developer and user interface specialist at the University of Illinois at Urbana-Champaign (UIUC) Library. From 2012 to 2014 he was a visiting metadata librarian for web scale discovery at UIUC responsible for metadata evaluation and workflows as they related to Primo Discovery Service.

INDEX